Serial Killers Identified by Their Handwriting

A LOOK AT 10 OF THE WORST

by John Racher

The contents of this work, including, but not limited to, the accuracy of events, people, and places depicted; opinions expressed; permission to use previously published materials included; and any advice given or actions advocated are solely the responsibility of the author, who assumes all liability for said work and indemnifies the publisher against any claims stemming from publication of the work.

All Rights Reserved
Copyright © 2023 by John Racher

No part of this book may be reproduced or transmitted, downloaded, distributed, reverse engineered, or stored in or introduced into any information storage and retrieval system, in any form or by any means, including photocopying and recording, whether electronic or mechanical, now known or hereinafter invented without permission in writing from the publisher.

Dorrance Publishing Co
585 Alpha Drive
Pittsburgh, PA 15238
Visit our website at *www.dorrancebookstore.com*

ISBN: 979-8-88925-055-5
eISBN: 979-8-88925-555-0

Serial Killers Identified by Their Handwriting

A LOOK AT 10 OF THE WORST

I DEDICATE THIS BOOK TO MY DAUGHTER LINDSAY, WHO CAME UP WITH THE IDEA THAT I EXAMINE THE HANDWRITING OF SERIAL KILLERS, TO MY BEST FRIEND/SPOUSE CINDY LOU, FOR HER UNWAVERING SUPPORT WHENEVER I STRUGGLED WITH WRITING THIS BOOK, AND TO MY SON-IN-LAW JAMIE WHO INSISTED THAT I WRITE SOMETHING ABOUT THE ZODIAC KILLER. MANY, MANY THANKS YOU GUYS!

Table of Contents

Chapter 1:
The Definition of a Serial Killer 1

Chapter 2: Gerard Schaefer:
An Unrepentant Sexual Deviant 9

Chapter 3: Aileen Wuornos:
A Horrible Upbringing with Horrible Consequences 27

Chapter 4: Ted Bundy:
Did He Have a Split Personality? 49

Chapter 5: Kendall Francois:
The Not-So-Gentle Giant 57

Chapter 6: Richard Cottingham:
The Oxymoron: A Serial Killer with a Normal Childhood 71

Chapter 7: Elizabeth Wettlaufer:
The Nurse Who Became a Serial Killer 87

Chapter 8: Dennis Nilsen:
A Scottish Serial Killer and Necrophile 99

Chapter 9: Dorothea Puente:
Death House Landlady 111

Chapter 10: Joseph DeAngelo:
The Burglar Who Became a Rapist Who Became a Serial Killer 127

Chapter 11: Samuel Little:
America's Secret Serial Killer 143

Chapter 12:
Handwriting Strokes Associated with Serial Killers 159

The Last Line of Defense 167
A Quick Look at 11 More Serial Killers 179
Hand Printing and the Zodiac Killer 191

Preface

Hundreds of books, articles and documents have been written about serial killers, and in many of these publications there have been examples of the serial killer's handwriting. What is surprising, however, is that very few of these specimens of handwriting have ever been carefully scrutinized to see if there were any signs that would identify the writer as a serial killer. This book seeks to rectify this situation.

There are a number of different methods that can be employed to analyze the cursive handwriting of serial killers to identify signs of their aberrant behavior. The technique used in this book is the trait-stroke process because it associates specific strokes with specific behaviors or personality traits. By way of example, whenever a writer makes their dots over the letters i and j as circles, this indicates that they seek to be different from other people in some way by responding to certain situations in an individualistic manner. This trait of idiosyncrasy can range from mild mannerisms to full blown eccentricity, and this range of behavior is related to the relative frequency of occurrence of the circles. Figure A01-05 in Appendix One provides an excellent example of what this stroke looks like.

Chapter 1 provides a clear definition of what a serial killer is, and how they are differentiated from mass murderers and spree killers. It also looks at the criteria that psychologists and law enforcement agencies use to categorize serial killers into five different types.

The next ten chapters provide in-depth analyses of ten serial killers. Each chapter starts with a detailed history about a serial killer and their crimes, followed by a brief discussion of their general personality profile as determined from an analysis of their handwriting. Each chapter is concluded with an in-depth discussion of the personality traits associated with what it is for them to be a serial killer and, most importantly, how they are identified as such by their handwriting. Flow charts outlining each killer's pathway to murder are provided.

Chapter 12 consolidates the detailed findings of the previous ten chapters and discusses the observation that there are a number of different handwriting strokes that can clearly be linked to the writers' activities as serial killers.

There are two traits that exist within everyone's personality that are used to control undesirable behaviors. Appendix One looks at these defense mechanisms and discusses their level of effectiveness in responding to a serial killer's predilections.

Having identified one handwriting stroke that all 10 of the serial killers exhibit, Appendix Two takes a quick look at 11 more serial killers' handwriting specimens to see if the initial finding in Chapter 12 can be validated.

All the analyses in this book looked at the cursive handwriting specimens of serial killers, but what about those murderers for whom we only have hand-printed specimens; can we still find the tell-tale strokes? Appendix Three looks at this situation and uses a specimen from the Zodiac Killer as an example.

Despite the public's perception that serial killers are overwhelmingly white American males, in reality they are a rather diverse group in terms of age, sex, ethnic background and nationality. Of the 22 serial killers featured in this book, five are women, two are people of color, two are Canadian, three are from the UK and the rest are Americans.

Chapter 1
THE DEFINITION OF A SERIAL KILLER

Because they've all killed more than one person, spree killers, mass murderers and serial killers all have that one thing in common, but what makes them different from one another? Law enforcement agencies and researchers all agree that it is the amount of time between killings that is the primary method for differentiating between each type, but this is where their unanimity ends.

Some authorities define a serial killer as someone who murders three or more people over more than a month and with a significant amount of time between the killings while they undergo a "cooling-off" period.[1] The Federal Bureau of Investigation (FBI) in the United States, however, defines serial killing as "… a series of two or more murders, committed as separate events, usually but not always by one offender acting alone."[2]

A spree killer is most frequently defined as a person who kills two or more people in a short time and in multiple locations:[3] they are occasionally described as being rampage killers. The FBI believes that the only way to differentiate between a spree and a serial killer is the former does not exhibit a "cooling-off" period. This definition, however, is not without its distractors. In their book *Controversial Issues in Criminology* (1999), John Fuller and Eric Hickey state that spree killers "… will engage in the killing acts for days and weeks."[3] Another set of authors carries the definition of spree killers to an even higher level of detail. In their book *Serial Murder, Third Edition* (2010), Ronald Holmes and Stephen Holmes define a spree murderer as someone who kills three or more people within a 30-day period. A recent and obvious example of a spree killer is Alek Minassian[4] who, in April 2018 drove down a sidewalk in Toronto, Canada and killed 10 people, injuring an additional 16. He wanted to kill 100 in order to set a world record but was said to have been satisfied with the 10.

There is less controversy around the definition of a mass murderer. While serial killers and spree killers clearly engage in separate acts of murder, mass murderers are defined as engaging in one incident with little to no time between killings. The FBI defines mass murder as killing a number of people either all at the same time or else over a very short period of time and in the same geographic location.[5] Mass murders can be committed by terrorist groups, religious cults or by individuals. In 1995 Timothy McVeigh detonated a bomb in front of a government building in Oklahoma City, United States, killing 168 people (19 of them children) and injuring more than 680 others.[6] McVeigh hoped to precipitate a revolution against the US government who, he felt, was the ultimate bully; McVeigh had been mercilessly bullied at school as he was growing up. A more recent example of mass murder is the July 07, 2005 bombings in London, England. Four radical Islamic suicide bombers killed 52 people and injured 784 others in closely coordinated attacks on three London Underground trains and a double-decker bus.[7]

Serial killers are most frequently placed into one of four broad categories based on what motivates them: Visionary; Mission-Oriented; Hedonistic; Power or Control.[8,9] However, there are some who cannot be so easily pigeon-holed, Elizabeth Wettlaufer, a Canadian nurse serial killer (See Chapter 07) being an obvious example.[10]

Visionary serial killers are typically found to suffer from psychotic departures from reality, occasionally believing that they are being instructed to kill by the Devil or God. The American Herbert Mullin[11] is a textbook example of this class of serial killers. He believed that his dead father was telling him to make a number of human sacrifices to Nature in order to prevent a massive earthquake from destroying California.

Mission-Oriented serial killers believe that they must eradicate "undesirables" from the earth. Their victims can be almost any group of people based on race, religion, economics or just because they are different from the perpetrator. These killers typically are mentally stable; many of them see themselves as conducting a cleansing action in society. A good example of this type of serial killer is Joseph Franklin,[12] an American white supremacist who roamed the East Coast during the late 1970s and early 1980s killing up to an estimated 28 or more individuals in an effort to eradicate people whom he considered to be inferior, notably Jews and blacks.

Power or Control serial killers' main objective is to gain power over their victim, frequently torturing or abusing them as a way of completely dominating them. Ted Bundy[13] is a classic example of this type of killer and his story is presented in Chapter 4.

Hedonistic serial killing is the fourth category and is subdivided into three sub-types, as follows:

a. **Lust**. Sex is the main reason for these types of serial killers, and their sexual gratification is largely derived from torture and mutilation. Between 1997 and 2003, Paul Durousseau[14] raped and strangled seven young women in the Southeastern United States. He was also suspected of killing several women in Germany when he was stationed there with the US Army in the early 1990s.

Jeffrey Dahmer[15] was a particularly horrific lust serial killer. Known as the Milwaukee Monster, Dahmer killed and dismembered 17 men and boys between 1978 and 1991. In a sickening display of sadism, he sought to create "living zombies" who would passively obey him by drilling a hole into his victim's head and poring acid into it. He also dabbled with cannibalism in order to be sure that his victims would always remain as a part of him.

b. **Thrill**. The motive of a thrill serial killer is to create pain and terror in their victim. The thrill of the kill is what is most important to this category, and once the kill has occurred, they lose all further interest in the victim. Robert Christian Hansen[16] killed at least 17 women between 1971 and 1983. He abducted many of his victims and then released them in the wilderness so that he could then hunt them down, rape and murder them. Most of his killings were in Alaska, United States (USA). Hansen grew up in Iowa, and, not receiving the attention he felt he deserved from attractive girls in school, he cultivated an intense hatred and a desire to extract revenge on any good-looking female.

c. **Comfort**. These serial killers are a rather pragmatic group because they are motivated by materialism. They seek a comfortable lifestyle through acquiring money and possessions by killing. Dorothea

Puente,[17] who we meet in Chapter 9, killed a number of residents at her boarding home in Sacramento, USA so that she could cash their social security or pension cheques.

Approximately 15% of serial killers are female,[18] and they are most frequently categorized as comfort murderers who have a fairly strong preference for using poisons to kill their victims and who usually are acquainted with the victims (e.g.: family, friends). Having said that, Aileen Wuornos[19] (See Chapter 3) is very much an exception since she used a gun to kill her victims who were strangers rather than people she knew.

How do people become serial killers? The FBI has studied this issue extensively, and their conclusion is that a predisposition to serial killing results from a combination of biological, social and psychological factors.[20] They go on to state that while they cannot describe with any real level of accuracy exactly what each of these factors need to be, they do observe that the right combination, or is it the wrong combination, occurs only rarely. Using a slightly different approach, it can be said that in order for an individual to become a serial killer, there must be the combined effect of three factors: nature, nurture and notion (the Three N's). Nature refers to genetics, nurture involves the individual's upbringing and social development (or lack thereof), and notion refers to the decision to actually proceed with killing. The "Three N's" are important and will be elaborated upon in Chapter 12 where we look at what handwriting tells us about a serial killer's personality.

A myriad of psychologists have also studied this issue, and one of the best predictors for an individual to evolve into a serial killer is the Trauma Control Model[1] (TCM). Most serial killers are found to have had significant problems during their childhood development, and the TCM seeks to analyze how this happens. Early childhood trauma, in essence, can doom a child to engage in socially unacceptable behaviors in later life, and the TCM indicates that one of the primary factors in determining whether or not a child's behavior will further develop into murderous activities is the quality of the child's early parental environment. Extreme parental neglect and/or abuse can irrevocably damage, if not destroy, a child's ability to develop healthy emotional attachments with their parents and then, by extension, to other members of society. This level of damage will almost guarantee that the child's ability to relate to and value other members of society is largely nonexistent. A particularly severe example of this dynamic is seen with the serial killer Aileen Wuornos[19] (See Chapter 3), who suffered from an absolutely horrific upbringing. This behavior is usually diagnosed as either an antisocial personality disorder[21] and/or a borderline personality disorder, and as we will see in many of the serial killer cases presented in this book, these diagnoses are a common feature.

References

1. Holmes, R and Holmes, S (1998) Serial Murder ISBN 978-0-7619-1367-2

2. Morton, R (2005) Serial murder multi-disciplinary perspectives for investigators. Federal Bureau of Investigation.

3. Fuller, J and Hickey, E. (1999) Controversial Issues in Criminology

4. Wilson, Codi (March 03, 2021) "Alek Minassian found criminally responsible for Toronto van attack, guilty on all 26 counts" CP24 CTV News

5. Aggrawal, A (2005) Encyclopedia of Forensic and Legal Medicine ISBN 978-0-12-547970-7

6. "McVeigh biographers share 'chilling audiotapes' : Authors Michel and Herbeck reflect on McVeigh, OKC anniversary" (April 15, 2010) NBC News

7. Campbell, Duncan and Laville, Sandra (July 13, 2005) "British suicide bombers carried out London attacks, say police" The Guardian

8. Chase, Jennifer (May 07, 2015) Examining Four Types of Serial Killers *jchasenovelist.com*

9. The Four Types of Serial Killers TIM – This Interests Me

10. Dubinski, Kate (June 01, 2017) "Ex-nurse Elizabeth Wettlaufer felt 'red rage' before killing elderly patients" CBC News

11. Scott, Shirley (October 21, 2012) "Herb Mullin" *trutv.com*

12. "Joseph Franklin, white supremacist serial killer, executed" (November 20, 2013) BBC News

13. Sullivan, Kevin (2009) The Bundy Murders: A Comprehensive History ISBN 978-0-786444-26-7

14. Bell, Rachael (March 26, 2013) Paul Durousseua. The Jacksonville Serial Killer. *Crime Library truTV*

15. Ellens, J. Harold (2011) Explaining Evil, Volume 1 ISBN 978-0-313-38715-9

16. Krajicek, David (August 30, 2014) "Robert (Bob the Baker) Hansen

blamed his tortured adolescence for the rape and murder of dozens of women in Alaska in 1970's" New York Daily News

17. Kulczyk, David (2013) California Fruits, Flakes, and Nuts: True Tales of California Crazies, Crackpots and Creeps ISBN 978-1-61035-213-0

18. Kelleher, D and Kelleher, C (1998) Murder Most Rare: The Female Serial Killer ISBN 978-0-275-96003-2

19. Reynolds, Joseph (2016) Dead Ends: The Pursuit, Conviction, and Execution of Serial Killer Aileen Wuornos ISBN 978-1-5040-38669

20. Serial Murder (October 28, 2010) Federal Bureau of Investigation

21. Millie, Andrew (2008) Anti-Social Behaviour ISBN 978-0-335-23762-3

Chapter 2
GERARD SCHAEFER

AN UNREPENTANT SEXUAL DEVIANT

Gerard Schaefer is one of the worst "lust" category of serial killers to have ever lived. Formally charged with the abduction, torture, rape and murder of two young ladies, Shaefer has also been directly linked to nine other murders, and authorities strongly suspect that he was involved in even more.

Shaefer was 23 years old when he committed his first murder; his victim was someone he knew from their high school years. At his trial for murder, the prosecuting attorney described him as "the most sexually deviant person" that he had ever met.[1] Convicted and sentenced to life in prison in 1973, Schaefer was murdered by a fellow inmate at the Florida State Prison in 1995 for being an informer, being stabbed over 40 times in the head and body; his throat was slashed.

Figure 02-01: Gerard Schaefer

Wilton Manors police applicant photo of Schaefer. September 16, 1970

BACKGROUND

Born in 1946 in Wisconsin, Gerard Schaefer was the first of three children; his mother was a homemaker, and his father was a travelling salesman. Over the next 14 years, the family moved to Tennessee and Georgia before finally settling in Florida. Shaefer's father was an alcoholic who often verbally abused his wife and children. Schaefer greatly resented his father because of his constant criticism and also because he believed that he favored his daughter over himself and his brother.

Schaefer's deviant sexual behavior began to manifest itself in his early teenage years, and in retrospect it was an eerie forecast of things to come. He developed sexual fantasies of abusing women, and these gradually evolved into an obsessive fixation on sadomasochism in which he would engage in autoerotic asphyxia while wearing women's underwear after tying himself to trees in rural locations. While in high school, Schaefer's abnormal sexual antics did not go unnoticed. Several female classmates avoided him whenever possible because, as one young lady once said, he would "practically stand on his head to look up a girl's skirt."[2] He also became a peeping tom and is now known to have developed the habit of cross dressing.

In 1964 at the age of 18, Schaefer entered a social sciences program at a local community college but then switched his interest into teaching. In 1968 he entered the Florida Atlantic University (FAU) with the intention of earning a degree in education. In December 1968, Schaefer married his FAU classmate, Martha Fogg, but the marriage lasted only 16 months when Fogg divorced Schaefer citing his extreme cruelty and obsessive demands for sex as the reason. A summary of these and other key milestones in Schaefer's life over the next four years is presented in Figure 02-02.

As part of his FAU degree program, Schaefer was required to gain teaching experience by serving as a student teaching intern at a local high school. In September 1969, when Schaefer was 23 years old, he started an internship at Plantation High School, but this lasted for just over six weeks, when he was fired for refusing to accept any advice from his teaching mentors and for persistently forcing his own moral and political opinions onto his students.[3] This latter behavior was so egregious that a number of parents of his students complained to the high school authorities. It was also during this short period of time that one of his known victims, Leigh Bonadies, disappeared. See Figure 02-02. Bonadies went missing on September 1969, but her badly decomposed body was not found until April 1978 at a construction site.[4] Bonadies and Schaefer attended the same high school and knew one another. A private investigator hired by her family learned that Schaefer had talked to her on the day of her disappearance.

Schaefer soon managed to obtain another student teaching internship, this time at Stranahan High School, but this one didn't last very long either. After just seven weeks on the job, he was let go, the primary reason being his arrogance towards the permanent staff.[2] The date of his firing was May 1970, the same month that Martha Fogg divorced him (See Figure 02-02). It was just prior to him starting this job, however, that another young woman went missing and who would, years later, be linked to Schaefer. Carman Hallock (22 years old) disappeared on December 18, 1969. Her body has never been located, but two of her teeth and a gold pin that she was wearing when she disappeared were found in Schaefer's home in April 1973.[4]

Perhaps realizing that a teaching career wasn't the best idea, Schaefer applied to join the Broward County Police Department in September 1970. He was eventually accepted, completed his training and was posted to the Wilton Manors detachment as a patrolman in September 1971. Schaefer's luck at holding down a job continued to elude him, however, because after just six months he was dismissed from his position. Apparently, his senior officer learned that he had been stopping young female drivers for minor traffic violations and then surreptitiously using their car license plate numbers to access their personal details and contacting them for a date.[5] It was on January 04, 1972 when Schaefer had been with the Wilton Manors police detachment for three months that Belinda Hutchens went missing; she had briefly dated Schaefer a few months earlier. Her body was never recovered, but the address book that she always carried with her was found in Schaefer's home in April 1973.

Figure 02-02: Key Milestones in Gerard Schaefer's Life

1968 - December	Marries Martha Fogg
1969 - September	Began working as student teaching intern at Plantation High School
	Leigh Bonadies disappears
1969 - November	Fired at Plantation High School
1969 - December	Carman Hallock disappears
1970 - April	Began working as student teaching intern at Stranahan High School
1970 - May	Fired at Stranahan High School
	Martha Fogg divorces Schaefer
1971 - September	Begins working as patrolman for Broward County Police Department at Wilton Manors
	Marries Teresa Dean
1972 - January	Belinda Hutchens disappears
1972 - March	Dismissed from Broward County Police Department
1972 - June	Begins working as deputy at Martin County Sheriffs Department
1972 - July	Abducts Nancy Trotter and Paula Wells. Ties them to trees and restrains them with hangman nooses. Girls manage to escape
	Dismissed from Martin County Sheriffs Department. Charged with abduction and aggravated assault of Nancy Trotter and Paula Wells
1972 - September	Susan Place and Georgia Jessup disappear. Remains found in April, 1973
1972 - October	Mary Briscolina and Elsie Farmer disappear. Remains found in early 1973
1972 - December	Sentenced to one year in jail for abduction and aggravated assault of Nancy Trotter and Paula Wells
1973 - January	Barbara Wilcox and Collette Goodenough disappear. Skeletal remains found in January, 1977
	Begins serving sentence for abduction and aggravated assault of Nancy Trotter and Paula Wells
1973 - April	Named as suspect in murder of Susan Place and Georgia Jessup. Police obtain warrant to search Schaefer's home and his mother's home. Evidence also gathered linking Schaefer to disapperance of Leigh Bonadies, Carman Hallock, Belinda Hutchins, Mary Briscolina, Barbara Wilcox and Collette Goodenough. Evidence also included 37 Polaroid photographs of women being hung and/or mutilated
1973 - May	Formally charged with murder of Susan Place and Georgia Jessup

Schaefer didn't waste any time obtaining a new job after his dismissal, and law enforcement was what he wanted to remain in. After forging a letter of recommendation from the senior police officer at Wilton Manors, Schaefer was offered a job as a deputy at the Martin County sheriff's department. Unbelievably, this job lasted only one month before he was dismissed for the abduction and assault of two young female hitchhikers.

On July 21, 1972, Schaefer encountered Nancy Trotter (age 18 years) and Paula Wells (age 17 years) as they were hitchhiking to Jensen Beach. He offered to drive them to their destination the following day and they accepted; after all he was a police officer and so had to be trustworthy. Sadly, instead of heading for the coast the next day, he drove them to a very secluded forest area where he handcuffed and gagged them, took them further into the woods and then informed them that he intended to rape and murder them. Both girls were tied up, made to stand on exposed tree roots, and forced to precariously balance themselves with a noose that Schaefer put around their necks and attached to an overhead branch of the tree. Figure 02-03 shows a reenactment of just how the girls were tied up.

Figure 02-03: Nancy Trotter Reenactment of How She Was Tied to a Tree

Martin County Police Photograph

Shortly after tying the girls to the trees, Schaefer received an urgent call ordering him to report to the police station. While he was gone, both girls were eventually able to free themselves from their nooses and ran for help. When Schaefer returned a couple of hours later and found that they had escaped, he immediately called his commanding officer and brazenly claimed that he had decided to teach a couple of foolish young female hitchhikers a lesson about the risks of hitchhiking but that he "overdid the job." The girls were quickly located and were taken to the police station where they provided a detailed statement about what had happened and identified Schaefer as their assailant. For his part, Schaefer continued to insist that he had merely overreacted in his efforts to teach the girls a lesson and pointed out that other than a good scare, no harm had come to either one of them. His explanation was not believed by his commanding officers; he was immediately fired from his position as a deputy and was formally charged with abduction and aggravated assault.[6] Two weeks after his arrest, he was released on bail and a court date was set for December 1972. See Figure 02-02.

If someone thought that this turn of events would have put a damper on Schaefer's deviant behavior, they'd be wrong. Unbelievably, just three or four weeks after getting out on bail, Schaefer struck again, and again, and again.

Between the time of his release on bail in early August and December 22, four young ladies—Susan Place, Georgia Jessup, Mary Briscolina and Elsie Farmer—disappeared. On December 22, the judge decided to postpone Schaefer's formal sentencing until after the Christmas holiday season, on January 15, 1973. In retrospect the judge made what was a disastrous decision because two more young ladies—Barbara Wilcox and Collette Goodenough—disappeared on January 11, 1973, just four days before Schaefer began his time in prison.

On September 27, 1972 two teenagers—Susan Place (aged 17 years) and Georgia Jessup (aged 16 years)—met a man who called himself Jerry Shepherd and who offered to drive them to Fort Lauderdale to go to the beach. While picking up a few things for the trip, Susan Place introduced "Jerry" to her mother, who was immediately wary of the situation. She didn't stop Susan from going, but she did write down Jerry's car license plate number. Four days later, neither Susan Place nor Georgia Jessup had returned home, and their parents reported them as missing.[7] The police investigation didn't yield anything, and by early 1973 the case became cold, but that changed on April 01, 1973 when the very decomposed bodies of two individuals were found and were eventually identified as Place and Jessup.[8] Both individuals had numerous knife and machete marks on their spines and other bones. Their jaws had been fractured, and they had been decapitated after death. Crime scene evidence indicated that had been suspended from tree branches prior to their deaths. One body was partially clothed and the other was completely nude.

Because of the similarity of the crime scene with that of the Trotter and Wells abduction and assault, and because Place's mother positively identified Schaefer as the man who called himself Jerry Shepherd, the police obtained a search warrant for Schaefer's home and the home of his mother. Jessup's purse was among a number of incriminating pieces of evidence gathered during the searches.

The April 06, 1973 police search of Shaefer's home and that of his mother's uncovered the disturbing level of depravity of Schaefer's character. A number of hunting and skinning knives were found along with handguns, rope and dozens of pornographic magazines which Schaefer had modified to accentuate pictures of women being hanged and/or tied with ropes. Even more disturbing were the 37 Polaroid pictures taken of women who were being hung and mutilated in a forested area, but because of the poor quality of the pictures, none of the women could be conclusively identified. Finally, there were the hundreds of pages of stories (occasionally accompanied by drawings) that Schaefer had written in graphic detail over the years about the abduction, rape, torture and murder of a number of teenagers and young women who were described as whores, sluts or harlots.

But what about the other four young ladies who had disappeared between early August and December 22? The decapitated bodies of Mary Briscolina (aged 14 years) and Elsie Farmer (aged 13 years) were found by construction workers early in 1973,[9] and a gold chain and medallion belonging to Briscolina was found in Schaefer's home. The skeletal remains of Collette Goodenough (aged 19 years) and Barbara Wilcox (aged 19 years) were not discovered until January 1977; they had been discarded along a canal bank in Saint Lucie County, Florida.[2] Barbara Wilcox's driver's license and Collette Goodenough's passport were found in Schaefer's home. At the time of the police search of his residence, Schaefer was serving his sentence in the Martin County jail for the abduction and assault of Trotter and Wells. It was here that he was informed of the pending charge of murder of Place and Jessup and the public defender that was assigned to his case would be Elton Schwartz. (As an aside, Schwartz provided Schaefer with a spirited defense, and even though Schaefer was eventually convicted of murder, Schaefer was appreciative and complimentary of his efforts; that is, until Schwartz married Schaefer's second wife—Teresa Dean—in December 1973.[1])

Schaefer was formally charged with the murders of Place and Jessup on May 18, 1973 and was transferred to the Florida State Hospital for psychiatric evaluations. The final report by the psychiatrist stated that there was "evidence of considerable paranoid feelings, hostility, and anger, which erupts with little stress," that he had a "character disorder" and a "very active fantasy life."[2] It was also stated that he saw himself as "an eliminator of women he deemed immoral."[2] Schaefer's trial began on September 17, 1973 and was concluded on September 26 with two verdicts of first-degree murder; it only took the jury a little over five hours to come to their decision. Upon hearing the verdict, Schaefer continued to proclaim his innocence while stating "that's the roll of the dice. I had a good defense."[10]

Over the next 20 years, Schaefer continued to proclaim his complete innocence in any crimes, though in a personal letter in 1992 to Sondra London, a true crime writer who co-authored two books with him, he explained that, "When I nabbed Jessup and Place, I had been in the ghoul game for almost ten years, so I knew what to expect from these juicy young creatures… Doing doubles is far more difficult than doing singles, but on the other hand it also puts one in a position to have twice as much fun… When you have a pair of lively teenage bimbolinas bound hand and foot and ready for a session with the skinning knife, neither one of the little devils wants to be the one to go first…"[11]

Figure 02-04: Schaefer Post-Mortem Photo

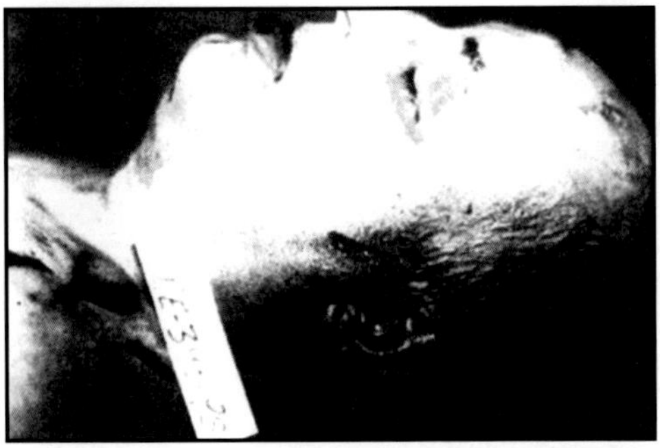

On December 03, 1995, Schaefer was killed by another inmate in his Florida State Prison cell. His throat had been slashed and he had been stabbed over 40 times in the face, neck and body; it was strongly suspected that he had been killed because he was deemed to be a prison informant.[12] The judge involved with his murder trial, having heard of Schaefer's death, was said to have exclaimed that "He's finally got the death sentence he ultimately deserved but couldn't be given,"[13] primarily because at the time of his trial Florida had banned the use of the death penalty.

HANDWRITING ANALYSIS - GENERAL PROFILE[14]

Schaefer's emotional makeup was one of moderation. He had a warm disposition and was not inclined to emotionally charged outbursts. He was also fairly intelligent with a good eye for detail and well organized in how he approached a problem. That being said, he was severely lacking in esteem, meaning that he had very little confidence in his own worth or his abilities. Low self-esteem is often linked to events in a person's upbringing such as unsupportive parents or stressful events such as divorce or numerous family moves to new locations. See Figure 02-05.

Figure 02-05: Basic Personality Traits[14]

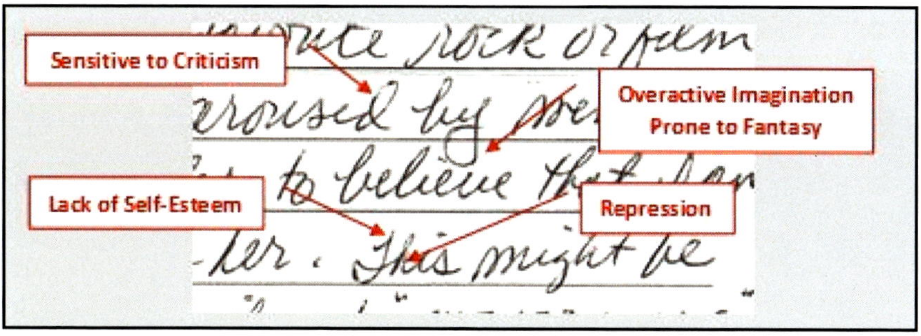

Note: Sensitive to Criticism – t and d stems that are looped. Overactive Imagination – Very wide loops on g, y, and j. Lack of Self-Esteem – Capital letters that are less than 2½ times the height of average lowercase letter. Repression – m, n and h letters that appear squeezed or pinched.

Schaefer's personality exhibited a fairly high degree of repression; 46% of his letters that can reveal this trait in fact did so. See Figure 02-05. With repression, an individual is unconsciously suppressing thoughts or memories that would otherwise make them feel emotional pain, embarrassment, guilt or shame. The unconscious is the area of the mind containing memories that are unavailable to voluntary recall, but they still influence behavior. Schaefer was also quite sensitive to criticism with an impressive 72% frequency score, which meant that he had a well-developed fear of disapproval and so was very quick to feel hurt or insulted. Unfortunately for Schaefer, his very overactive imagination intensified the effect of his sensitivity to criticism by causing him to imagine slights and then magnify them. See Figure 02-05.

Schaefer had a rather unusual combination of five traits, four of which were also very strong in their impact on his personality. See Figure 02-06. These traits worked synergistically and resulted in his extreme arrogance and his almost total refusal to take direction from others or adhere to basic social norms. Schaefer was very narrowminded (i.e.: 80% frequency of occurrence), extremely obstinate (i.e.: 90% frequency of occurrence) and totally opposed to listening to anyone who he perceived to be trying to exert any influence over him (i.e.: Defiance—100% frequency of occurrence). And if this were not enough, he was 100% determined to form his own conclusions with no regard to the views of others or society as a whole when it came to what he was planning to do (i.e.: Independent Thinking—100%). The net result of the combination of these behaviors was to create a mental cocoon for his thinking that completely insulated him from being influenced by what society would otherwise condemn him for doing. And what this collage of traits couldn't effectively deal with, his repression of uncomfortable feelings of guilt or shame kicked in and removed them from conscious thought.

Figure 02-06: Personality Traits Associated with Arrogance[14]

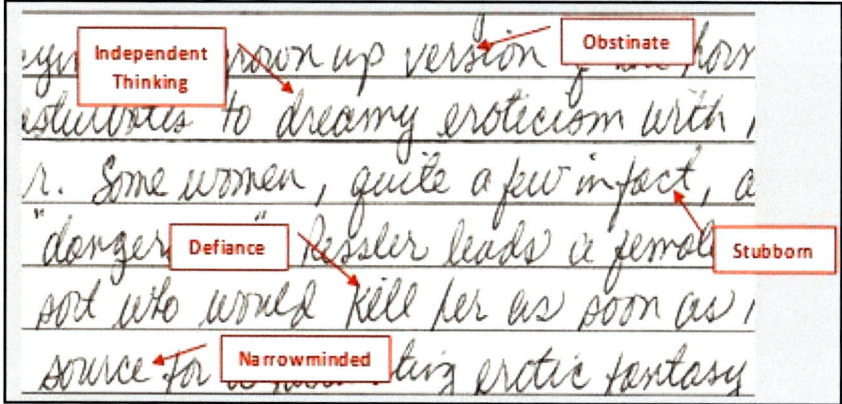

Note: Obstinate – Letter s with point at top. Narrowminded – Letter e that is narrow or completely closed. Defiance – Buckle of letter k higher than the height of average lowercase letter height. Stubborn – Wedge configuration in the base of d and t stems. Independent Thinking – Height of d and t stems are less than twice the height of average lowercase letters.

Schaefer was untrustworthy by nature. Of the six most commonly seen handwriting strokes associated with untrustworthiness,[15] he exhibited five of them. See Figure 02-07. The combined effect of these five strokes amounted to an overall frequency of occurrence rate of 25%, meaning that Schaefer could not be relied upon to be honest or truthful, and this was quite obvious throughout most of his life. Schaefer was quite smooth in his ability to conceal or cover up the truth (i.e.: Cap Stroke) and very adept at circumventing the truth without actually telling a lie, when it suited his purposes to do so (i.e.: Evasive). Deceit came naturally to Schaefer, and he would often scheme and distort the truth as part of his action plan (i.e.: Tear Drop Stroke). He was adeptly manipulative as he sought to unscrupulously control a situation or another individual. He was also quite capable of playing innocent or dumb or to inappropriately blame others in order to protect himself. All of these individual traits were on display in Schaefer's personality.

Figure 02-07: Trait of Untrustworthiness[14,15]

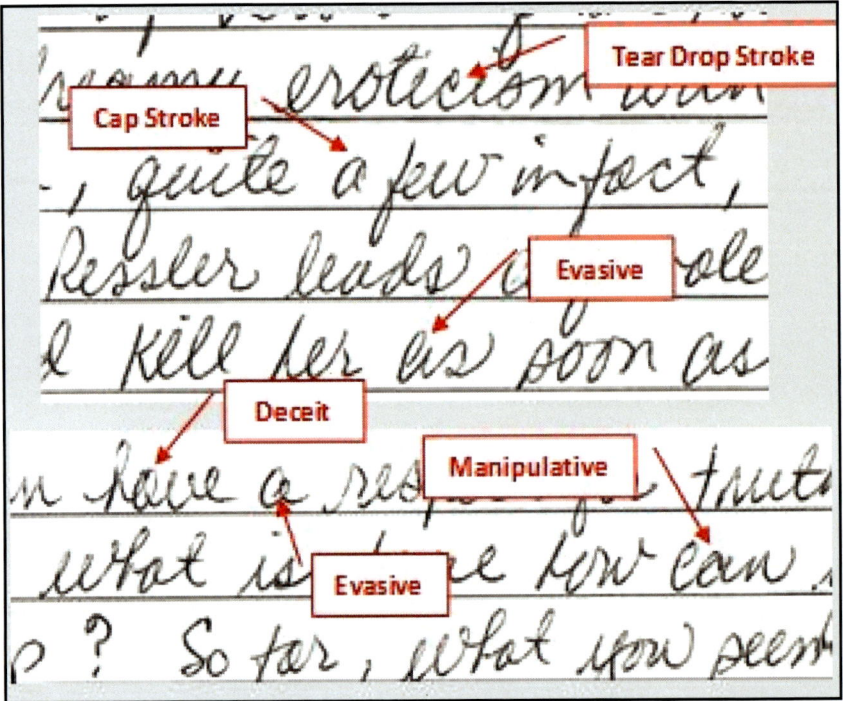

Note: Cap Stroke – Downward stroke of circle letters starts beyond the mouth of the letter. Evasive – Rounded hook that is interior and at the top of circle letter. Deceit – Approach stroke and final stroke in circle letters both form internal loops. Tear Drop Stroke – Tear drop configuration formed by counterclockwise stroke within a circle letter or letter c. Manipulative – Loop on interior, left hand side of lowercase circle letter combined with an interior hook.

HANDWRITING ANALYSIS - SERIAL KILLER PATHWAY[14]

Like so many other serial killers, Schaefer was consumed with anger, as evidenced by the high level of resentment strokes (18% frequency of occurrence) seen in his handwriting, as well as harpoon strokes and dot grinding. See Figure 02-08.

In Schaefer's personality, the anger associated with his feelings of resentment were made even worse by his overactive imagination (See Figure 02-05), and the presence of harpoons is especially worrisome, since they are a combination of a resentment stroke with a temper tick added in; it is for this reason that the presence of harpoon strokes is indicative of a person who is prone to acts of physical aggression.

The focus of all this anger is revealed by Schaefer's muddy writing and his need to dominate and domineer. See Figures 02-09 and 02-10. Muddy writing is produced by people with very significant sensory appetites, and we know that for Schaefer this was sexual. Being sensual is not a bad thing in-and-of-itself, but when there is an inclination of serious overindulgence, then this is when muddy writing strokes begin to emerge in handwriting. The dark side of this overindulgence becomes apparent with the presence of dominating and domineering strokes. Schaefer's need to take control of young women in order to satisfy his sexual urges became all the more deviant due to his overactive sexual fantasies that had masochistic overtones ever since he was a young man.

Figure 02-08: Negative Personality Traits[14]

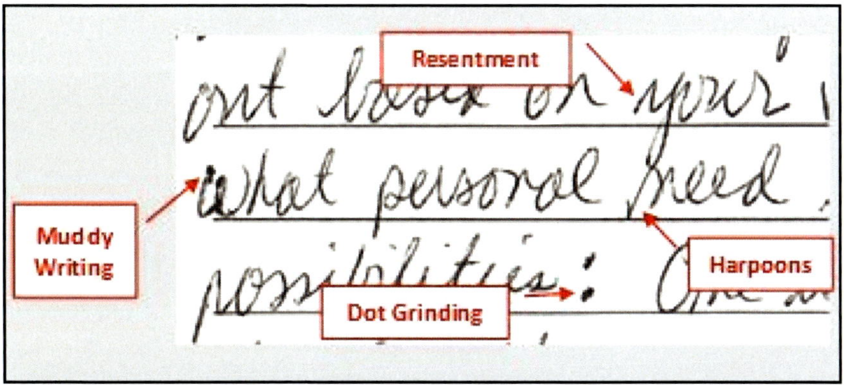

Note: Dot Grinding – Heavy pressure applied to punctuation. Resentment – Straight approach stroke starting at or below baseline. Harpoon – Resentment stroke that begins with a hook or temper tick. Muddy Writing – Blobs, blotches, cross-outs and partially filled-in circles and loops.

Figure 02-09: Personality Traits Associated With Schaefer's Pathway to Murder[14]

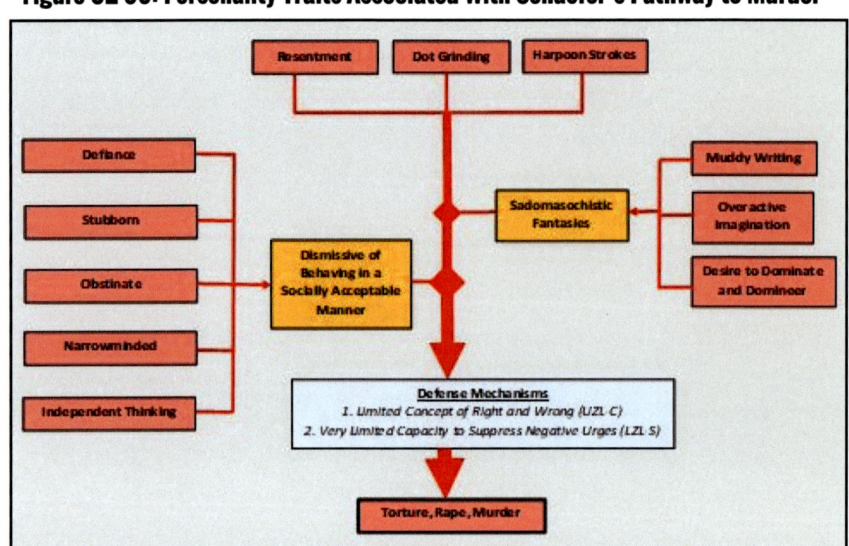

Schaefer's unbridled sadomasochistic inclinations were more than amply fueled by the large reservoir of anger that resided in his personality, and they found expression because of his complete ambivalence towards what society regarded as acceptable behavior (See Figure 02-06 and 02-09) and his weak defense mechanisms. See Figures 02-09 and 02-11.

Figure 02-10: Negative Personality Traits[14]

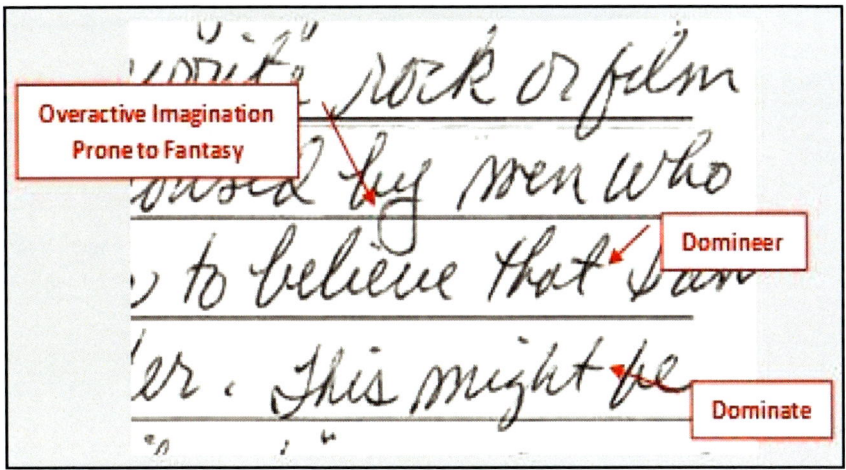

Note: Overactive Imagination – Very wide loops on g, y, and j. Dominate – Downward pointing t-bar with a blunt end. Domineer – Pointed t-bar that slopes downward.

As discussed in greater detail in Appendix One, a person's mind has two different types of defense mechanisms to prevent them from engaging in a socially unacceptable way. Conscientiousness is evaluated by the length of upper zone strokes (ie: UZL-C) and is expressed in their understanding and response to the concepts of good versus evil. Sublimation is evaluated by the length of lower zone strokes (i.e.: LZL-S) and acts like a sort of gate-keeper, rechanneling the energy associated with negative thoughts and urges into a behavior that is more socially acceptable. When the upper and lower zone lengths are two or more times the average height of the middle zone letters, then it can be said that these defense mechanisms are at normal strength. If the ratios are less than two, these mechanisms are said to be stunted in their effectiveness. Schaefer's scores were UZL-C = 1.8 and LZL-S = 1.2, indicating that he had a diminished capacity to curtail his abusive and murderous desires.

Figure 02-11: Defense Mechanism Personality Traits[14,16]

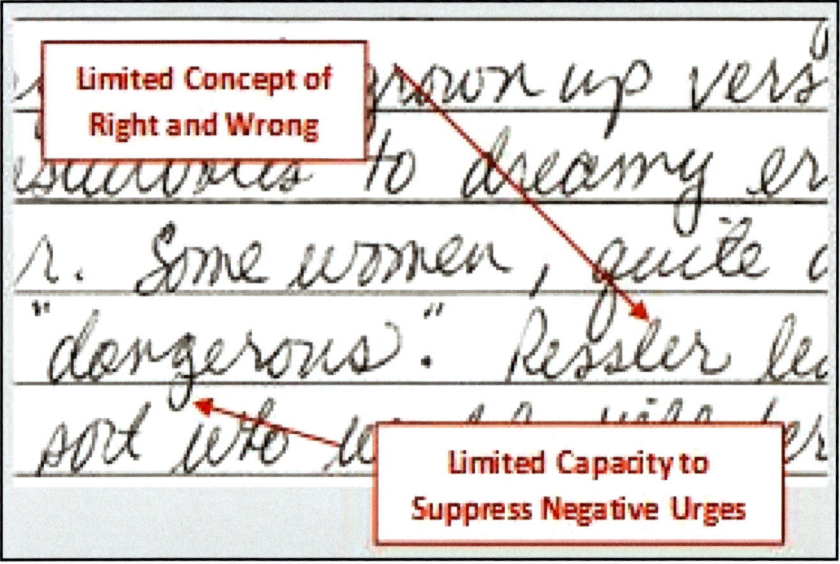

Note: Limited concept of right and wrong – Upper zone strokes in b, k, l and h are less than two times the average middle zone letter height. (i.e.: UZL-C). Limited capacity to suppress negative urges – Lower zone strokes in g, y, j and q are less than two times the average middle zone letter height. (i.e.: LZL-S)

Schaefer was a manipulative, conniving sexual deviant who cared about nothing other than satisfying his selfish desires. This was made even worse by his need to terrorize, humiliate and torture his victims. His crimes against a number of young women were abhorrent, more so because he refused to confess to any of them. No wonder he was compared to Britain's notorious serial killer, Jack the Ripper.[2]

References

1. Treadway, Tyler (November 28, 2010) Treasure Coast Newspapers
2. Kendrick, Patrick (2020) American Ripper: The Enigma of America's Serial Killer Cop ISBN978-1-604-52163-4
3. Campbell, Jean (July 11, 2021) "He Wore the Uniform of a Cop, but his True Passion Was Being a Serial Killer" *frontpagedetectives.com*
4. Cawthorne, Nigel (1993) Killers: Contract Killers, Spree Killers, Sex Killers, the Ruthless Exponents of Murder, the Most Evil Crime of All ISBN 978-0-752-20850-3
5. Cole, Catherine (2011) True Crime: Florida The State's Most Notorious Criminal Cases ISBN 978-0-8117-4439-3
6. Boyson, Mara (March 19, 2017) New York Daily News
7. Ellison, Jayne (April 06, 1973) The Palm Beach Post
8. Lane, Brian (1992) Real-Life Crimes ISBN 978-1-856-29736-3
9. Murder Database: Gerard Schaefer *web.ukonline.co.uk* (April 14, 2000)
10. Schaefer Guilty: "Off the Streets" (September 28, 1973) Fort Lauderdale News
11. London, Sondra "Killer Cop" *sondralondon.com*
12. Barker, Tom (2020) Aggressors in Blue: Exposing Police Sexual Misconduct ISBN 978-3-030-28440-4
13. "Killer Who Preyed on Women is Slain in Prison" (December 05, 1995) Tampa Bay Times
14. Racher, John (2022) Advanced Graphology: An Encyclopedia of Personality Traits Revealed in Handwriting ISBN 978-1-7773610-1-3
15. Racher, John (Spring 2022) *Traits of the Untrustworthy* The Graphologist - The Journal of the British Institute of Graphologists

Chapter 3
AILEEN WUORNOS

A HORRIBLE UPBRINGING WITH HORRIBLE CONSEQUENCES

The combination of paranoia, a persecution complex, a "powder keg" explosive temper and a pistol can never be good.

Aileen Wuornos was a hedonistic-comfort serial killer (See Chapter 1) who murdered seven men in Florida within the span of twelve months in 1989 and 1990; she was 33 years old when the killings took place. All of her victims were men who had engaged her services as a prostitute but who all got much more than they bargained for. Wuornos was convicted of six of the seven murders and spent twelve years on Florida's death row before being executed by lethal injection.

Figure 03-01: Aileen Wuornos

BACKGROUND

It could be said that Aileen Wuornos was doomed even before she was born. Her mother was only 14 years old when she married, and Aileen was her second child, born when her mother was 16.[1] After two years of marriage, she divorced her husband, who was diagnosed with schizophrenia and eventually committed suicide while in prison.[2] When Aileen was not quite four years old, her mother abandoned her children and left them with her alcoholic parents. She was often sexually assaulted and beaten by her grandfather and sadly, at what should have been an age of innocence, at the age of 11 she was trading sex at her school in exchange for cigarettes, drugs and food.[3] In 1970 when she was 14 years old, she became pregnant[4] after having been raped by an acquaintance of her grandfather.[5] At the age of 15, her grandfather threw her out of the house, and she began supporting herself through prostitution.[2]

Given this horrific childhood, it comes as no surprise that Wuornos was eventually diagnosed with an antisocial personality disorder and a borderline personality disorder, which also involved the repression of the myriad of overwhelmingly painful memories. While the concept of repression is not unanimously accepted within the field of psychiatry, the most common belief is that when it is severe enough it can result in the distortion of reality which then leads to illogical and anti-social behaviours.[6] Wuornos's tumultuous history adds credence to this observation about individuals suffering from significant repression. Her suffering also extended into recurrent attempts to end her own life; during the 1970s she had done so on six different occasions,[7] the last attempt in 1978 when she deliberately shot herself in the abdomen.

Wuornos's adulthood was dominated by two recurrent themes: violent outbursts involving physical assaults due to a hair-trigger and explosive temper,[8] and a morbid fascination with guns.

At the age of 18, she was arrested for disorderly conduct. When she was 20 years old, she was jailed for assault in a local bar in Florida and for beating her recently married, 69-year-old husband with his cane. The marriage was annulled in 1976 after only nine weeks. Later that same year, she was arrested again, this time for assaulting a bartender. In January 1986, Wuornos was charged with, among other things, resisting arrest and the obstruction of justice in Miami. In 1988 she was involved in an altercation with a bus driver.

Wuornos's first episode with a gun occurred in 1974 when she was arrested for firing a small caliber pistol from a moving car. In 1981 she was arrested for the theft of money and cigarettes from a convenience store while brandishing a gun, and in 1985 she was implicated for stealing a revolver and ammunition. The following year she accosted a male acquaintance and demanded money while pointing a gun at him.

Wuornos's pathway to murder (See Figures 03-02 and 03-05) began in November 1989 when she shot and killed Richard Mallory (See Figure 03-03), a man who was known to approach prostitutes, was a convicted sex offender and someone who, during his incarceration for rape in Maryland, was described as displaying serious sociopathic behavior. At her trial for Mallory's murder, Wuornos claimed that he had violently beat, raped and sodomized her after taking her to a secluded location for sexual services. It has been suggested that Mallory's brutal attack on Wuornos triggered an even more violent reaction on her behalf, culminating in her shooting him[9] in self-defense and her subsequent realization that his murder had no real effect on her in terms of remorse or regret. If this is correct, this realization then allowed her to proceed with other murders of men who were seeking sexual services from her as a means of obtaining their money, possessions and cars.

Figure 03-02: Crime Scene Photograph

Photo from blogspot.com

Wuornos's next murder occurred approximately six months later when she shot David Spears six times with a small caliber handgun. About one month after this murder, Wuornos shot Charles Carskaddon nine times, wrapped his body in an electric blanket and discarded it along a countryside road. One month after Carskaddon's murder, Wuornos killed Peter Siems, took his car and sold some of his possessions to a pawn dealer. It was this murder that eventually led to her arrest. She was seen abandoning his car,[10] and her fingerprints were found in it. Because she had a number of prior convictions in Florida, her fingerprints were on file and this led to the issuance of a warrant for her arrest that eventually occurred in January 1990.[11] Sadly, during the five-month period between when the arrest warrant was issued and the time of her apprehension, she murdered three other men: Troy Burress, Charles Humphreys, and Walter Antonio. See Figure 03-03.

Figure 03-03: Wuornos's Victims

RICHARD MALLORY DAVID SPEARS CHARLES CARSKADDON PETER SIEMS

TROY BURRESS CHARLES HUMPHREYS WALTER JENO ANTONIO

Wuornos was arrested as part of the police investigation of the disappearance of Peter Siems and because she was definitively linked to the sale of some of his possessions. However, the initial charge did not include murder because his body had not been found. The break in this case and also for the other murders came about only because Wuornos's long-time, live-in partner Tyria Moore agreed to cooperate with the police and elicit a confession from Wuornos in exchange for immunity from prosecution; she had been involved with the illegal sale of some of the victims' possessions. Armed with the information provided by Moore, the police were eventually able to get Wuornos to confess to the murders of the seven men mentioned above. Ironically perhaps, Wuornos was never charged and convicted of the murder of Peter Siems, the case that first led to the discovery of her killing rampage.

The reason was two-fold: his body was never found, and authorities already had enough evidence to convict Wuornos for the other six killings.

It was during Wuornos's trials and her time on death row that the sheer magnitude of her paranoia and feelings of persecution became evident. She initially claimed that all seven men had raped her and she had shot them in self-defense,[12] but then she changed her story and said that it was only Mallory who had raped her and that the others "only began to start to.[9]" Later on, she dropped the self-defense story and said, perhaps rather pragmatically, that her motive was robbery and the fact that she didn't want to leave any witnesses. In 2001 when all of her appeals had been denied, she told the Florida Supreme Court that, "I killed those men…robbed them as cold as ice…and I'd do it again too…[because] I have hate crawling through my system."[13] She also provided a long litany of grievances about people who she said were out to punish, torment or kill her. At various times and under different circumstances, she accused the mafia, government agents, the prison guards, the police, the "system" and even the biographer who had been interviewing her for a book and movie. During the last interview before her execution, she claimed that her head was being crushed by "sonic pressure" and said, "Thanks a lot, society, for railroading my ass."[14]

Wuornos was executed on October 09, 2002 and her ashes were, according to her last wish, scattered beneath a tree in Michigan where she grew up.

HANDWRITING ANALYSIS - GENERAL PROFILE[15]

When Wuornos was not in an angry mood (which by all accounts wasn't often), she could be quite personable. In fact, the biographer who had a number of one-on-one interviews with her said that "when she wasn't in those extreme moods, there was an incredible humanity to her."[8] This was validated by her handwriting, which indicates that she had the capacity to be sensitive to and considerate of other people's feelings. Unfortunately, people who have been diagnosed with an anti-social personality disorder are often aggressive and hostile, with poorly regulated tempers, and can lash out violently with little provocation or frustration.[8]

Wuornos had a fairly high intellectual effectiveness score. She could quickly comprehend situations and would assimilate information rapidly; see Figure 03-04. She was quite decisive and rather well organized in her thought processes. She had a natural ability to come quickly to the point in terms of her thinking and acting, and this trait worked to positively reinforce her decisiveness. Wuornos's directness, that is, her desire to save time by getting straight to the point, was a double-edged sword of sorts. While it did add to her quick intellect, it also reinforced her well-documented inclination towards angry responses to people who annoyed or offended her (intentionally or not). People like Wuornos who have a strong trait of directness (See Figure 03-04) are often irritated by people who are not, such as indecisive individuals or those who want to talk around a subject and engage in long-winded commentaries before saying what's really on their mind. Wuornos's quickness to anger was only made worse by her directness, and this trait is seen in her handwriting with a 50% frequency of occurrence.

Like many other serial killers, Wuornos had very little self-esteem and an overabundance of obstinance. In fact, in terms of the latter there is a 100% frequency of occurrence rate, which is highly unusual. As seen in Figure 03-04, every letter "s" has the diagnostic stroke of a sharp pointed tip. This level of obstinance made Wuornos extremely hard to deal with because she would flatly refuse to be persuaded about something that was contrary to what she believed in, regardless of the amount of evidence that was provided. This one trait significantly reinforced her paranoia and her feelings of persecution.

Perhaps surprisingly, Wuornos had a fairly well-developed sense of dignity, as evidenced by the number (i.e.: 69% frequency) of retraced "d" and "t" stems; see Figure 03-04. The strength of this trait enabled her to strive to maintain an inner sense of worthiness, even in the face of her very challenging life.

Wuornos was rather vain, especially when it involved her personal demeanor and how she looked. Vanity is evidenced by "d" and "t" stems that are greater than 2.5 times the average middle zone letter height; see Figure 03-04.

Figure 03-04: Wuornos's Handwriting[15]

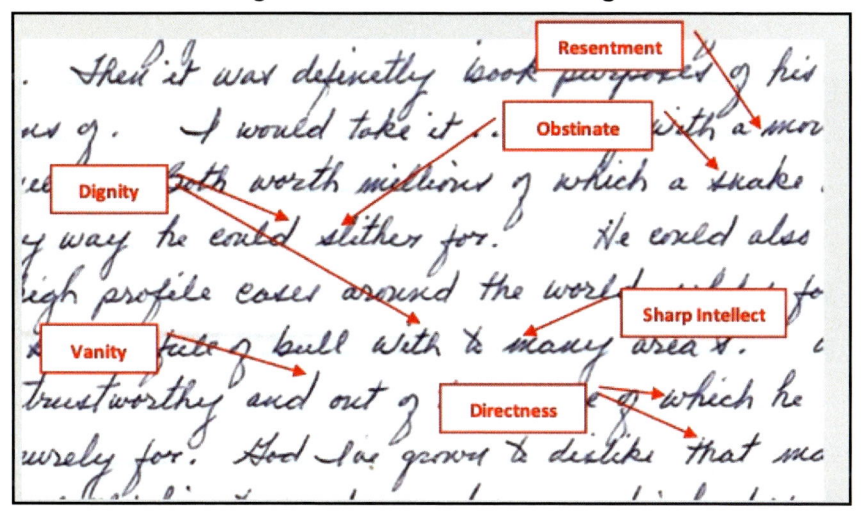

NOTES: Resentment – Straight approach stroke starting at or below baseline. Obstinate – Letter s with point at top. Dignity – Retraced t and t stems. Direct – Absence of approach strokes. Sharp Intellect – Humps on m and n letters are pointed, with some retracing. Vanity – Height of d and t stems are greater than 2.5 times the average middle zone letter height.

HANDWRITING ANALYSIS - SERIAL KILLER PATHWAY[15]

Of the four personality traits that contributed to Wuornos's serial killer activities, three of them are rarely seen. In Figure 03-04 we see an example of her resentment stroke, and the analysis of the entire specimen yielded a 20% frequency of occurrence rate, a rate significantly higher than what is typically seen in the population, but which is quite common with serial killers. The power of this negative trait within Wuornos's personality is amplified by her vanity, directness and her very strong material imagination (i.e.: the high frequency of lower zone loops). With her vanity, the resentfulness was made even worse in reaction to anyone who belittled the high opinion she had for herself, and through the synergistic combination of resentfulness and strong directness, Wuornos had absolutely no patience for anyone who she perceived to be a waste of her time.

As seen in Figure 03-05, the three very rare traits seen in a serial killer's pathway to murder are shark teeth strokes (See Figure 03-06), X-strokes (See

Figure 03-07) and strokes indicative of repression (See Figure 03-08). In a database of over 200 individual handwriting specimens, shark teeth and X-strokes were only detected once (not in the same specimen) and only occurred 1-2 times in each of the specimens. In Wuornos's handwriting, the shark teeth occurred 8.6% of the time, and the X-strokes were seen in 8.3% of all words. Shark teeth strokes are associated with individuals who are described as two-faced backstabbers who strike out without warning. X-strokes are seen in individuals who utilize conflict and confrontation to take advantage of others.

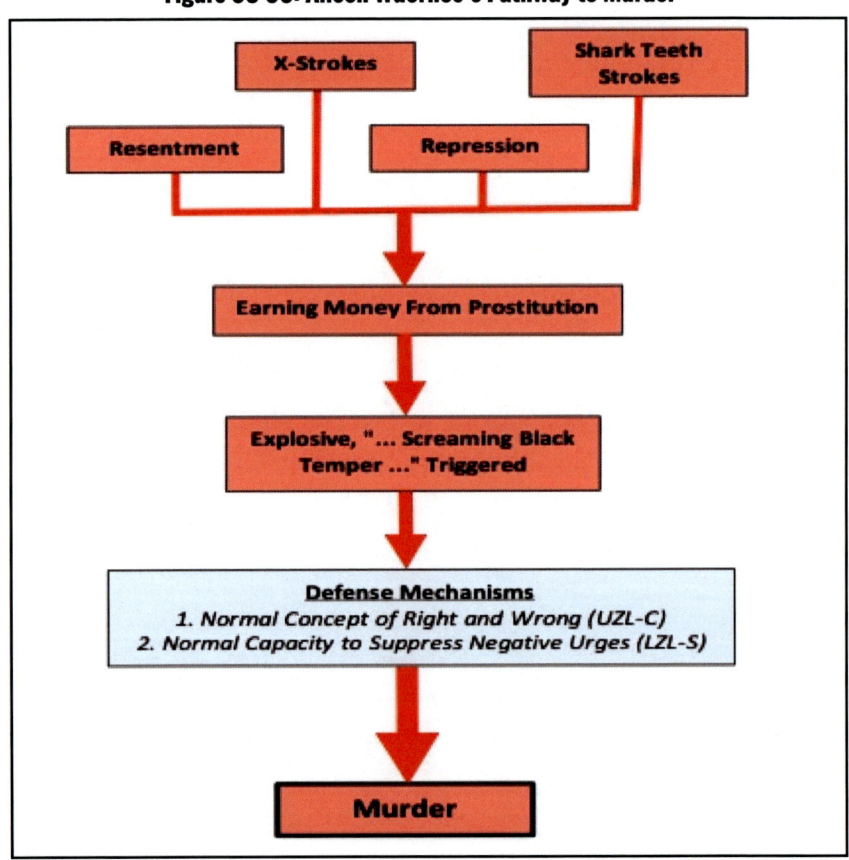

Figure 03-05: Aileen Wuornos's Pathway to Murder[15]

```
    X-Strokes              Shark Teeth Strokes
         │                        │
  Resentment     Repression
         │           │
         └─────┬─────┘
               ▼
   Earning Money From Prostitution
               ▼
   Explosive, "... Screaming Black
         Temper ..." Triggered
               ▼
         Defense Mechanisms
   1. Normal Concept of Right and Wrong (UZL-C)
   2. Normal Capacity to Suppress Negative Urges (LZL-S)
               ▼
            Murder
```

Figure 03-06: Shark Teeth Stroke[15]

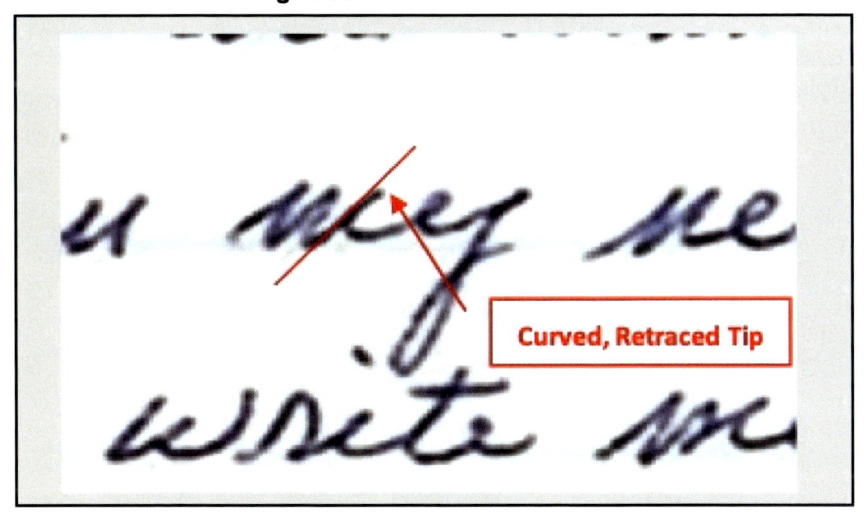

Curved, Retraced Tip

NOTES: Shark Teeth Stroke – Retraced hooks on mounds of m, n, h.

Figure 03-07: X-Stroke[15]

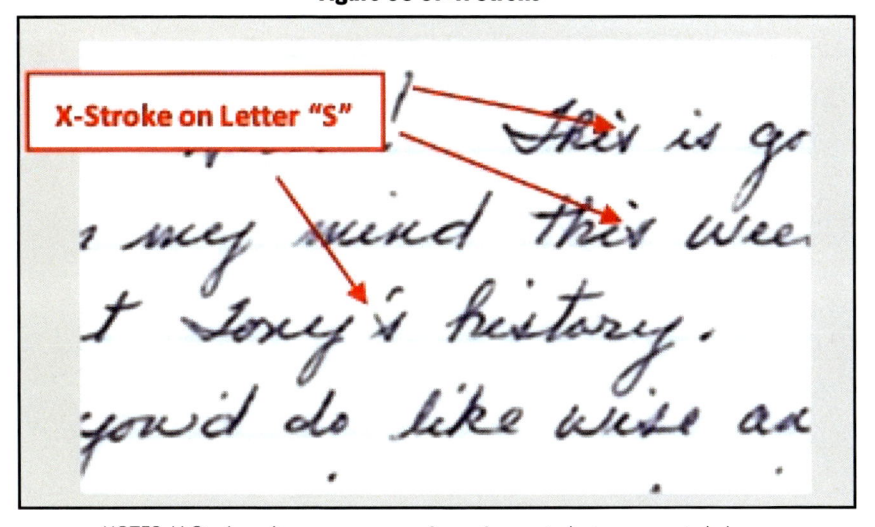

X-Stroke on Letter "S"

NOTES: X-Stroke – Any cross or some form of an x-stroke in unexpected places.

Repression is a trait used to avoid or reject memories that are emotionally painful to the individual and is actually on a continuum of behavior with suppression and the associated effects that they have in the personality. Suppression is conscious and sporadic whereas repression is unconscious and frequent. The relationship between the two traits and their impact on a personality is best explained by way of an analogy. A low level of suppression is like having a benign lump just under your skin. It is harmless in that it is localized and non-cancerous. High levels of suppression or low levels of repression are like having a small, single nodule on your kidney. The nodule is cancerous, but it is confined to the nodule; it isn't spreading. A significant level of repression such as what Wuornos exhibited with a 42% frequency of occurrence is equivalent to having metastatic lung cancer. The cancer is spreading throughout the body, much like how severe repression negatively affects the entire personality.

Figure 03-08: Repression Strokes[15]

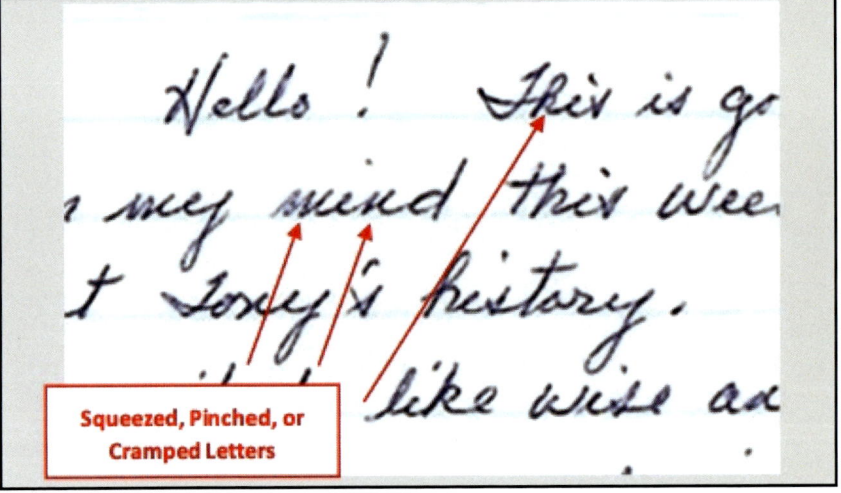

Squeezed, Pinched, or Cramped Letters

NOTES: Repression – Letters are squeezed, causing upstrokes to retrace downward strokes in m, n, h, r letters.

The combined effect of these four negative traits were obviously significant enough to overwhelm Wuornos's defense traits of conscientiousness and sublimation (See Appendix One), even though their respective scores were UZL-C = 2.3 and LZL-S = 2.8 respectively. For a normal, healthy personality these scores would be indicative of someone whose defense mechanisms for controlling undesirable behavior would be adequate. However, given all of Wuornos's strong negative traits that were made even stronger from reinforcing traits such as directness, defiance and vanity, she was unable to contain her murderous impulses.

In Chapter 1, we learned that in order for an individual to become a serial killer there must be the combined effect of three factors: Nature, Nurture and Notion (the Three N's). As one can imagine, it is very difficult to describe what these factors are for any one individual serial killer because having the appropriate information is almost impossible to definitively obtain in retrospect. In Wuornos's case, however, it seems that we can get at least a glimpse into what each of these three factors were.

With regards to nature, we need only to look at Wuornos's father's diagnosis of schizophrenia to see the possibility of a genetic factor coming into play. Her horrific early childhood in which she was abandoned by her mother, sexually abused by her grandfather, and the callous disregard for her safety by her grandmother who ignored the abuse that was constantly going on, all contributed to the serious damage inflicted upon how she was *nurtured*. The third factor—*notion*—can perhaps be identified as the time when Wuornos was beaten, raped and sodomized by the violent sociopath Richard Mallory.[16] As was suggested previously, it was at this time that Wuornos discovered that committing murder was not nearly so emotionally traumatic as one might otherwise think it would be, and so she incorporated into her behavior pattern on a go-forward basis. Once she had committed that murder, it is rather telling that the next six killings all occurred within the next twelve months.

References

1. Reynolds, Joseph (2016) Dead Ends: The Pursuit, Conviction, and Execution of Serial Killer Aileen Wuornos. ISBN 978-1-5040-3866-9

2. Howard, Amanda and Smith, Martin (2004) River of Blood: Serial Killers and Their Victims ISBN 978-1-58112-518-4

3. Howard, Peter (2007) Female Serial Killers: How and Why Women Become Monsters. ISBN 978-0-425-21390-2

4. Macleod, Marlee (June 02, 2009) "Aileen Wuornos: Killer Who Preyed on Truck Drivers – A Poor Beginning". *Crime Library*

5. Silvio, Heather; McCloskey, Kathy; Ramos-Grenier, Julia (May – June 2006) "theoretical consideration of female sexual predator serial killers in the United States" Journal of Criminal Justice

6. Repression *PsychologyToday.com*

7. Myers, Wade; Gooch, Erik; Meloy, J. Reid (May 2005) "The Role of Psychopathy and Sexuality in a Female Serial Killer". Journal of Forensic Sciences

8. Millie, Andrew (2008) Anti-Social Behaviour ISBN 978-0-3352-3762-3

9. "Aileen Carol Wuornos" The Clark County Prosecuting Attorney (September 14, 2008)

10. Macleod, Marlee (2003) "Aileen Wuornos: Killer Who Preyed on Truck Drivers" *Crime Library* Court TV

11. Kennedy, Dolores and Nolin, Robert (1994) On a Killing Day: The Bizarre Story of Convicted Murderer Aileen Carol Wuornos ISBN 978-1-56171-293-9

12. Dwyer, Kevin and Fiorillo, Jure (November 06, 2007) True Stories of Law & Order: SVU ISBN 978-0-425-21735-1

13. Zarrella, John (October 15, 2002) "Wuornos' last words: 'I'll be back' " CNN

14. Cheshire, Gidfrey (January 14, 2004) "Charlize Thernon's career-making performance anchors a harrowing tale" *Indy Week*

15. Racher, John (2022) Advanced Graphology: An Encyclopedia of Personality Traits Revealed in Handwriting ISBN 978-1-7773610-1-3

16. Aileen C. Wuornos v. State of Florida. (November 19, 2004) Florida Supreme Court.

Chapter 4

TED BUNDY

DID HE HAVE A SPLIT PERSONALITY?

A co-worker thought he was "kind, solicitous and empathetic."[1] She was wrong.

Ted Bundy was born on November 24, 1946 to Eleanor Cowell at the Elizabeth Lund Home for Unwed Mothers in Burlington, Vermont, USA. His early childhood was spent being raised by his maternal grandparents who treated him as their son; he was told that his mother was his older sister. By all accounts, life was not easy in this household. His grandfather was an ill-tempered bigot who occasionally talked to spirits and frequently beat his wife, his dog and physically abused his children.[2,3] His grandmother was a timid soul who often had to undergo electroconvulsive therapy for depression.

Bundy grew up to become what the author Ann Rule described as "a sadistic sociopath who took pleasure from another human's pain and the control he had over his victims, to the point of death and even after."[1] Bundy was also a career thief. He shoplifted almost everything he ever owned,[4] and when he couldn't steal the item itself, he purchased it using money or credit cards that he stole from women's purses left unattended in shopping carts at grocery stores.[5] The actual possession of stolen items was very important to Bundy, and this obsession with possessing things was also a key motivation for the rape and murder of many of his victims. As he described to one of the police investigators involved in his case, sexual assault fulfilled his urge to "totally possess" his victims. He went on to say that the "ultimate possession was…the taking of life and then…the physical possession of the remains."[6] One of his defense lawyers felt that he was consumed by rage against women and that he viewed their murders as "his life's accomplishments."[3] Bundy was convicted of three murders in Florida[7] and was executed in January, 1989 by electrocution at the age of 43. (See Figure 04-01.) Just prior to his death, he confessed to 30 murders (20 of which were eventually confirmed), but he was suspected of having killed many more. Most of his assaults occurred in California, Colorado, Utah and Oregon.

Figure 04-01: Ted Bundy Autopsy Photograph

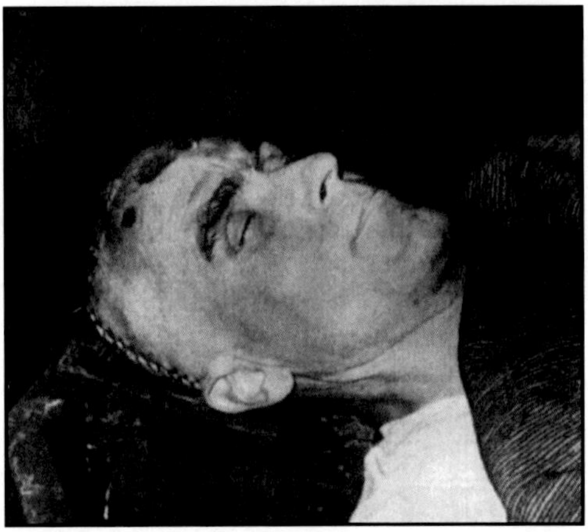

NOTE: Bundy was executed by electrocution. (See marks on forehead.)

BACKGROUND

A host of psychiatry experts had an opportunity to examine Bundy, and it is interesting that they struggled to pin down exactly what sort of disorder he was suffering from. The majority tended towards a diagnosis of antisocial personality disorder (ASPD) because he displayed a number of personality traits commonly found in ASPD patients. For instance, even though he would appear to be personable he had no true personality. He had the ability to tell the difference between right and wrong, but this had no real effect on his behavior, and he would not feel any guilt or remorse about his actions. Dr. Dorothy Lewis, a professor of psychiatry and an expert on violent behavior, struggled with deciding what Bundy's problem was.[2,3] While she eventually settled on ASPD as the most likely diagnosis, she did also consider the possibility that he had a multiple personality disorder, otherwise known as dissociative identity disorder[17] (DID).

In the early stages of Bundy's evolution as a serial killer, he tended to engage in violent attacks on his sleeping victims.[5] These attacks were brutal and occasionally involved a sexual assault using a foreign object. Many of these victims were killed, though a few survived with permanent and life-altering injuries. As Bundy grew more confident in his predator abilities, he would typically lure his victims to his vehicle where he would then suddenly and violently beat them into unconsciousness with a club, a crowbar or some other instrument, handcuff them and then drive them to a secondary location that he had carefully preselected, where he would then beat and strangle them as he raped them. Their clothing was often removed and occasionally replaced with other apparel. A number of times he would, over a period of time, revisit the corpse and perform sex acts on them.[8] In approximately twelve instances, he decapitated the corpse and kept the heads in his apartment before eventually discarding them.

Bundy was at his most predatory worst in the Northwest United States, especially Colorado and Utah. After having attracted enough attention by the police to lead to his arrest, he managed to escape and then fled to Florida. It was there that his final acts of depravity were to occur, but perhaps because he was a fugitive and was relatively unfamiliar with the area, he reverted to only violent attacks on his victims.[2] It was in Florida where he was apprehended and charged, convicted and executed for three murderous assaults.

In amongst Bundy's numerous murders and assaults, there are two episodes that stand out for their audaciousness. July 14, 1974 was a sunny, hot day, and so the beach at the Lake Sammamish State Park in Washington state was crowded with young people and families. According to a number of eye witnesses, a young man with a pleasing demeanor and his arm in a sling was seen approaching young women, asking them if they would help unload his sailboat from his car. A number of them refused, but one young lady, 23-year-old Janice Ott, agreed.[9] About four hours later, 19-year-old Denise Naslund was seen going to the washroom but she never returned.[5] Towards the end of the day, both were reported as missing, but a massive search revealed nothing. (See Figure 04-02.) On September 06, a pair of hunters made a grisly discovery along a service road approximately three kilometers from the Lake Sammamish State Park: the skeletal remains of two young women who were eventually identified as Ott and Naslund.[10] In addition to their remains, investigators also found human bones from two other individuals.[11]

Figure 04-02: Janice Ott, Ted Bundy and Denise Naslund

On January 15, 1978, at a little after 2:00 A.M., Bundy broke into a women's residence at the Florida State University (FSU) and, over the span of just fifteen minutes, viciously assaulted four young ladies while they slept, killing two.[5,12,13] Margaret Bowman was beaten with a large stick and strangled to death with a nylon stocking. Lisa Levy was beaten and strangled to death. She also had bite marks on her body and had been sexually assaulted with a hair spray bottle. Kathy Kleiner was attacked and was left for dead with a broken jaw and deep cuts on her shoulder. Karen Chandler was also attacked but survived, though she had a concussion, a broken jaw, a loss of teeth and a broken finger. As if these attacks weren't enough (See Figure 04-03), after leaving the sorority house, Bundy broke into Cheryl Thomas's apartment and attacked her, leaving her with a broken jaw, a fractured skull and a dislocated shoulder. She survived the attack but was left with permanent damage.[5]

Figure 04-03: Crime Scene Photograph In Women's Residence, FSU

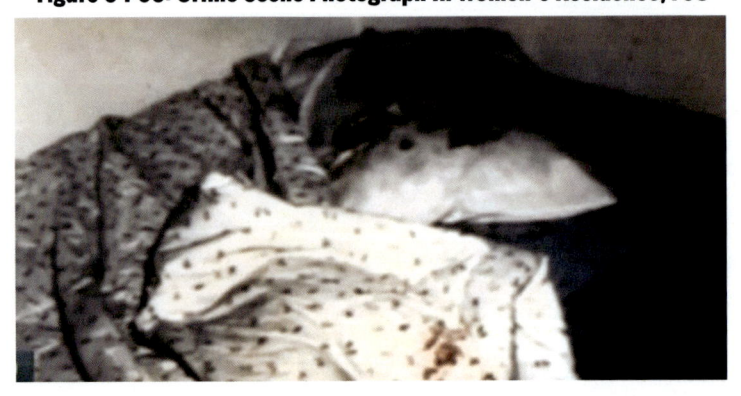

One month later, Bundy was arrested for driving a stolen vehicle.[2] In the car police found a number of stolen credit cards, a stolen television set and three identification cards belonging to the FSU students who had been assaulted the previous month. This brought his killing rampage to an end.

An important point to be made about Bundy was the fact that he was not a threat to all women. Over the years, he had a number of close female acquaintances and was romantically involved with at least four of them. None of these women ever became a victim; he only attacked young, attractive women who he had never met and did not know beforehand at all. Bundy's romantic relationships appear to have all been rather platonic; in at least one instance two of these relationships were occurring simultaneously. Just prior to his execution, Bundy explained to Elizabeth Kloepfer, whom he had been involved with since 1969, that whenever he started to feel the urge to kill, he deliberately stayed away from her.[2]

HANDWRITING ANALYSIS - GENERAL PROFILE[14]

Bundy's emotions were dominated by strong urges that would predispose him to react immediately and without thinking. These were reinforced by his stronger than normal depth of feeling, meaning that he found it difficult to forget the details of an emotionally charged situation. Bundy had a natural exuberance about him that people found to be infectious.

Bundy was a careful thinker, and, before making a decision or drawing a conclusion about something, he wanted to gather enough information and then "mull it over." He was naturally curious about most things, and while he was gathering information prior to making a decision, he characteristically had a lot of questions of clarification. Because of this rather methodical approach to problem solving, Bundy was rarely the first to speak up in a group situation, and this was reinforced by his strong reticence. The flip side to this is, when he did speak up, he would do so with a lot of enthusiasm which bolstered people's confidence in him. See Figure 04-04. Bundy's intellectual effectiveness rating was at a moderate level due in part to his good attention to little details and his capacity to think for himself and not be swayed by what others might be saying or doing.

Like so many other serial killers, Bundy had very low self-esteem. In his own mind he had no self-respect; this condition is often linked to events in a child's upbringing such as unsupportive parenting.

In dealing with others on a day-to-day basis, Bundy was quite careful about what he said and how he said it. This was part of his desire to conceal the truth from others, just as his ability to be frustratingly evasive when responding to questions that he didn't want to answer truthfully. Bundy was extremely narrowminded and obstinate. See Figure 04-04. These two traits were so pervasive within his personality that he had absolutely no respect for people's ideas that differed from his own and would cling tenaciously to an opinion or course of action despite common sense or reason. These personality shortcomings were in full display during his trial in Florida for the FSU assaults and murders. Despite having five court-appointed lawyers as his defense team, Bundy insisted on unilaterally orchestrating his legal defense. As one of these lawyers would say later about Bundy's behavior, "all that mattered to him...was that he be in charge."[3]

Figure 04-04: Personality Traits[14]

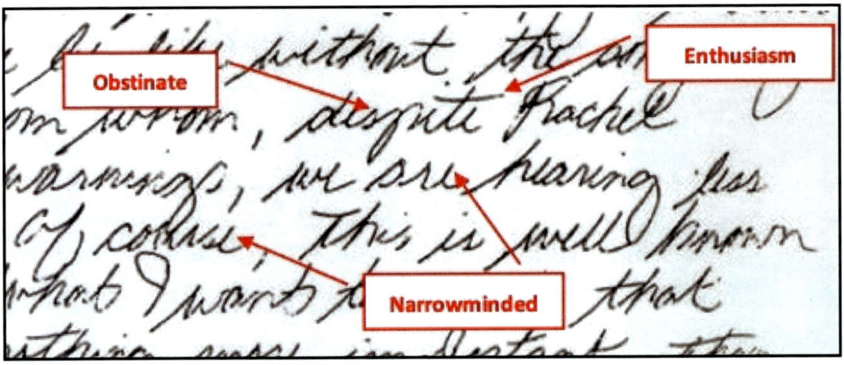

NOTE: Obstinate – Letter s with point at top. Enthusiasm – t-bars longer than average middle zone letter width. Narrowminded – Letter e that is narrow or completely closed.

HANDWRITING ANALYSIS - SERIAL KILLER PATHWAY[14]

One of the defense lawyers assigned to Bundy's case described him as "the very definition of heartless evil."[3] You would think that someone as bad as that would obviously have defense mechanism scores[15] that would be very, very low. See Appendix One. You would be mistaken however, because his UZL-C score was 2.0 and his LZL-S score was 2.2. See Figure 04-05. How could this be?

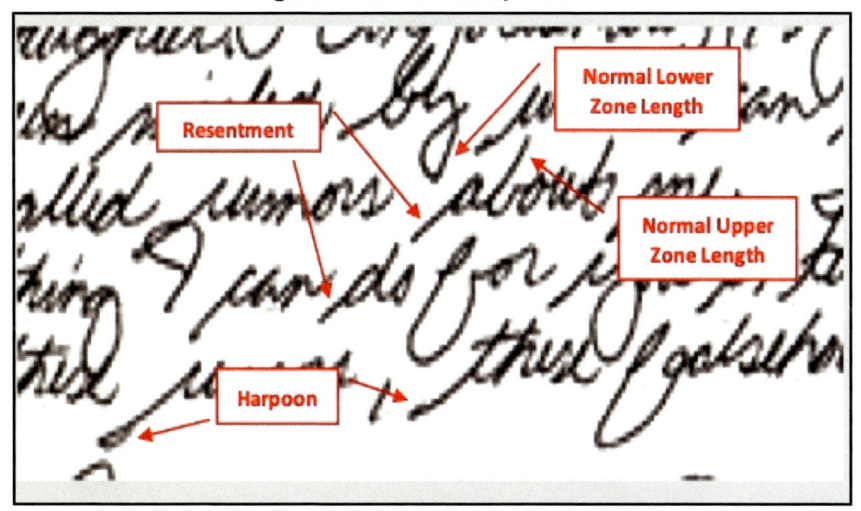

Figure 04-05: Personality Traits[14,15]

NOTE: Resentment – Straight approach stroke starting at or below baseline. Harpoon – Resentment stroke that begins with a hook or temper tick.

Bundy's case is, from a graphological perspective at least, very revealing when it comes to understanding the limitations of a personality's defense mechanisms. Under normal circumstances with a typical human being, his defense mechanism scores would have been enough to curtail any socially unacceptable behaviors. Bundy, however, was anything but normal because he had some monstrously negative traits dwelling within his very dark basement.[23] Bundy's handwriting (See Figure 04-05) shows an astonishingly high level of resentment; 43.8% of the words he wrote had the resentment stroke. And if that were not enough, an additional 19.6% of his words had the harpoon stroke. Harpoon strokes look like resentment strokes that begin with a temper tick. Whenever you see a harpoon, you know that you are dealing with a person who has major resentfulness and who is capable of acts of physical aggression. Even the presence of just a few harpoons is to be taken seriously, and Bundy had an almost unprecedented number of them. And then there were the maniac "d" strokes. In a specimen of Bundy's writing, the slant of two of the 18 "d" letters was markedly more pronounced (i.e.: greater than 10%) than the average degree of slant of the rest of his writing. When a maniac "d" is seen it is indicative of a person who can have sudden, uncontrolled and violent actions followed by a rapid return to normal behavior, and this is an almost exact description of the assaults that Bundy would engage in. When one considers the combined effect of these three extremely negative traits, it should be of no surprise that Bundy's defense mechanisms were overwhelmed. See Figure 04-06.

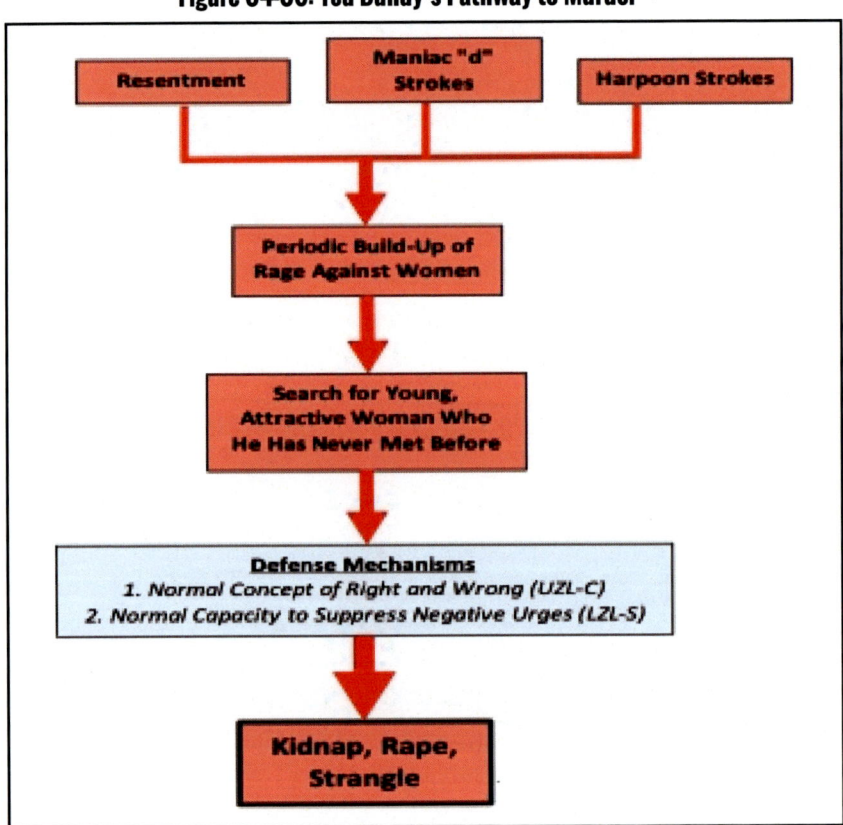

Figure 04-06: Ted Bundy's Pathway to Murder[14,15]

```
    Resentment        Maniac "d" Strokes        Harpoon Strokes
                             │
                             ▼
              Periodic Build-Up of Rage Against Women
                             │
                             ▼
              Search for Young, Attractive Woman Who
                     He Has Never Met Before
                             │
                             ▼
                     Defense Mechanisms
        1. Normal Concept of Right and Wrong (UZL-C)
        2. Normal Capacity to Suppress Negative Urges (LZL-S)
                             │
                             ▼
                   Kidnap, Rape, Strangle
```

HANDWRITING ANALYSIS - SPLIT PERSONALITY OR SUBPERSONALITY?

There has been a myriad of examples of Bundy's handwriting available for scrutiny and they are all very similar…except for one.

Graphologists who have taken an interest in Bundy's handwriting will tell you that his handwriting is quite recognizable for a variety of reasons, but mostly because of the highly unusual frequency of resentment and harpoon strokes. This characteristic has been noted and remarked upon by a number of authors over the years. Figure 04-07a is a fairly typical example. There are slight fluctuations in slant, baseline and the frequency of a number of trait strokes, but this is to be expected due to the natural variation that you will find when you look at someone's handwriting. But then there's the specimen of Bundy's handwriting as shown in Figure 04-07b. It doesn't take a trained graphologist's skills to see that the specimens in Figures 04-07a and 04-07b are noticeably different. The difference between the two can't be explained as being due to natural variation because the differences are too many and too extreme, and because both specimens were written within a relatively short period of time when Bundy was in a Florida prison awaiting execution.

What exactly are the similarities and differences between the two specimens? Chart 04-01 lists many of the more significant differences and Chart 04-02 highlights the major similarities. Specimen #1, which represents Bundy's most frequent writing style, shows high frequencies of resentment and harpoons, but Specimen #2 has no harpoons and a significant reduction in the frequency of resentment strokes. This might suggest that Specimen #2 shows a less vicious type of personality and that would be correct, if not for the anti-social behavior stroke data. There are no such strokes in Specimen #1, but Specimen #2 shows an alarming level of frequency. Being anti-social means that the writer is against the usual rules of society, and in significant cases this attitude will manifest itself in disruptive acts. Specimen #2 reveals a writer who is vain and craving the attention of others, while Specimen #1 has nothing. Specimen #2 also shows that the defense mechanism of sublimation[15] (See Appendix 01) is significantly restricted with a LZL-S score of only 1.4. This writing suggests a writer who has little working for him to control undesirable impulses.

And then there are the two very different personal pronoun "I" configurations.[23] In Specimen #1 (See Figure 04-08a), the configuration is quite different from the more classical configuration seen in Specimen #2 (See Figure 04-08b).

All these differences could potentially be taken for evidence that we are actually looking at two different writers, were it not for the similarities that tell us that the author of the two specimens is likely the same person. Especially telling are the very similar frequencies for attention to detail and self-castigation.

Both specimens display an unusually high level of narrowmindedness, and this is a well-documented trait of Bundy. In addition to the data in Chart 04-02, there are other similarities to be found, not the least of which is the degree of slant to Bundy's writing. In Specimen #1, 87% of his letters have a right-handed slant of between 125 – 145 degrees; in Specimen #2 the frequency is 82%.

So how can we possibly explain these two very different handwriting specimens, both allegedly generated by the same person within a relatively short period of time and under very similar conditions (i.e.: prison environment).

Bundy underwent numerous psychiatric examinations, and one diagnosis (later retracted) included the possibility of a multiple personality disorder. This assessment was not without some supporting evidence. A family member described an incident when she saw Bundy "turn into another, unrecognizable person" who she was immediately frightened of.[3] There was an incident with a prison guard who described a time when Bundy "became weird on me" and that there was an "almost complete change of personality."[3] And then there were comments from Bundy himself. On more than one occasion, Bundy made reference to his "dominant personality" and his inner "entity."[16,17]

Split personality disorder, or more accurately described as dissociative identity disorder (DID) is rather controversial within the field of psychiatry,[18] not the least because it is so difficult to accurately diagnose. There is, however, some consensus on what one typically sees in patients with true DID, and Bundy does not meet the majority of these criteria.[19]

Figure 04-07a: Bundy Specimen #1

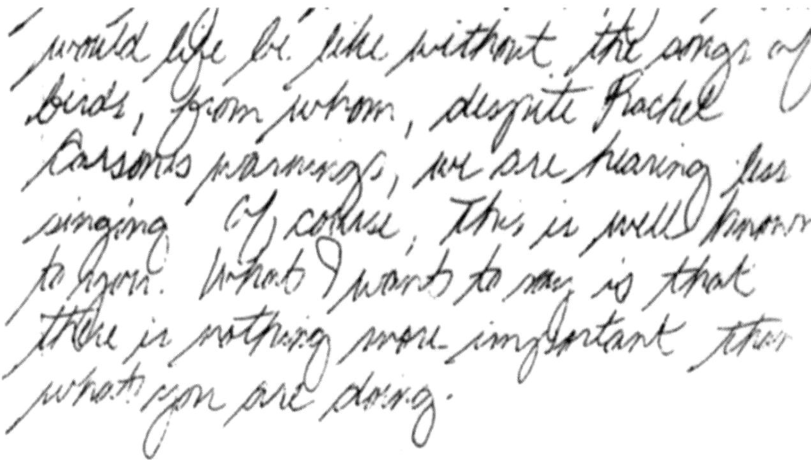
would life be like without the songs of
birds, from whom, despite Rachel
Carson's warnings, we are hearing less
singing. Of course, this is well known
to you. What I want to say is that
there is nothing more important than
what you are doing.

Figure 04-07b: Bundy Specimen #2

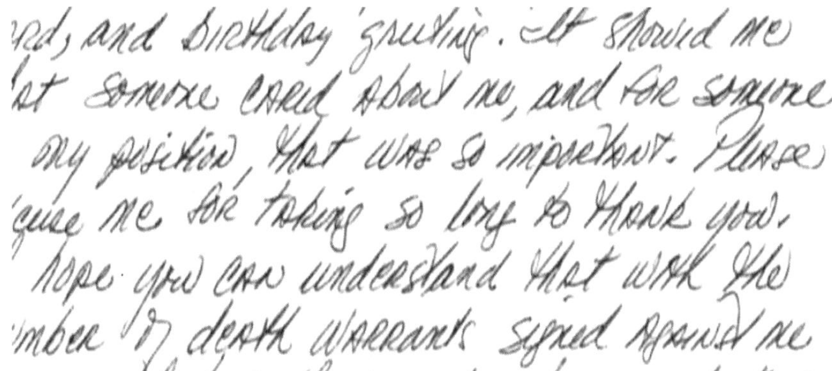
rd, and birthday greeting. It showed me
at someone cared about me, and for someone
my position, that was so important. Please
cuse me for taking so long to thank you.
hope you can understand that with the
mber of death warrants signed against me
1986, I have had a very busy and trying

Something more mainstream than DID within the field of psychiatry is the concept of subpersonalities in which people normally have a number of personality "modes[21]" that are all quite similar in nature and are activated when the person is confronted by certain types of psychosocial situations.[20] For instance, a boy who is easy going and often uses either complete avoidance or gentle persuasion to diffuse tense or angry situations, when confronted by a schoolyard bully, might rise to the occasion and face down his tormentor. This mode of action is a subpersonality being activated. Typically, subpersonalities are well integrated into the overall "self"; they are like various shades of gray, and most people have about a dozen of them.[21] Occasionally, however, sub-personalities are not at all cohesive with each other.

Bundy's mind does not seem to fit the typical mold of subpersonalities because the differences revealed through graphology and outlined in Chart 04-01 would suggest that what we're seeing in Specimen #2 (See Figures 04-08a and 04-08b) is too far along in development and differentiation.

Chart 04-01: Major Variations of Trait Frequencies[14,15]
Frequency of Trait (% of Words or Letters)

Personality Trait	Specimen #1	Specimen #2
Anti-Social Behaviour Stroke	0%	39%
Attention, Desire For	0%	13%
Dignity	89%	53%
Directness	5%	61%
Harpoons	20%	0%
Independent Thinking (d-Stems)	95%	14%
Irritation (i,j)	37%	77%
Loner Stroke	0%	22%
Maniac "d" Stroke	11%	0%
Obstinate	83%	14%
Resentment	44%	16%
Self-Consciousness	6%	26%
Self-Esteem	0%	53%
Simplicity	3%	17%
Stubborn	35%	6%
Vanity	0%	38%
Defense Mechanisms	**Score**	**Score**
UZL-C	2	2.5
LZL-S	2.2	1.4

Chart 04-02: Major Similarities in Trait Frequencies[14]

Personality Trait	Specimen #1	Specimen #2
Attention to Detail	92%	93%
Decisiveness	89%	79%
Defiance	50%	50%
Evasiveness	8%	7%
Imagination, Abstract	14%	14%
Narrowmindedness	98%	80%
Reticence	78%	83%
Self-Castigation	13%	16%
Willpower *(Normal Levels)*	97%	92%

Frequency of Trait (% of Words or Letters)

Fortunately, there may be a more likely explanation of Bundy's situation. The psychologist Richard Schwartz[22] observed over the years that he spent as a family therapist that people often described their inner lives as being "parts," particularly when the parts or subpersonalities were conflicted. Schwartz developed the Internal Family System[22] (IFS) as a type of psychotherapy to address multiple and disparate subpersonalities within an individual's mental system. He conceived the mind as a family and the parts as family members interacting with one another. What is particularly noteworthy about Schwartz's operating premise was his view that DID alternate personalities are at one end of a continuum with subpersonalities at the other end. The only difference between the two is that DID alternate personalities are more remote from and isolated from the rest of the holistic self. If Schwartz's hypothesis is correct, then what we are probably seeing in Bundy's specimen #2 is an entity that has moved along the continuum from being a simple subpersonality towards being more like a distinct and separate personality.

Figure 04-08a: Bundy Specimen #1[15,23]

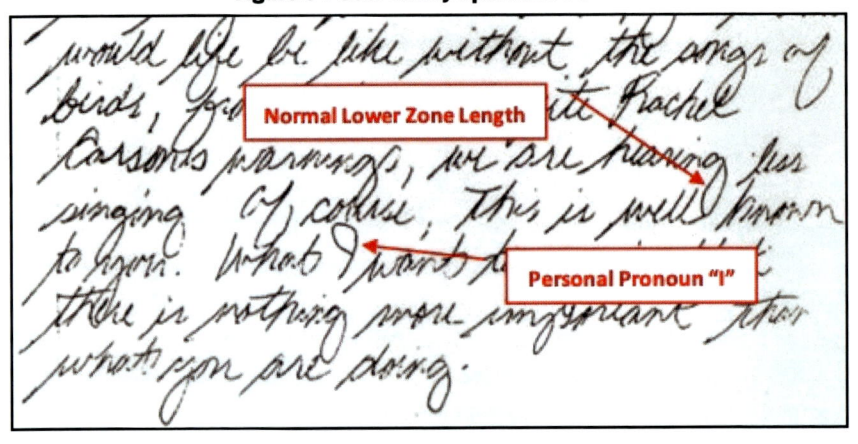

[Handwriting specimen with annotations: "Normal Lower Zone Length" and "Personal Pronoun 'I'"]

Figure 04-08b: Bundy Specimen #2[14,15,23]

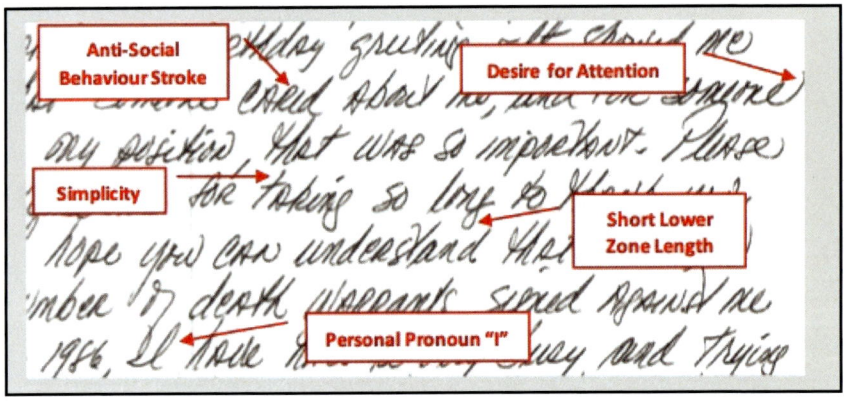

[Handwriting specimen with annotations: "Anti-Social Behaviour Stroke", "Desire for Attention", "Simplicity", "Short Lower Zone Length", and "Personal Pronoun 'I'"]

NOTE: Anti-Social Behavior Stroke- Capitalized letters in place of lowercase letters. Simplicity – Letters such as b, l, f and t that are made with a single downstroke instead of a loop. Desire for Attention – Final letters at the end of words made with a final stroke that is abnormally long, often curves backward and finish higher than the height of lowercase letters.

    In Bundy's case, graphology has been able to recognize and quantify the differences and similarities of personality evidenced by the two handwriting samples as shown in Figure 04-07. These findings are in no way psychologically diagnostic, nor can they even begin to compete with the educated assessments by professional psychotherapists, but it does provide an interesting glimpse into what might have been going on in Bundy's mind.

References

1. Rule, Ann (1980; Revisions – 1986, 1989, 2000, 2008) The Stranger Beside Me ISBN 978-0-393-05029-5

2. Michaud, Stephen and Aynesworth, Hugh (1983; Revision – 1999) The Only Living Witness: The True

3. Nelson, Polly (1994) Defending the Devil: My Story as Ted Bundy's Last Lawyer ISBN 978-0-688-10823-6

4. Kendall, Elizabeth (1981) The Phantom Prince: My Life With Ted Bundy ISBN 978-0-914842-70-5

5. Rule, Ann (2009) The Stranger Beside Me ISBN 978-1-4165-5959-7

6. Michaud, Stephen and Aynesworth, Hugh (1989) Ted Bundy: Conversations With a Killer ISBN 978-0-451-16355-4

7. Hagood, Dick (February 10, 1980) "Bundy Jury: Death" *Florida Times Union*

8. Keppel, Robert (2010) The Riverman: Ted Bundy and I Hunt for the Green River Killer ISBN 978-1-4391-9434-8

9. Keppel, Robert (2005) The Riverman: Ted Bundy and I Hunt for the Green River Killer ISBN 978-0-7434-6395-9

10. Dental Records Establish Identities of Two Women (September 11, 1974) *The Bulletin – Associated Press*

11. Keppel, Robert and Michaud, Stephen (2011) Terrible Secrets: Ted Bundy on Serial Murder ISBN 978-1-928704-97-3

12. Foreman, Laura (1992) Serial Killers – True Crime ISBN 978-0-7835-0001-0

13. Rule, Ann (1989) The Stranger Beside Me ISBN 978-0-451-16493-3

14. Racher, John (2022) Advanced Graphology: An Encyclopedia of Personality Traits Revealed in Handwriting ISBN 978-1-7773610-1-3

15. Racher, John (Autumn 2022) *Conscientiousness, Sublimation … and Serial Killers* The Graphologist - The Journal of the British Institute of

Graphologists

16. Enns, Gregory (May 21, 1989) "Bundy's Mystic Lives On" *Anchorage Daily News*

17. Tron, Gina (November 20, 2020) Why One Psychiatrist Believes Ted Bundy May Have Had Multiple Personalities *Oxygen True Crime*

18. Brand, B; Loewenstein, J: Spiegel, D (2014) "Dispelling Myths About Dissociative Identity Disorder Treatment: An Empirically Based Approach" *Psychiatry*

19. Johnson, J. (July 14, 2020) "Split personality disorder: Signs, Symptoms, Causes, Diagnosis, and More *Medical News Today*

20. Fall, Kevin (2003) Theoretical Models of Counseling and Psychotherapy ISBN 1-58391-068-9

21. Rowan, J. (1990) Subpersonalities: The People Inside Us ISBN 978-041-504329-8

22. Schwartz, R. (2001) Introduction to the Internal Family Systems Model ISBN 978-0-9721-14800-9

23. Lowe, Sheila (2007) The Complete Idiot's Guide to Handwriting Analysis, Second Edition ISBN 978-1-59257-601-2

Chapter 5
KENDALL FRANCOIS

THE NOT-SO-GENTLE GIANT

Kendall Francois was born and raised in Poughkeepsie (pronounced "poh-kip-see"), where he killed eight women over the span of just under two years (1996 – 1998) when he was 25 – 27 years old. All of his victims were sex workers, and Francois was convicted in August 2000 of murdering them. He died in prison[5] in 2014 at the age of 43; the cause of death was HIV-related.

Figure 05-01: Kendall Francois

BACKGROUND

Based on an almost total lack of information to the contrary, it would appear that Francois had an unremarkable childhood and, apart from being bullied during his younger years because of his size (i.e.: at the age of 14 he was 6'4" and 250 lb.—seriously obese) he was quiet, had few friends and pretty well kept to himself. His parents held respectful jobs, and when Francois was four years old, they bought a modest home in an average middle-class neighborhood; see Figure 05-02. They resided there until 1998 when it was discovered to be a crime scene and the family had to vacate the premises. Apart from a two-year stint in the army, Francois had always lived in his parents' home along with his three sisters, two of whom had moved out by 1998.

First appearances aren't necessarily reflective of reality however. When the police obtained a search warrant in 1998 for the home (i.e.: 99 Fulton Avenue) what they found, apart from eight corpses stored in the attic and in a crawlspace under the front veranda of the house,[1] was an unbelievable level of squalor. Investigating officers discovered that the house was full of garbage, there were no doors on any cabinets, bedsheets covered the windows instead of curtains, broken furniture and old newspapers were everywhere, clothes were piled up in every room, used syringes were lying about, the kitchen was full of rotting food and maggots were in the sinks. This level of uncleanliness strongly suggests that something was seriously wrong in the house and had been that way for quite some time.

Figure 05-02: 99 Fulton Avenue, Poughkeepsie

Poughkeepsie Journal photo of police forensic investigator

Francois graduated from Arlington High School in Poughkeepsie in 1989 and joined the army. He was stationed in Honolulu, Hawaii for approximately three years but was discharged because of his weight. Francois returned to Poughkeepsie to live with his parents and struggled to find steady employment. He had several jobs but wasn't able to stay with any of them for very long, for whatever reason. In 1996 (the year he began killing) he found a job at his old high school, first as a janitor and then as a "school monitor." Francois was not liked by the staff at Arlington High School. A number of teachers complained that he acted inappropriately towards the female students, touching their hair and telling off-color jokes to them. The students themselves were rather derisive towards him, calling him "Stinky" because he exhibited very poor personal hygiene and constantly had a bad odor about him.

When he wasn't working or attending the local community college on a part-time basis, Francois was often seen frequenting the downtown area of Poughkeepsie along Main Street where sex workers were most likely to be found. In fact, what appears to be a rather regular routine was for Francois to drop his mother off at work in the morning and then go downtown to pick up a prostitute and take her back to his house.

As it turns out, Francois was a "regular" and was well known amongst the local sex workers and to the police, primarily because of his preference for what was euphemistically referred to as "rough sex."[9] Many of the prostitutes put up with his roughness, but occasionally he would be too aggressive with the wrong person, and that would lead to a complaint to the police. This occurred with sufficient regularity that Francois was familiar with the routine of being taken to the police station for questioning. Charges were rarely laid, but the files about the assaults were kept, therefore the police were quite aware of Francois's proclivities.

Francois committed his first murder on October 24, 1996. Wendy Meyers accompanied Francois back to his home as she had done so on a number of times, but unfortunately for her, things didn't go as well as they had on previous occasions. For whatever reason, Francois became angered and choked her into unconsciousness. He told police investigators that she fought hard and "wouldn't die." Once unconscious, Francois took her to the bathroom, placed her face down in the tub and filled it with water. After she had drowned, he took her body up into the attic and left it there. Her badly decomposed body remained there for almost two years before being discovered by the police. Just one month later, Francois killed again. In this case he met Gina Barone, a sex worker who had been in the business for approximately ten years. While having sex with her in his car in a parking lot, Francois alleged that Barone was in a bad mood, complaining about how heavy he was and how it was taking so long for him to finish. This criticism angered him to the point where he choked her so that she'd be quiet and he could finish. The initial choking didn't kill her however, and when she regained consciousness, he strangled her to death, dumped her body in the trunk of the car and took it home to store it in the attic along with Wendy Meyer's body.[2]

Another month passed and another sex worker disappeared off the streets. All the Poughkeepsie police had to go on were missing person reports from worried family members, but they nevertheless became sufficiently concerned that they started to investigate any "Johns" who were reputedly into rough sex, and Francois's name came up. At this stage however, because the police didn't know that anyone had been killed, they were just listed as missing. They assigned some resources to see if Francois was into something more than rough sex, but surveillance wasn't 24/7 and nothing came of it during that time.

In March 1997, a relative of a sex worker—Catherine Marsh—called the police to say that she hadn't heard from her daughter since last November. The police contacted the Federal Bureau of Investigation, but because there weren't any bodies or a crime scene, they were not able to help. However, to the Poughkeepsie police department's credit, they were sufficiently concerned that they took the unusual step of creating a task force. Normally that doesn't happen until there is some sort of evidence that crimes had been committed, but they were convinced that some form of criminality had occurred. That was the good news. The bad news was that the police assumed that whoever it was they were looking for, he would be a white male. That being the case, and despite Francois's name cropping up again and again from the sex worker community as being into rough sex, they were disinclined to investigate him to any great degree.

In October 1997, Michelle Eason was reported as missing. That same month another sex worker—Mary Giaccone—was reported as having been last seen back in February of that year. By this time, the police had begun an active search for bodies, employing helicopters to search the Hudson River, which flowed through Poughkeepsie. As the task force accelerated their investigation of all these missing women, the decision was made to take a closer look at Francois, particularly because he had just been arrested for assaulting a sex worker in May 1998. In the arrest documentation, the complainant stated that Francois had taken her to his home, but when they got into an argument because he didn't want to pay, he punched her in the face and began to choke her. The issue of payment was set aside; she agreed to have sex with him and then he let her go. Francois pleaded guilty to the charge and spent fifteen days in jail, but less than two weeks later another sex worker was reported missing, and her car was found abandoned less than three blocks away from his house.

On September 01, 1998, Francois's luck ran out. A sex worker, Christine Sala, accused Francois of attacking her. The police took him in for questioning and, during the course of the interrogation, informed Francois that they had obtained a search warrant for his house. It is at this point that Francois apparently decided that his situation was untenable, so he told the police investigators that he wanted to "talk to the chief prosecutor of the missing women and [he'd] tell…what happened."[6] A few hours later, the police were flabbergasted; a single charge of assault had morphed into a full-blown case of a serial killer with Francois providing a full confession.

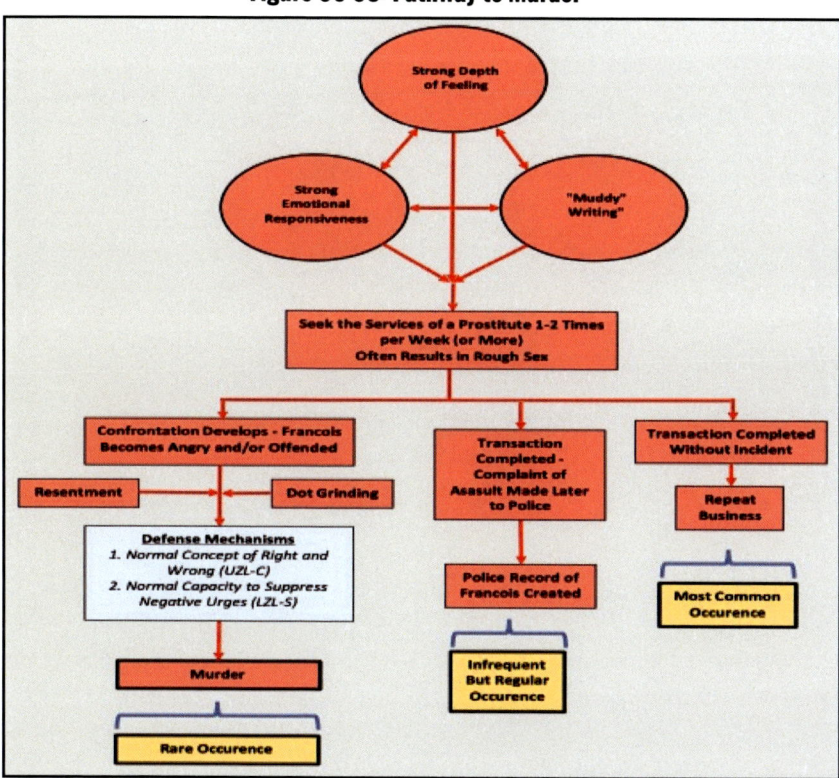

Figure 05-03: Pathway to Murder[12]

Within 24 hours of the confession, the authorities assembled a multi-jurisdictional team of investigators and forensic specialists and arrived at 99 Fulton Avenue shortly before midnight. They advised Francois's parents and sister that the house was a crime scene, and they would have to leave immediately. They were taken to the police station and were questioned about the bodies that the police were expecting to find. The police were astounded that the family claimed no knowledge whatsoever about the bodies or about Francois's criminal behavior. What made the police even more incredulous about the family's claims was the fact that the entire house reeked of human feces and rotting flesh.[8] However, given the huge amount of garbage and filth throughout the house, perhaps one more source of nasty odors could go unnoticed. Regardless, no legal action was pursued against the family, and they moved out of Poughkeepsie shortly thereafter.

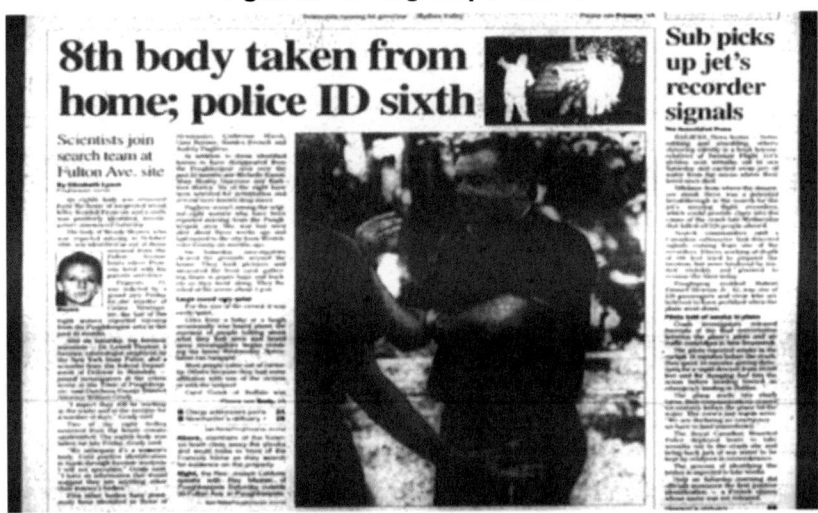

Figure 05-04: *Poughkeepsie Journal*

It took the authorities three days to locate the eight bodies in the two-and-a-half-story home. See Figure 05-04. Three partially dismembered bodies were wrapped in plastic and stored in the attic. Also in the attic was a body left to rot in a child's wading pool and covered with clothes and blankets. The fifth body in the attic was in a garbage can. The remaining three bodies had been partially buried under the floor of the veranda at the front of the house.

On October 13, 1998, Francois was formally charged with eight counts of murder and one count of attempted assault. Even though he had originally pleaded not guilty, in order to escape the death penalty Francois changed his mind and pleaded guilty; by taking this route Francois received life without parole.

HANDWRITING ANALYSIS - GENERAL PROFILE[12]

Francois routinely experienced very strong and long-lasting emotional reactions to almost everything that was happening either around him or to him, as indicated by a pronounced right-hand slant to his writing and its very "heavy" or thick-looking appearance; see Figure 05-05. While it's quite common for people to show some degree of a right-hand slant in their writing, Francois's was quite significant and therefore not often seen. 73% of his letters had a slant of between 125 to 145 degrees, and 18% exceeded 145 degrees. This strong emotional responsiveness was compounded by the heavy writing, the combination of which is quite uncommon. When this thickness of writing is seen, you know that the writer has particularly deep feelings regarding sensory stimuli (e.g.: food, music, sex) and will react quickly and vigorously over stressful situations or events that anger or annoy them. The interesting thing about Francois, however, is that he was able to contain his reactions the vast majority of time because of his very strong need to appear poised and in control of himself. This outer image of objectivity and proper behavior didn't negate the deep and often dark feelings however; the feelings were still there, and in Francois's situation it was a bit like trying to keep a lid on a boiling pot of water; eventually the lid comes flying off.

Francois was rather vain, especially when it came to his manners in public and how he expressed his personality. This trait only added to his need to be seen behaving appropriately in public. Not that he would say much in public anyway; he was very, very disinclined to say much of anything to anyone, and would typically only respond to direct questions, and when he did, he would do so with as few words as possible.

In a letter that Francois wrote to an acquaintance while in prison,[3] he described himself as "a pretty good thinker" and his handwriting seems to bear this out. He exhibits a high degree of curiosity, good analytical thinking and an unusual level of attention to detail; this latter trait is exhibited by his i-dots being placed very close to the i-stems; see Figure 05-05. Also contributing to his intellectual effectiveness was Francois's degree of open-mindedness; 85% of his "e" letters were well rounded. This trait meant that he would be tolerant of other people's opinions, and this enabled him to appreciate both sides of an argument and so able to learn from that insight. The only major detractor from Francois being very intellectually effective was his almost complete inability to organize his thoughts; the letter "f" in his handwriting is never properly formed.

Figure 05-05: Personality Traits[12]

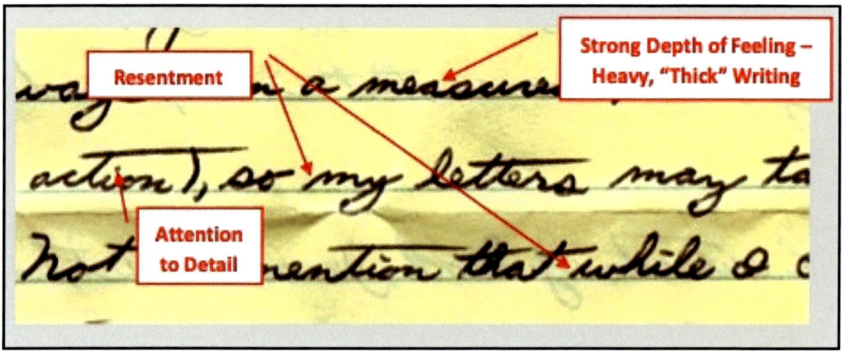

NOTES: Resentment – Straight approach stroke starting at or below baseline. Attention to Detail – i and j dots placed close to stem. Strong Depth of Feeling – unusually thick lines of writing.

HANDWRITING ANALYSIS - SERIAL KILLER PATHWAY[12]

As mentioned earlier, Francois had a very strong and deep-seated emotional make-up to begin with, and while this is not by itself a cause for worry, whenever you see muddy writing in addition to these two other traits, then there is cause for concern. Figure 05-06 is an example of Francois's muddy writing, and Figure 05-03 identifies the interplay between the three traits.

Muddy writing is said to exist when blobs and blotches are present, and these strokes are indicative of an individual who has very significant sensory appetites and a concurrent build-up of emotional pressure. People with strongly slanted and heavy writing like to indulge their senses, and this becomes a liability when muddy writing is seen because it is an indication that over-indulging is occurring, as is seen in Francois's history of frequently accessing the services of sex workers and his preference for rough sex.

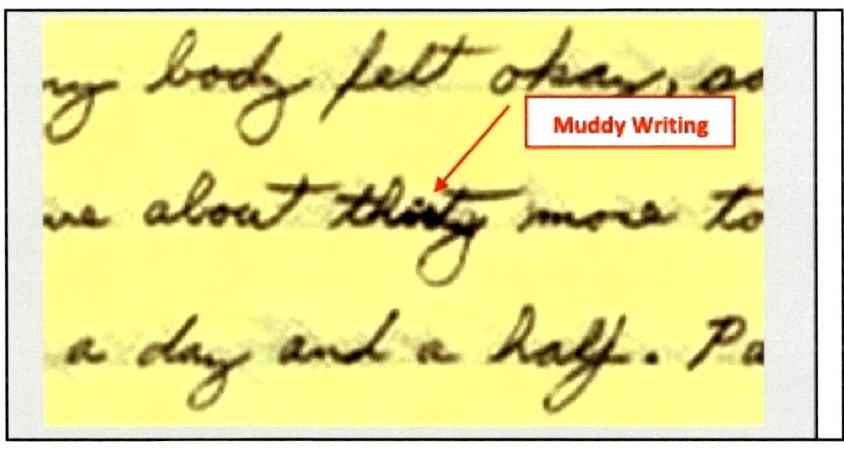

Figure 05-06: Personality Traits[12]

NOTES: Muddy Writing – Blobs, blotches, cross-outs and partially filled-in circles and loops.

Another very clear indication of Francois's obsession with sex (consensual or not) occurred during his time in prison. The author Claudia Rowe spent almost four years corresponding with Francois and occasionally visiting him in prison. The relationship was professional because Rowe was gathering information about him that she would eventually publish in her book,[4] *The Spider and The Fly: A Reporter, A Serial Killer, and the Meaning of Murder*. At the end of one of the face-to-face meetings between Rowe and Francois, he reputedly said to her in a matter-of-fact fashion, "I was thinking, I want to throw you down on this table and fuck your brains out."

Francois's handwriting is dominated by indications of the negative trait of resentment; 45.1% of all words start with the indicator stroke. (See Figure 05-05). This unusually high degree of negativity was made even worse by the presence of dot grinding; see Figure 05-07. Writers who display dot grinding are obsessively resentful because they believe that they are being forced to accept something that they do not like, and the feelings of painful bitterness can manifest themselves in destructive behaviors. It is interesting to note that some graphologists have stated that dot grinding is seen in the handwriting of individuals who were the victim of some form of emotional or physical abuse, and there is some hint of the possibility of that in Francois's childhood environment. Francois's feelings of resentment were also reinforced by his very overactive imagination, his pronounced sensitivity to criticism and his strong trait of irritability; see Figure 05-08.

When all of these traits are looked at together, they cumulatively result in an extremely strong negative force. As highlighted in Figure 05-03, Francois's pathway to murder came about when he and the sex worker he was with at the time found themselves in some sort of confrontation, as was the case with Gina Barone when her complaints about his weight and sexual performance probably triggered his sensitivity to criticism and irritability. This, along with his very powerful baseline feelings of resentment towards anyone he felt might be trying to take advantage of him, resulted in his murderous behavior.

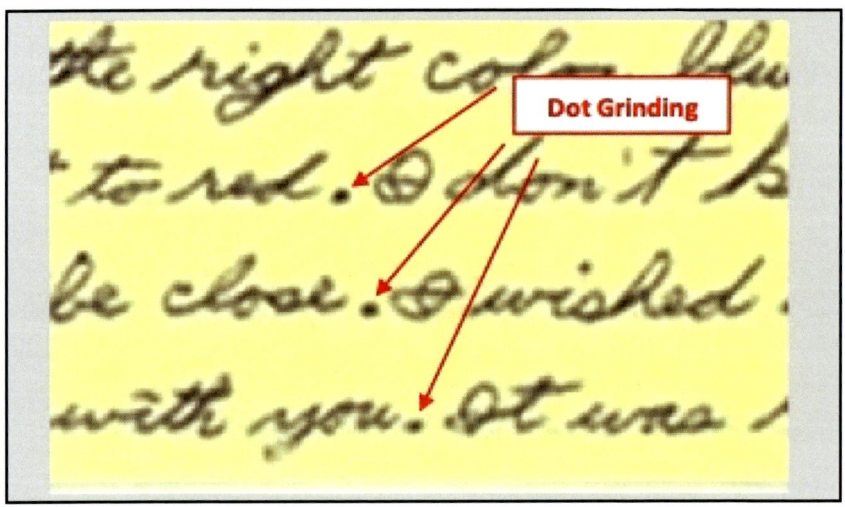

Figure 05-07: Personality Traits[12]

NOTES: Dot Grinding – Heavy pressure applied to punctuation.

Figure 05-08: Personality Traits[12]

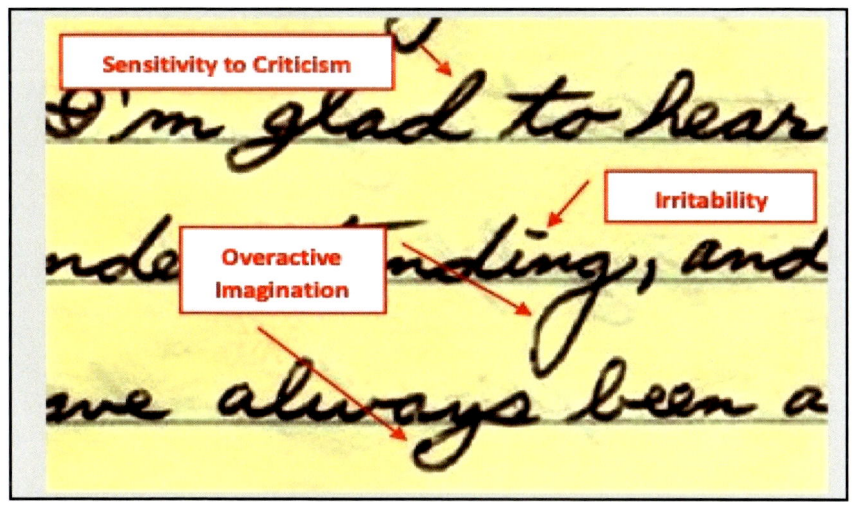

[Handwriting sample with annotations: "Sensitivity to Criticism", "Irritability", "Overactive Imagination"]

NOTES: Sensitivity to criticism indicated by d- and t-stems that are looped. Irritability is indicated by i- and j-dots that look like slashes. An overactive material imagination is indicated by inflated lower zone loops on letters such as g and y.

The overall strength of Francois's negative personality traits appears to have been enough to overwhelm his defense traits of conscientiousness and sublimation (See Appendix One for an in-depth description of these traits) even though he had normal scores of UZL-C = 2.2 and LZL-S = 2.5. In one of the many interviews with the police, Francois callously stated that he felt that all of his victims deserved to die, and Casey Jordan, a criminologist and lawyer who met numerous times with him, said that Francois "felt no guilt, no remorse, about killing them."[7] His total lack of empathy towards his victims and their families was in full display when, during the sentencing phase of his trial, when the families of his victims were giving their impact statements, he astonishingly giggled at what was being said.[8]

Kendall Francois is a bit of an enigma. He killed eight people; the manner in which he treated their bodies bordered on the macabre, yet he is, for the most part, completely unknown to the general public and to most serial killer aficionados. Case in point, Dennis Rader[11] was a serial killer who murdered only slightly more people than Francois (i.e.: 10), yet his antics were covered by the international news media. So, what made Radar a media sensation and Francois a virtual unknown? The answer, it seems, is because Francois was black.

Allan Branson, a criminal justice professor wrote an article in 2013 entitled "African American Serial Killers: Over-Represented Yet Underacknowledged" in which he said that one key reason for this disparity is because "the predominant media portrayals of serial murderers are white male perpetrators." He goes on to state that the "media show little reticence in portraying black males as low-level criminals, but rarely portray them as serial killers."[10] Unfortunately, this myopic view was not confined to the general public, but was widely held by law enforcement agencies. Remember that the Poughkeepsie police, even though they were quite aware of Francois's history of assaults towards sex workers, nevertheless automatically assumed that they were looking for a white male. The unfortunate consequence of this narrow point of view, as Branson points out, is that it most probably creates a situation where more people may die unnecessarily before a black killer is eventually captured.

References

1. Rosen, Fred (2015) Body Dump: Kendall Francois, the Poughkeepsie Serial Killer ISBN 978-0-0624-9762-8

2. Gado, Mark (2011) Nightcrawler ISBN 978-0-7953-2315-7

3. "Francois letters: Inside the mind of a remorseless killer" (October 11, 2014) The Poughkeepsie Journal

4. Rowe, Claudia (2017) The Spider and the Fly: A Reporter, a Serial Killer, and the Meaning of Murder ISBN 978-0- 0624-1614-8

5. Ferro, John (September 12, 2014) "Serial Killer Kendall Francois dies in prison" Poughkeepsie Journal

6. Kendall Francois – The Poughkeepsie Killer (February 10, 2020) Criminal Discourse Podcast

7. Sedlak-Hevener, Amanda (October 23, 2018) 11 Grisly Details About Kendall Francois, An Unrepentant Serial Killer *Ranker Unspeakable Crimes*

8. Serial Killer (February 06, 2021) *Killer Queens: A True Crime Podcast*

9. Marco Margaritaff (January 11, 2022) Meet Kendall Francois, The "Poughkeepsie Killer" Who Monitored Students by Day and Brutalized Sex Workers by Night *Allthatsinteresting.com*

10. Branson, Allan (February 2013) "African American Serial Killers: Over-Represented Yet Underacknowledged" The Howard Journal of Crime and Justice

11. Hickey, E (2012) Serial Murderers and Their Victims ISBN 978-1-285-40168-3

12. Racher, John (2022) Advanced Graphology: An Encyclopedia of Personality Traits Revealed in Handwriting ISBN 978-1-7773610-1-3

Chapter 6
RICHARD COTTINGHAM

AN OXYMORON: A SERIAL KILLER WITH A NORMAL CHILDHOOD

Richard Cottingham is a typical power or control type of serial killer in that his primary objective was to completely dominate and control his victims. A police investigator once explained that when he asked Cottingham what motivated him he was told that "he got his kicks…not necessarily by murdering women, but by getting them to do what he wanted…"[1] In another interview he said, "It's God-like, almost. You're in complete control of somebody's destiny."[3]

Between 1981 and 1984, Cottingham was convicted in three separate trails for the murder of five women and was sentenced to life in prison with no chance of parole. However, beginning in 2009, almost 30 years after being imprisoned, he began to confess to another seven murders, all of which had been cold cases and so had never been linked to him; it was not until this time that the full depravity of the man was ascertained.

What makes Cottingham so intriguing is the fact that there seems to be nothing in his life history that would even remotely explain why he became a serial killer. As explained by the director of the Serial Killer Database Research Project, "serial killers' psychological dysfunction often correlates strongly to some kind of horrendous home situation.[2]" However, crime historian Peter Vronsky (who had interviewed Cottingham for over 50 hours) has stated that Cottingham's childhood was "absolutely idyllic"[2] with three sisters who were all well-adjusted and who adored their brother, a mom who was your typical homemaker housewife, a father who was an executive with a life insurance company and "no reports of family dysfunction."[2] The New York Daily News described him as "too ridiculously normal to be a serial killer."[4] So just what did happen that pushed this young man to become a serial killer? Vronsky has floated one possible explanation—a brain injury.[2]

Figure 06-01: Richard Cottingham

Bergan County Sheriff's Office, May 1980

BACKGROUND

Richard Cottingham grew up in New Jersey, not far from New York City (NYC). By all accounts he had a normal, nondescript childhood, he participated in sports while in high school, and when he graduated, he went to work in the mail room at Metropolitan Life's head office in NYC where his father was a vice-president. A few years later, he got a job as a computer operator for Blue Cross Blue Shield Association, also based in NYC and remained in their employ right up until the time of his arrest in 1980.

There are two very distinct components to Cottingham's criminal activities. See Figure 06-02. Between 1970 and 1980, he committed five murders, for which he was found guilty and sentenced to life in prison. But then there were seven other murders that he was never connected to. These seven murders all became cold cases and were not linked to Cottingham until he formally began to confess to them 30 years later.

Police records from the 1970s show that Cottingham first came to their attention in September 1973 when he was charged with sexual assault and robbery of a sex worker in NYC. By this time, he had been married for three years, and even though his home was in Lodi, New Jersey, he maintained an apartment in downtown NYC, close to where he worked, because after working night shifts he told his wife that the commute home was just too tedious. The reality was, however, the freedom of his own apartment allowed him to easily access the night life in NYC with all its bars, sex shops and sex workers. The September 1973 case went to court, but because the complainant failed to show up, the charge was dropped.

Cottingham's next run-in with the police occurred in March 1974. The charge was similar to the first—robbery and unlawful imprisonment of a sex worker—but the outcome was the same. The complainant was a no-show at court so the charge was dropped.

It was over the next three years that Cottingham committed five murders and a number of violent assaults, which ultimately were all linked to him by 1980.

The body of Maryann Carr, a 26-year-old x-ray technician, was found on December 15, 1977 in the back seat of her car in the parking lot of a Quality Inn motel. She had been beaten and had numerous bites and small cuts on her body, indicating that she had been tortured before being strangled to death. Her murder was linked to Cottingham in 1980 when he was arrested for assault on a sex worker and a subsequent search of his car and home yielded evidence that linked him with Carr.

On December 02, 1979, NYC firemen responded to a call at the Travel Inn motel near Times Square.[6,7] What they encountered were two burning mattress in one of the motel rooms, each of which had a nude body on it. As if seeing the burnt bodies was not bad enough, when the firemen attempted to rescue them they discovered, to their horror, that they had both been decapitated and their hands had been cut off; the body parts were never found. Investigators revealed that both bodies had knife wounds and that there were words carved into both victims' backs.[6] One of the women was eventually identified as Deedeh Goodarzi, a known sex worker, but the other woman has remained unidentified to this day. These murders were eventually linked to Valerie Street's murder (see below) which in turn was linked to Cottingham in 1980.

Valerie Street was a 19-year-old sex worker whose nude body was found on May 05, 1980 in a room in a Quality Inn motel in New Jersey. Her hands were handcuffed behind her back, she had been severely beaten, numerous knife wounds were found on her breasts and she also had bite marks on her.[3] She had been strangled to death. This was the same Quality Inn where Maryann Carr's body had been found in the parking lot, and where Leslie O'Dell (see below) was assaulted later that same month, on May 22. Unbeknownst to Cottingham, the net was starting to tighten around him; one of his fingerprints were found on the handcuffs,[5] and it was matched when Cottingham was arrested on May 22.

Figure 06-02: Key Milestones in Richard Cottingham's Criminal Life

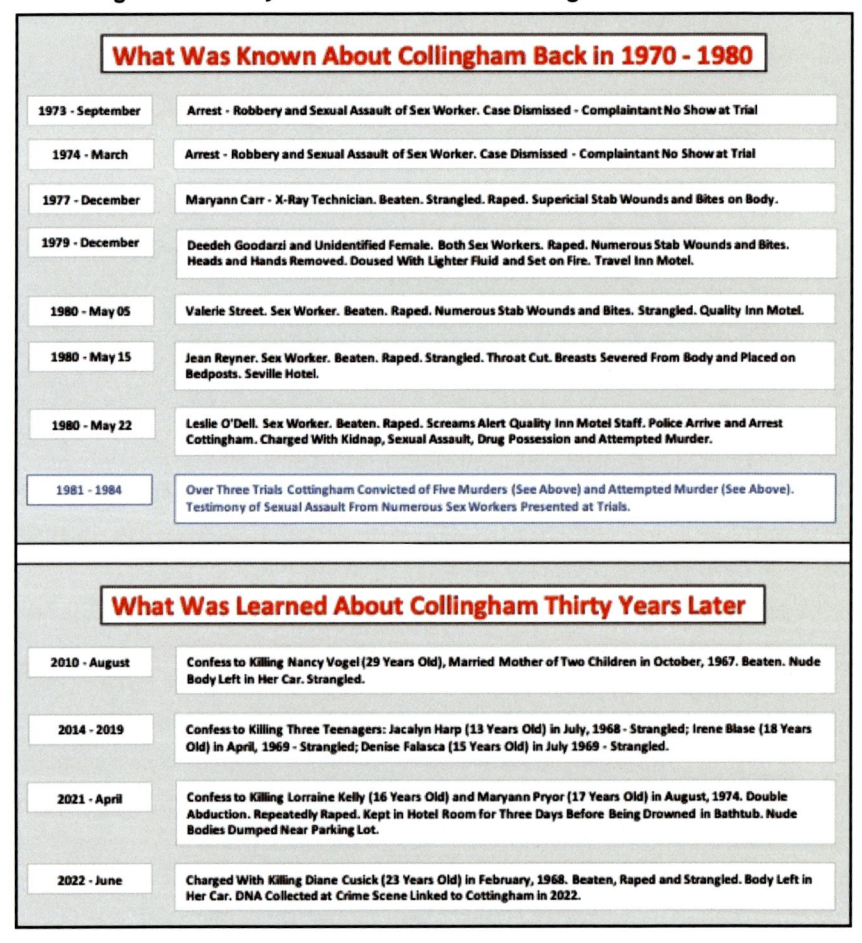

What Was Known About Collingham Back in 1970 - 1980

1973 - September	Arrest - Robbery and Sexual Assault of Sex Worker. Case Dismissed - Complaintant No Show at Trial
1974 - March	Arrest - Robbery and Sexual Assault of Sex Worker. Case Dismissed - Complaintant No Show at Trial
1977 - December	Maryann Carr - X-Ray Technician. Beaten. Strangled. Raped. Supericial Stab Wounds and Bites on Body.
1979 - December	Deedeh Goodarzi and Unidentified Female. Both Sex Workers. Raped. Numerous Stab Wounds and Bites. Heads and Hands Removed. Doused With Lighter Fluid and Set on Fire. Travel Inn Motel.
1980 - May 05	Valerie Street. Sex Worker. Beaten. Raped. Numerous Stab Wounds and Bites. Strangled. Quality Inn Motel.
1980 - May 15	Jean Reyner. Sex Worker. Beaten. Raped. Strangled. Throat Cut. Breasts Severed From Body and Placed on Bedposts. Seville Hotel.
1980 - May 22	Leslie O'Dell. Sex Worker. Beaten. Raped. Screams Alert Quality Inn Motel Staff. Police Arrive and Arrest Cottingham. Charged With Kidnap, Sexual Assault, Drug Possession and Attempted Murder.
1981 - 1984	Over Three Trials Cottingham Convicted of Five Murders (See Above) and Attempted Murder (See Above). Testimony of Sexual Assault From Numerous Sex Workers Presented at Trials.

What Was Learned About Collingham Thirty Years Later

2010 - August	Confess to Killing Nancy Vogel (29 Years Old), Married Mother of Two Children in October, 1967. Beaten. Nude Body Left in Her Car. Strangled.
2014 - 2019	Confess to Killing Three Teenagers: Jacalyn Harp (13 Years Old) in July, 1968 - Strangled; Irene Blase (18 Years Old) in April, 1969 - Strangled; Denise Falasca (15 Years Old) in July 1969 - Strangled.
2021 - April	Confess to Killing Lorraine Kelly (16 Years Old) and Maryann Pryor (17 Years Old) in August, 1974. Double Abduction. Repeatedly Raped. Kept in Hotel Room for Three Days Before Being Drowned in Bathtub. Nude Bodies Dumped Near Parking Lot.
2022 - June	Charged With Killing Diane Cusick (23 Years Old) in February, 1968. Beaten, Raped and Strangled. Body Left in Her Car. DNA Collected at Crime Scene Linked to Cottingham in 2022.

Yet another sex worker, Jean Reyner, was found murdered on May 15, 1980 in the Seville Hotel in downtown NYC.[5] Her throat had been slashed and she had been strangled. In a macabre act, her breasts had been cut off and carefully positioned on the headboard of the bed before the bed was set on fire, much like what happened with Deedeh Goodarzi and the unidentified sex worker at the Travel Inn motel near Times Square.

Cottingham's life as a rampaging serial killer came to a rather abrupt end one week later, on May 22, when he picked up Leslie O'Dell and took her to the same Quality Inn motel in New Jersey where he had murdered Valerie Street 17 days earlier and where he had dumped Maryann Carr's body back in December 1977. Cottingham handcuffed O'Dell and began torturing her, but despite being gagged, her screams of pain were loud enough to attract the attention of the motel staff, who called the police. Cottingham was caught trying to escape. He was charged with kidnapping, sexual assault, attempted murder and possession of drugs.[8] Upon his arrest, search warrants were obtained for his car and his home, where various items from previous victims were discovered.

Over the next three years—1981 to 1984— Cottingham was, over the course of three separate trials, convicted of five murders and sentenced to serve life in prison. In all the trials, Cottingham consistently pleaded his innocence and claimed he was being "framed." Numerous women testified that they had been drugged by Cottingham and taken to hotel rooms where they were viciously assaulted, some being so badly beaten that they were left for dead.[6] Interestingly, however, he did claim at one of his trials that "the whole idea of bondage had aroused and fascinated me since I was very young."[6]

Thirty years later, an elderly Richard Cottingham (See Figure 06-03) began to change his tune…

Up until 2009, Cottingham continued to proclaim his innocence, but then he suddenly changed his tune and actually admitted having committed the murders[9] he had been convicted of. When asked why he waited for so long to confess, he explained that by insisting he was innocent he was hoping that his family would not give up on him. Then, in August 2010 Cottingham started to shock the authorities by confessing to other murders that had never been associated with him at all.

Figure 06-03: Richard Cottingham – 74 Years Old – 2020

His first confession, in August 2010, was about a 29-year-old homemaker and mother of two, Nancy Vogel, who was last seen on October 28, 1967 when she was headed out to meet some friends and go play bingo at a neighborhood church. However, instead of going to bingo, she decided to go to a local mall to purchase a pair of shoes. While in the mall, she was approached by Cottingham who, masquerading as a store security officer, accused her of theft and took her away. Three days later, her nude body was found in the back of her car that was abandoned in a nearby town.[10] It is interesting to note that when Cottingham committed this, his first murder, he was only 21 years-old, a young age for a serial killer to start murdering. It wasn't until three years later that he became married.

From 2014 to 2019 Cottingham then confessed to killing three teenage girls:[10]

1. On July 17, 1968, Jacalyn Harp, a 13-year-old, was walking home after an evening band practice at her school when a man in a car pulled up beside her and asked her if she wanted a ride. She refused and started to walk away, but the man got out of the car and chased and caught her. She was dragged into some bushes and was strangled.
2. In April 1969, Irene Blase, an 18-year-old was last seen shopping in a mall where a man asked her to go for a drink. The next day she was found face down in the Saddle River in New Jersey. She had been strangled.

3. On July 14, 1969, Denise Falasca, a 15-year-old, was walking to a friend's house in Emerson, New Jersey when she disappeared. Her body was found the next day by the side of a road; she had been strangled.

**Figure 06-04: Discovery of Bodies – August 1974
Lorraine Kelly and Maryann Pryor**

New York Daily News, August 15, 1974

In April 2021, Cottingham next confessed to the brutal slaying of two teenaged girls in August, 1974: Lorraine Kelly (16 years old) and Maryann Pryor (17 years old). See Figure 06-04. These two young ladies were on their way to the mall to buy bathing suits when a man offered to give them a ride. Once in the car, Cottingham took them to a hotel where, for the next three days, he repeatedly beat, tortured and raped them. On the third day, he then forcibly drowned them in the motel room bathtub and then dumped their bodies in a nearby wooded area.

When Cottingham began to voluntarily confess to being the murderer responsible for the above-mentioned cold cases, the early speculation was that he had somehow mellowed in his old age and was hoping to bring some comfort to the aggrieved families by giving them some closure regarding the deaths of their loved ones. "He's not in great shape and it appears his heath is failing," stated a news reporter.[4] "I think that played a role in him admitting to additional murders, because he knows he's getting close to the end." Rod Leith, a former police intelligence officer who spent years investigating and writing about Cottingham, strongly disagrees, however. This isn't about some new-found compassion and remorse as far as he was concerned. He knows Cottingham to be a "very psychologically ill sadist," the "confessions" being nothing more than a self-serving attempt to obtain what he considered to be his "long-denied attention."[4] Robert Anzilotti, a New Jersey police investigator who spent decades on cold cases and who spent hours meeting with Cottingham, agrees. Anzilotti said this about Cottingham:[1] "I find him to be without a soul. Depravity comes to mind as a word." He then goes on to say that "he's a major control freak."[1]

On June 22, 2022, Cottingham, as he lay in a hospital prison bed and barely able to speak, was formally indicted for the killing 23-year-old Diane Cusick back in February 1968. A dance teacher, Cusick had gone to a local mall to do some shopping, only to be found hours later beaten and raped, with duct tape wrapped around her mouth and neck; she died from asphyxiation. With this indictment, Cottingham perhaps did get some of the press coverage that he craved, though the nature of the media attention wasn't exactly what he was seeking. This case was solved through DNA testing of specimens that had been collected and then preserved since the murder occurred, 54 years ago. Acting on a hunch that Cusick's case might be linked to Cottingham, the police submitted a specimen for testing and, amazingly, got a match. At a press conference, the police described the DNA test results as being noteworthy because it was one of the oldest DNA hits in the US[11] to have ever occurred.

HANDWRITING ANALYSIS - GENERAL PROFILE[12]

Cottingham's handwriting indicates that in many respects he was an ordinary, everyday sort of guy. He was emotionally expressive by nature, but not overly so, therefore he could interact with others without overwhelming them by being impulsive or high-strung. His handwriting is a little heavier than what you normally encounter (See Figure 06-05), and this indicates that his response to sensory stimuli such as food, music and sex was a bit on the exuberant side. These traits, combined with his strong willingness to be cooperative and accommodate the wishes of others (See Figure 06-05 - Amenable; 67% Frequency of Occurrence [FOO]) and his optimism (See Figure 06-05) made it easy for people to like him. With his natural enthusiasm (See Figure 06-05), people's opinion of him would be one of an upbeat, likeable, neighborly type of person. Perhaps that's why Leslie O'Dell thought "he seemed like just a nice, quiet guy who only wanted to party with a pretty prostitute before going back to his humdrum suburban life"[6] That is, until he turned on her.

Like most everyone else, however, Cottingham wasn't totally perfect. He had a rather restricted point of view on most topics (See Figure 06-06 – Narrowminded; 79% FOO) and so was intolerant of opinions that differed from his own. This would become particularly evident if and when Cottingham chose to articulate his position, because when he did so, it would be done with quite a bit of vigor. (See Figure 06-06 - Argumentative; 100% FOO).

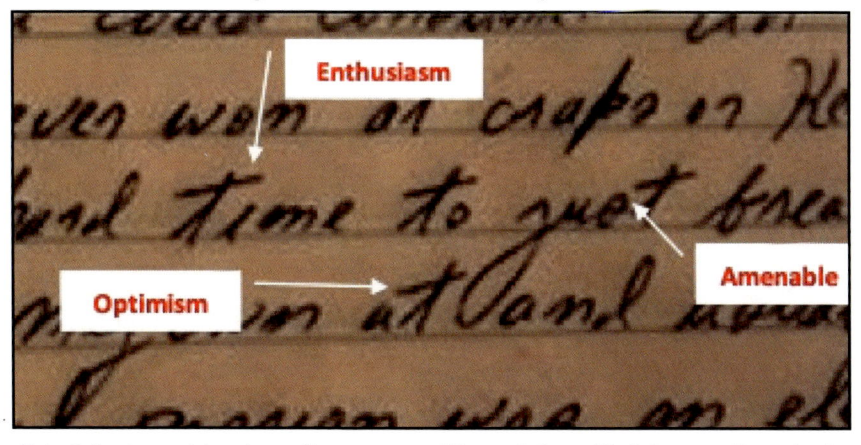

Figure 06-05: Basic Personality Traits[12]

Note: Enthusiasm – t-bars longer than average middle zone letter width. Optimism – Upward inclination of words, lines of writing and t-bars. Amenable – Letter s that has rounded upper tip or a printed letter configuration.

Cottingham's very strong vanity only made things worse when he got into an argument because his exaggerated opinion of himself made it almost impossible to reason with him at these times.

Figure 06-06: Basic Personality Traits[12]

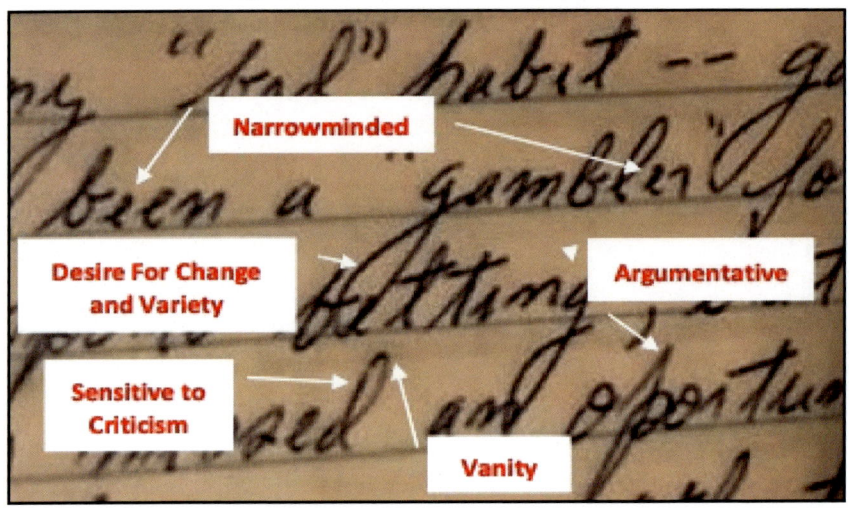

Note: Sensitive to Criticism – t and d stems that are looped. Argumentative – The beginning of the downstroke on letter p starts at a point higher than the loop. Narrowminded – Letter e that is narrow or completely closed. Vanity – Height of d and t stems are greater than 2.5 times the average middle zone letter height. Desire for Change – Length of downstroke on g, y, j is three or more times the average height of lowercase letters. Desire for Variety – Lower loop width of g, y, j is greater than 0.5 times the average width of lowercase letters.

As noted in Cottingham's background, he worked as a computer operator for the Blue Cross Blue Shield Association based in NYC. A position like this requires a great deal of focus on fine details and adherence to strict protocols in order to do a good job, but there's a lot in Cottingham's personality profile that suggests he would not excel at this work. First and foremost is his strong lack of attention to detail. See Figure 06-07. 88% of the handwriting strokes that should show some level of attention to detail are completely devoid of that stroke, meaning that Cottingham had little ability to pay attention to the fine points of any work he was to perform. And then there was his limited ability to maintain his focus on working toward his assigned tasks. This lack of determination (See Figure 06-07; 68% FOO), otherwise known as "stick-to-it-ness," would further erode his capacity to be a high performer.

As if these two weak personality traits did not do enough to thwart Cottingham in any attempt to be a high-quality performing computer operator, there was his rather strong dislike for repetition (See Figure 06-07 – Desire for Change; 73% FOO) coupled with his intense need to constantly seek new and varied experiences. See Figure 06-07 – Desire for Variety; 100% FOO. Given all of these factors working against him, it is easy to speculate that Cottingham was a mediocre performer who didn't like his job and therefore sought stimulation and fulfillment in his outside activities. This grim reality is perhaps one reason why he was such a prolific and ruthless criminal.

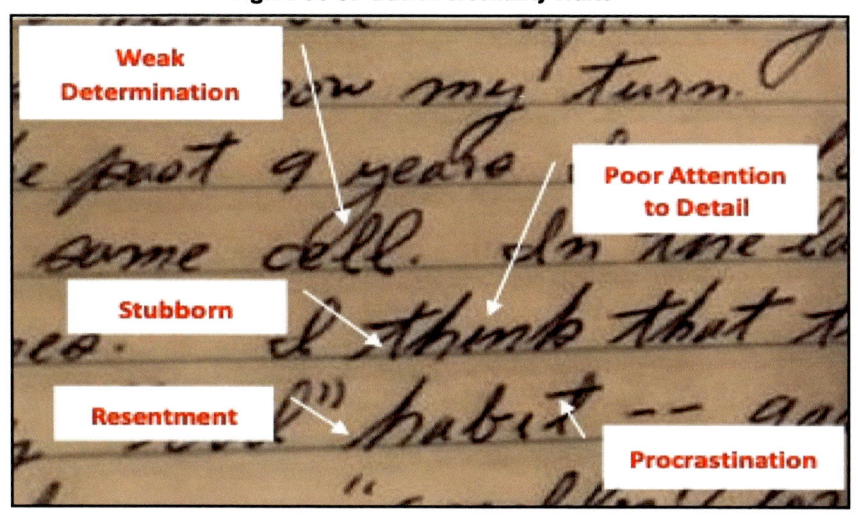

Figure 06-07: Basic Personality Traits[12]

Note: Resentment – Straight approach stroke starting at or below baseline. Stubborn – Wedge shape formation at bottom of d and t stems. Weak Determination – Downstroke in g, y, j, and q is not straight down but bends to the left in a curved fashion. Procrastination – t-bars are positioned left-of-center on the stem. Poor Attention to Detail - i and j dots placed far from their stem or else missing entirely.

HANDWRITING ANALYSIS - SERIAL KILLER PATHWAY[12,13]

Cottingham harbored a great deal of anger and rage in his soul, as evidenced by the fact that 54% of the words in his handwriting show the resentment stroke. See Figure 06-07. In the general population, 47% of people exhibit no resentment strokes in their handwriting at all, and for those who do, the average rate of occurrence of the stroke is just 13%. Figure 06-08 outlines how

Cottingham's deep-seated anger manifested itself in his behavior, especially in terms of how it led to assaults on women. Even though Cottingham's defense mechanisms were in the normal range,[13] they obviously were not effective in curtailing his criminal behavior. Refer to Appendix One for an in-depth discussion of defense mechanisms.

As mentioned previously, one of the more peculiar aspects of Cottingham's case is the fact that he became a serial killer despite the fact that his upbringing was quite benign. Peter Vronsky spent over 50 hours interviewing him and says that he, "uncovered nothing in [Cottingham's] youth that points easily to a life of extreme violence."[2] Vronsky did, however, uncover something in his interviews with Cottingham that might explain his behavior; he, "was hit by a car as a four-year-old and suffered brain damage to his frontal lobe – an area of the brain associated with the desire to commit acts of aggression…"[2]

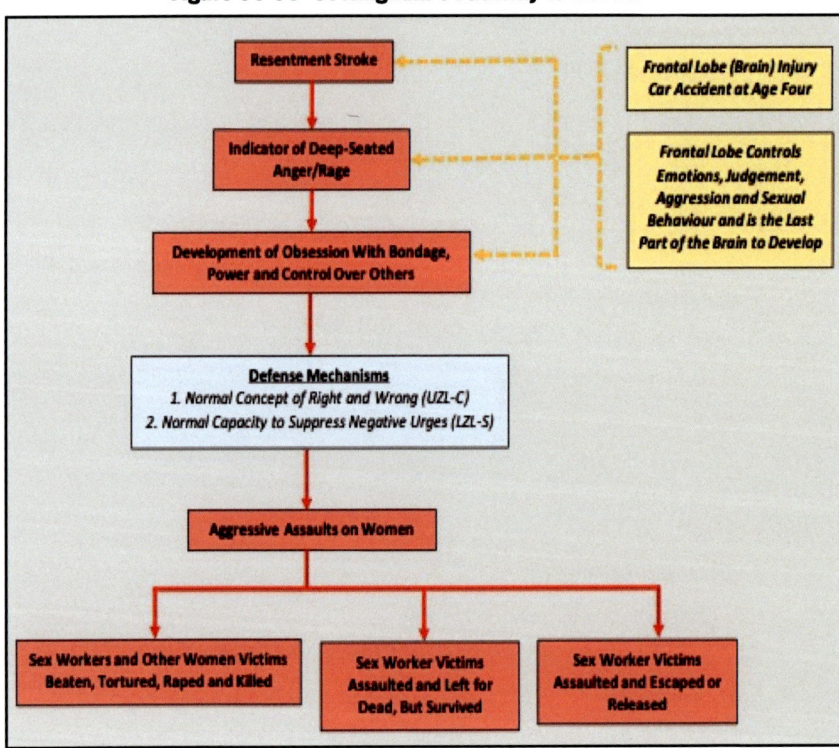

Figure 06-08: Cottingham's Pathway to Murder[12,13]

There are no references available to verify the fact that Cottingham did suffer frontal lobe damage, but if this is correct, then there is some substance to the suggestion that it, at the very least, contributed to the manifestation of Cottingham's serial killer proclivities. A study reported in 2001 in the Journal of Neurological and Neurosurgical Psychiatry[14] investigated the link between frontal lobe damage and violent and criminal behavior. What the authors found was that "focal orbitofrontal injury is specifically associated with increased aggression."[14] A report by the Brain Injury Institute[15] provides additional supportive information, stating that "the most common cause of frontal lobe disorders is a closed head injury like an accident." The report goes on to explain that symptoms of frontal lobe damage are behavioral, such as "difficulty in the preservation of social inhibition" and emotional, such as "difficulty controlling anger" and "difficulty in understanding others' opinions." This last point is particularly interesting because it could well explain Cottingham's strong narrowmindedness.

There are also some additional hints in Cottingham's background that might lend support to the possibility of a brain injury being the cause of his murderous behavior. One is seen in his statement that he became fascinated with bondage at a very young age. The other is the fact that he began his serial killer activities at the young age of 21, a rarity for serial killers. Both of these observations could be said to be linked to his early childhood brain injury.

So, do we know for sure why Cottingham became a serial killer? No. All we know for sure is that he definitely was a vicious one.

References

1. Ehrlich, Brenna (February 05, 2022) "Darkness Enveloped My Soul"; The Final Confessions of the Torso Killer. *Rolling Stone Magazine*

2. Janos, Adam *(September 05, 2019)* How to Explain Serial Killers Who Come from Good Homes. *True Crime Blog: Stories & News*

3. The Story of Richard Cottingham, "The Times Square Torso Ripper." (December 12, 2021) *AllThatsInteresting*

4. Ponti, Crystal *(December 16, 2021)* What Is "Torso Killer" Richard Cottingham's Life Like Today? *True Crime Blog: Stories & News*

5. Vanapalli, Viswa *(December 29, 2021)* Where is Richard Cottingham Now? *TheCinemaholic*

6. Bovsun, Mara and Dominguez, Robert *(May 02, 2021)* "Torso Killer" Richard Cottingham left a bloody trail of victims 30 years ago – and the body count is still rising. *New York Daily News*

7. Raab, Selwyn *(December 10, 1979)* "Mystery Man Sought in 2 Hotel Slayings" *The New York Times*

8. Banks, Anthony *(March 03, 2019)* "The Torso Killer: Richard Cottingham" *Criminally Intrigued*

9. Fezzani, Nadia (2015) Through the Eyes of Serial Killers: Interviews with Seven Murderers. Dundurn Press ISBN 978-1-45972467-9

10. Mulraney, Frances *(December 28, 2021)* "Manhatten Ripper" Inside chilling story of the Times Square "Torso" Killer feared to have slaughtered 100 Women and mutilated their bodies. *The U.S. Sun*

11. Farberov, Snejana *(June 22, 2022)* "Torso Killer" Richard Cottingham indicted in 1968 Long Island slaying: report. *New York Post*

12. Racher, John (2022) Advanced Graphology: An Encyclopedia of Personality Traits Revealed in Handwriting ISBN 978-1-7773610-1-3 *www.volumesdirect.com*

13. Racher, John (Autumn 2022) *Conscientiousness, Sublimation ... and Serial Killers* The Graphologist - The Journal of the British Institute of

Graphologists

14. Brower, M and Price, B. (December, 2001) Neoropsychiatry of frontal lobe dysfunction in violent and criminal behaviour: a critical review. *J Neurol Neurosurg Psychiatry*

15. Frontal Lobe Damage. Brain Injury Institute. Accessed November, 2022

Chapter 7
ELIZABETH WETTLAUFER

THE NURSE WHO BECAME A SERIAL KILLER

Canadians are generally regarded internationally as nice people, so you'd think that a Canadian nurse would be extra nice, wouldn't you? Then again, maybe not.

Elizabeth Tracy Mae "Bethe" Wettlaufer (nee: Parker) was born on June 10, 1967 and grew up in Woodstock, Ontario, Canada.[1] She voluntarily confessed[2] in 2016 to killing a number of elderly patients in long-term care institutions while working as a registered nurse, and ultimately was charged with eight counts of murder,[3] four counts of attempted murder and two counts of aggravated assault. The crimes were committed between 2007 and 2016 when Wettlaufer was in her forties. What made this case so sensational was the fact that all these crimes went completely unnoticed;[4] all the deceased were thought to have died of natural causes. In June 2017, Wettlaufer confessed to all charges, obliviating the need for a trial and was sentenced to life in prison.

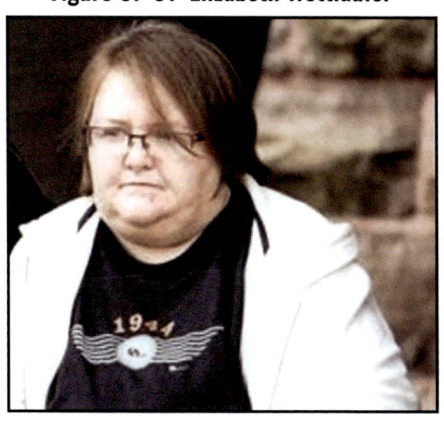

Figure 07-01: Elizabeth Wettlaufer

BACKGROUND

Elizabeth Parker was born and raised in the Woodstock, Ontario area in a fundamentalist Baptist family, the father of whom was an elder in the church and who held, amongst other things, very strong anti-gay[4] attitudes. Parker's parents were described by people within the community as "very controlling" of their children. While in high school, Parker became conflicted when she realized that she had an attraction to a teenage girl in her neighborhood. Her advances were rejected, but the feelings continued. After graduating from high school, she attended the London Baptist Bible College, eventually earning a degree in religious education and counselling. All did not go well while in college. When Parker was discovered to be attending a gay-friendly church with a girlfriend, her parents coerced her into undergoing a process of conversion therapy to attempt to rid her of her lesbian urges. She described the entire experience as contributing to her bouts of depression, self-loathing and self-doubt.[4]

Even though she was not diagnosed at the time, psychiatrists retrospectively determined that Parker so resented her upbringing in a rigid Baptist home environment that she began to develop an antisocial personality disorder (APD) when she was approximately 15 years old.[4] APD is described as an instability in moods, behaviors and functioning, with one of the more common symptoms being a disregard of the rights of others.

After graduating from Bible college, Parker decided to go into nursing. In 1995 she graduated as a registered nurse and began to pick up jobs in the Woodstock area. She continued to experience sexual identity confusion, but in order to do what was expected of her, she married Donnie Wettlaufer in 1997.[3] The relationship didn't last long; her husband discovered that she was reaching out to women via the internet and this led to their separation and divorce in 2007. Shortly thereafter Wettlaufer pursued a romantic relationship with a female friend. They moved into an apartment together and were briefly engaged. Her parents refused to acknowledge the reality of this and future other lesbian relationships by rationalizing Wettlaufer's love interests as just boarders whom she was helping out during financially hard times.

It was also between 1996 and 2007 that Wettlaufer developed a host of other problems. She was diagnosed as having a borderline personality disorder and she developed a severe drug and alcohol addiction.[4] On one occasion, her nursing registration had a restriction placed on it after she was caught stealing an opioid (i.e.: hydromorphone) while at work.

In 2007 Wettlaufer was hired on a full-time basis at Caressant Care,[3] a long-term care (LTC) home in Woodstock and worked there until 2014 when she was fired. Seven of the eight murders that she committed occurred during her employment there.

Hydromorphone was Wettlaufer's drug of choice,[4] and she was taking large doses several times per month. She has explained why she was a regular user; she needed it to relax while at work. Because she always felt like she had to be constantly on top of her game and consequently felt stressed and anxious as a result of this self-imposed expectation, she found that by taking one to three pills she became calmer and felt relieved of the pressure to perform. Hydromorphone is a commonly prescribed drug in many LTC facilities to manage pain and shortness of breath and because the standard of care in LTC facilities at that time did not require a rigorous inventory control of opioids, they were relatively easy to obtain for nefarious purposes. Wettlaufer had a number of ways to unobtrusively obtain this powerful medication. She would substitute dementia patients' hydromorphone with laxatives because they wouldn't notice; she took the unused prescriptions of patients who had died; she would even open hydromorphone capsules, swallow the contents and then give the empty pill cases to the patients.[4]

As Wettlaufer would later describe to police, it was in 2007 that she began experiencing dark feelings that she described as "red surges.[2]" Just a few days after being hired at Caressant Care, she was in a general state of anger and decided that God probably wanted Clotilde Adriano, an 88-year-old with dementia, to be with Him. She stated that, "I honestly thought that God wanted to use me." Wettlaufer, as was to become her usual practice, injected Adriano with a large dose of insulin in a discreet spot on her body where a needle prick would be difficult to detect. Fortunately for Adriano, another nurse noticed that she was exhibiting signs of extremely low blood sugar levels and took the necessary actions to reverse the condition. Because insulin overdoses are very difficult to detect and the victims were elderly, Wettlaufer's actions went undetected because the patients were routinely assumed to have died of natural causes.

Three months later, Wettlaufer killed her first patient, James Silcox[8], an 84-year-old who had previously experienced a stroke. On August 11, 2007,

Silcox was behaving in an agitated fashion; he was relatively unaware of his surroundings and he was repeatedly calling out for his wife. Wettlaufer said that she experienced a "red surge" and became so angry with Silcox that she "wanted him to die." She injected him with a massive dose of insulin, and he died a few hours later. Afterwards Wettlaufer said she felt that "a pressure had been relieved from me."[4]

In March 2014, Caressant Care terminated Wettlaufer's employment because of repeated episodes of showing up drunk for work and a number of medication-related errors, the final straw being a serious incident in which she gave the wrong medication to a patient. Fascinatingly, none of these incidents were related to her assaults and murders.

After leaving Caressant Care, Wetlaufer bounced from job to job for the next two years. She was fired from two of them, one for stealing medication and the other for making a medication error while high. During this time, she assaulted three patients with insulin overdoses, one of whom died. It was during this period of time that Wettlaufer tried to get help with her opioid addiction by checking herself into a rehabilitation facility in Port Colborne, Ontario. The intervention proved to be unsuccessful. It was also during this time that she really began to feel conflicted about her religion because she was confused about why God wanted her to kill when she knew it was wrong.

Wettlaufer's downward spiral came to an end when, in 2016, she "started to believe I was the devil."[4] This led her to believe that she desperately needed psychiatric help and so, on September 16 she voluntarily entered an inpatient rehabilitation program at the Centre for Addition and Mental Health (CAMH), a psychiatric hospital in Toronto, Ontario. Over the next month, she confessed to CAMH staff about killing patients. When asked why she did it, Wettlaufer explained that she was acting out her really bad anger issues on the patients. This led the hospital to contact the Toronto Police Service[3] who initiated what was to become one of the most exhaustive murder investigations to occur in Canada.

Wettlaufer confessed to all the murder and assault charges that were filed against her, and on June 26, 2017 she was sentenced to eight concurrent life terms in prison with no possibility of parole for 25 years.

At first glance one of the more perplexing aspects of Wettlaufer's case was her repeated confessions of her murders. Starting as early as 2008, she alluded to her crimes at various times to ex-girlfriends, a male acquaintance, her pastor, a student nurse, a criminal lawyer and a Narcotics Anonymous sponsor.[7]

While it seems peculiar that none of these people took her seriously enough to report her to the authorities, it has also been suggested that these "confessions" were actually half-hearted attempts by Wettlaufer to exercise some form of self-control through self-intimidation in order to get herself to stop; she really didn't want to face justice, she just wanted to stop killing. For instance, when Wettlaufer was told by the student nurse that she was going report what she had heard, Wettlaufer talked her out of it by saying that her employer would never take the student's word over hers.

HANDWRITING ANALYSIS - GENERAL PROFILE[5]

Even though Wettlaufer's reactions to emotional situations could range from being unresponsive to very responsive, her most frequent behavior was warm and not overly reactive. She could be sensitive to and considerate of other people's feelings and, for the most part, would be able to exercise good judgement in her behavior towards others. That being said, she was subject to many mood changes due to an underlying current of instability, as indicated in her handwriting by the wavy, uneven and irregular baselines[9] and a significant variation in letter sizes within the same word[9]. (Figures 07-02, 07-03, 07-04). Wettlaufer's emotional instability appeared in her teenage years (Figure 07-02) and got progressively worse as she got older (Figure 07-03).

Figure 07-02: Wettlaufer (nee: Parker) Signature[5,9] (Age ~17 years)

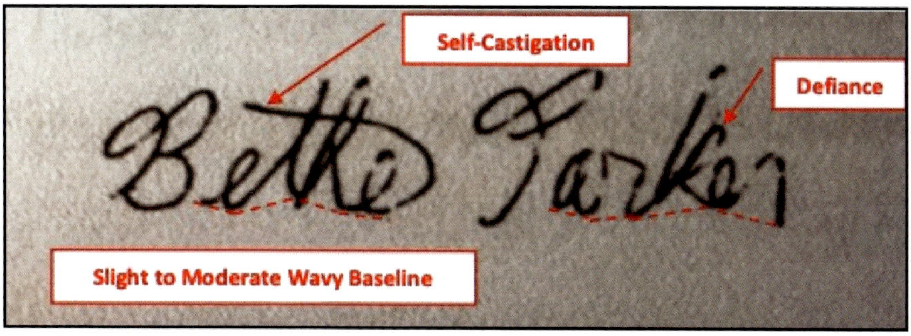

Figure 07-03: Wettlaufer Signature[5,9] (Age ~47 years)

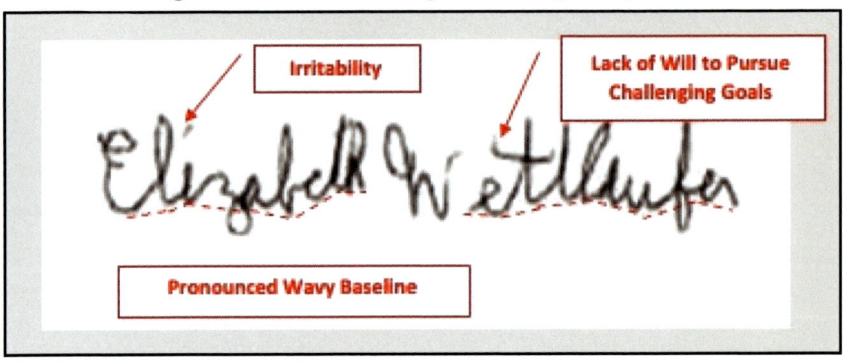

[Signature image annotated with: Irritability, Lack of Will to Pursue Challenging Goals, Pronounced Wavy Baseline]

Wettlaufer was above average in intelligence. She had a natural curiosity that was reinforced by her methodical way of examining and analyzing situations. She had a good grasp of theoretical and philosophical issues and her open-mindedness about most things gave her the ability to learn from new experiences. Wettlaufer had an above average attention to detail, having the ability to focus her mind on every aspect of a situation no matter how small the details were. She was very organized in her thinking and managing her life, though her ability to focus on long-term projects would often begin to wane after a little while.

Figure 07-04: Wettlaufer's Emotional Instability and Resentment[5,9]

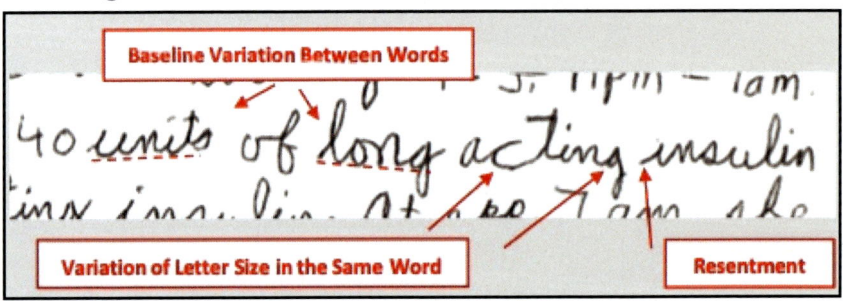

[Handwriting sample annotated with: Baseline Variation Between Words, Variation of Letter Size in the Same Word, Resentment]

In her teenage years, Wettlaufer tended to over-indulge in self-blame and to take on guilty feelings, even when they may not have been justified, as evidenced by the self-castigation stroke (Figure 07-02). This is a "backslash stroke" on t-stems when the pen stays on the paper and crosses back over the t-stem by making a stroke that is upward and facing to the left. She was also quite self-conscious, spending an excessive amount of time worrying about how others judged her appearance and behavior. This personality trait is identified by the mounds in the letters "m" and "n" that are higher than the rest of the letter. (Figure 07-05). As if her life wasn't challenging enough, Wettlaufer also suffered from very low self-respect (i.e.: self-esteem).

In order to deal with her above-mentioned insecurities, Wettlaufer developed a number of other traits. She developed the ability to resist any effort by people to exert what she considered to be an undue influence over her (i.e.: Defiance; Figure 07-02). This behavior was reinforced by a strong sense of resentment (Figures 07-02 and 07-05) and an even stronger inclination to adhere to an opinion or a course of action despite common sense or reason (i.e.: Obstinate – Sharp tipped letter "s"; Figure 07-05). Wettlaufer could also be rather stubborn when she wanted to me. This trait (Figure 07-05) is seen when there is a wedge (i.e.: an inverted "v") in the base of the letter's "d" and "t". Finally, Wettlaufer also suffered from an unconscious desire to avoid thinking about unpleasant realities. This trait of self-deceit (Figure 07-05) allowed her to delude herself of things that would otherwise cause her emotional anguish; it is a form of denial.

When it comes to Wettlaufer's "public face" there are a number of noteworthy traits. She was seen by many as a nice person, but she did have her rough edges. Wettlaufer was more known for her frankness rather than her diplomacy. Her candor was reinforced by her directness, that is, her ability to come straight to the point. Such bluntness can be "off putting" to many people, but fortunately for Wettlaufer she was quite reticent by nature, and this disinclination to talk freely undoubtedly helped to keep her from inadvertently ruffling feathers due to blurting out unpleasant truths or observations.

HANDWRITING ANALYSIS - SERIAL KILLER PATHWAY[5]

Wettlaufer's activities as a serial killer were simple in some ways and very complicated in others. As outlined in Figure 07-06, Wettlaufer's actual approach to murder was straight-forward: an unruly and/or irritating elderly patient would annoy her, which in turn triggered a "red surge" of anger, which she then dealt with by injecting the patient with a massive overdose of insulin that, more often than not, resulted in their death. What was complicated about these actions was the presence, absence and/or magnitude of the various triggering forces.

Figure 07-05: Wettlaufer's Handwriting[5]

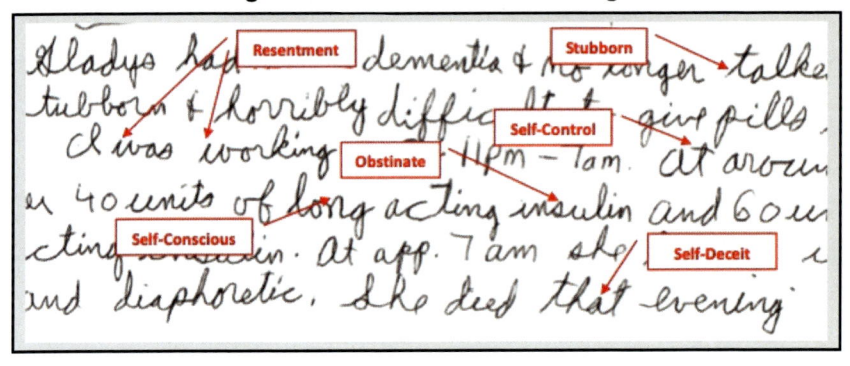

[Handwritten note with annotations: "Gladys had dementia & no longer talks. Stubborn & horribly difficult to give pills. I was working 11pm – 7am. At around 40 units of long acting insulin and 60 u cting in. At app. 7 am she and diaphoretic. She died that evening" — labeled with: Resentment, Stubborn, Self-Control, Obstinate, Self-Conscious, Self-Deceit]

Most healthcare workers who have dealt with elderly patients, and especially those patients with dementia, will tell you that they can routinely be uncooperative, belligerent and/or physically aggressive. What seems to have set Wettlaufer apart from most other healthcare workers in terms of her response to these patients was her emotional instability coupled with her relatively high level of resentment, both of which are revealed in her handwriting.

Emotional instability, as discussed previously, is shown by very wavy baselines (Figure 07-04). What handwriting cannot tell you, however, is what kind of emotional turmoil the writer is suffering from and whether or not it could be expressed through aggressive or harmful actions. With Wettlaufer however, the reinforcing trait of a deep-seated anger due to resentment comes into play.

In Wettlaufer's case, her resentment came from a feeling that she was being unreasonably imposed upon by unruly patients. It is a decidedly negative trait because it involves the persistent suspicion that one is being unfairly "used." The trait is indicated whenever there is a straight, rigid stroke at the beginning of a word that starts at or below the baseline (Figure 07-03, 07-05). To be fair, the presence of the occasional resentment stroke is not that uncommon and is not alarming in-and-of itself. What set Wettlaufer apart however was the frequency of the strokes; in her handwriting they appear in approximately 23% of her words, and that is an abnormal level that is concerning.

Figure 07-06 reveals the full complexity of Wettlaufer's situation due to a myriad of situational factors, all of which exacerbated her emotional stability problems. Key amongst these factors was her long-standing abuse of alcohol and opioids. Hydromorphone was Wettlaufer's "go to" drug, and she routinely consumed large quantities. A little known and uncommon side effect of long-term abuse of hydromorphone is seeing, hearing or feeling things that are not real. It seems possible that Wettlaufer was experiencing this symptom when she felt that God was endorsing her decision to inject patients with insulin overdoses. What is not clear is whether or not this was reinforcing what she was already experiencing from her mental health issues, or if it was the sole source of the feelings/voices. Regardless, Wettlaufer has been very clear about receiving these messages, and her tendency to self-deceit made it even easier to act on her impulses. As seen in Figure 07-05, self-deceit is seen in handwriting when there is a small loop on the interior, left side of lowercase letters such as "o"" "a", "d" and "g."

Wettlaufer wasn't always at the mercy of her urges, as the trait stroke of self-control reveals (Figure 07-05). Whenever you see a t-bar that is bent so that the ends turn downward, you are seeing a writer who is exerting a conscious effort to contain a behavior that is causing them emotional pain. As we have seen from her history, Wettlaufer was trying to control or at least contain her murderous intentions, but tragically she was also plagued by a counter force that worked to sap the energy from her efforts to control her anger. In Figure 07-03, we see a t-bar in which the ends turn upward. When this particular stroke is seen in handwriting, we know that the writer is not able to successfully pursue anything resembling a significant goal if it requires the expenditure of a lot of emotional energy.

Wetlaufer's case was very unusual in three different ways.

First, there were Wettlaufer's numerous admissions of killing patients to a variety of people over the span of approximately eight years. While it appears that most of these were more an attempt by Wettlaufer to pressure herself to stop killing as opposed to seeking justice, they are unusual within the realm of serial killers because of their forthrightness. A number of serial killers want the attention of the public, but they are, for the most part, extremely careful not to either name themselves or to provide any information that would lead the authorities to suspect them. Wettlaufer, on the other hand, came right out and named herself. It is unfortunate that none of these people took her admittedly "off the wall" admissions seriously.

Then there was Wettlaufer's almost unheard-of action of turning herself in to the authorities.[4] It has been suggested that a number of serial killers either consciously or unconsciously want to be caught and for that reason become careless in the commission of their crimes, enough so that they ultimately leave enough clues for the police to track the crime back to them. What differentiates Wettlaufer from these types of serial killers is the fact that while their actions were passive in nature, Wettlaufer was purposefully active by directly approaching the authorities. Because CAMH has a stellar reputation for professionalism, Wettlaufer knew that by voluntarily checking herself into this psychiatric hospital and confessing to her crimes the police would undoubtedly be alerted. What makes her actions even more remarkable is the fact that there was absolutely no external pressure that was driving her to surrender. None of her murders were even suspected by the police; there was no active police investigation that was driving her to confess because the police were closing in on her. The truth of the matter is that she had committed the perfect crime (actually the perfect crimes) and so, had she not actively sought out incarceration, she would have remained free of any suspicion. Wettlaufer's confession demonstrates that she must have had a functional sense of morality. In her confession to the police, she categorically stated that she "knew right from wrong"[7] yet she obviously couldn't control her urge to kill. When you look at her defense mechanism[6] scores however, the situation becomes clear. (See Appendix 1 for an in-depth discussion of defense mechanisms.) Her UZL-C score was 2.1 and her LZL-S score was 1.3. Her UZL-C score validates what she acknowledged in her confession, that she did really understand the difference between good and bad. Her LZL-S score indicates that there was little in the way of sublimation of her drives. Wettlaufer had a history of mental instability, had a great deal of anger (a whopping 23% of her handwritten words showed the resentment stroke) and she was subject to what she called "red surges" of rage. Wettlaufer was a bit of an oddity, a serial killer with a conscience.

Figure 07-06: Pathway to Murder[2,5,6]

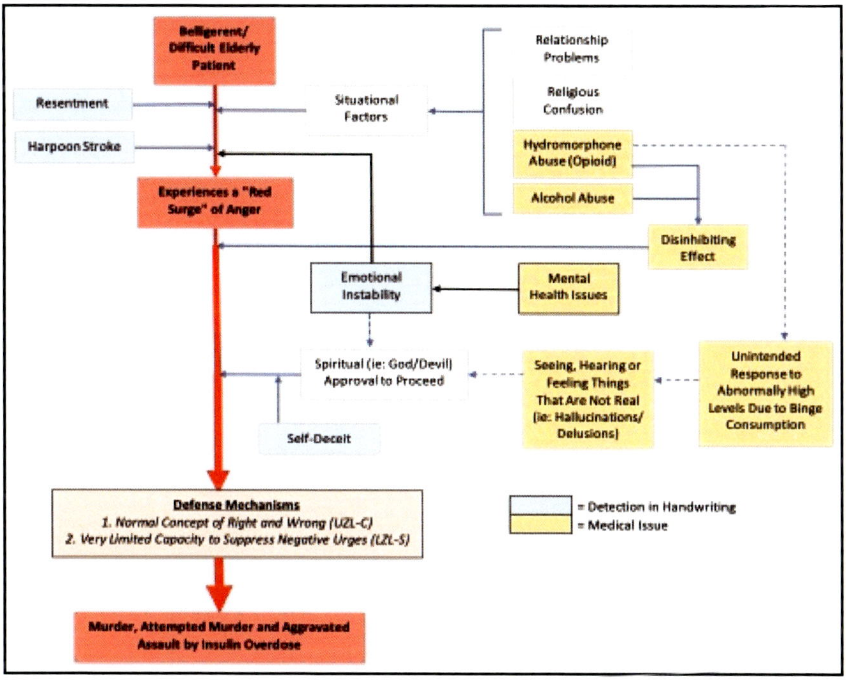

```
                    Belligerent/
                    Difficult Elderly                    Relationship
                    Patient                              Problems

   Resentment                      Situational          Religious
                                   Factors              Confusion

   Harpoon Stroke                                       Hydromorphone
                                                        Abuse (Opioid)
                    Experiences a "Red
                    Surge" of Anger                     Alcohol Abuse

                                                                          Disinhibiting
                                                                          Effect
                           Emotional              Mental
                           Instability            Health Issues

                           Spiritual (ie: God/Devil)   Seeing, Hearing or    Unintended
                           Approval to Proceed          Feeling Things       Response to
                                                        That Are Not Real    Abnormally High
                                                        (ie: Hallucinations/ Levels Due to Binge
                           Self-Deceit                   Delusions)          Consumption

                    Defense Mechanisms
                    1. Normal Concept of Right and Wrong (UZL-C)    ☐ = Detection in Handwriting
                    2. Very Limited Capacity to Suppress Negative Urges (LZL-S)   ☐ = Medical Issue

                    Murder, Attempted Murder and Aggravated
                    Assault by Insulin Overdose
```

Finally, there's the fact that Wettlaufer pleaded guilty to all charges and waived her right to a trial.[8] There have been those serial killers who have been surprisingly candid and forthcoming regarding the scope of their activities once caught, but for the most part they still insisted on going to trial to have their guilt proven in a court of law. Wettlaufer's action was almost unprecedented and has left a number of observers wondering that if she had gone to trial, her very serious addiction problems and psychiatric challenges might have been taken into full account and her prison sentence adjusted accordingly. Unfortunately for her, we will never know.

References

1. Baum, Kathryn; White, Patrick (October 25, 2016) "Friends of former Ontario nurse charged with murder stunned by allegations" The Globe and Mail

2. Dubinski, Kate (June 01, 2017) "Ex-nurse Elizabeth Wettlaufer felt 'red surge' before killing elderly patients" CBC News

3. Gillis, Wendy; Siekierska, Alicja; Goffin, Peter (October 29, 2016) "From caring nurse to accused serial killer: who is Elizabeth Wettlaufer?" Toronto Star

4. Lancaster, John (October 07, 2017) "Seeing Red: How did a mild-mannered nurse from small-town Ontario become one of Canada's worst serial killers?" CBC News

5. Racher, John (2022) Advanced Graphology: An Encyclopedia of Personality Traits Revealed in Handwriting ISBN 978-1-7773610-1-3

6. Racher, John (Autumn 2022) *Conscientiousness, Sublimation … and Serial Killers* The Graphologist - The Journal of the British Institute of Graphologists

7. Fraser, Laura (June 02, 2017) "Here's what ex-nurse Elizabeth Wettlaufer confessed about killing 8 patients" CBC News

8. "Timeline of events in case of former Ontario nurse Elizabeth Wettlaufer" (June 01, 2017 Global News The Canadian Press

9. Lowe, Sheila (2007) The Complete Idiot's Guide to Handwriting Analysis, Second Edition ISBN 978-1-59257-601-2

Chapter 8
DENNIS NILSEN

A SCOTTISH SERIAL KILLER AND NECROPHILE

"I wished I could stop, but I couldn't. I had no other thrill or happiness."[11]

Dennis Andrew Nilsen (See Figure 08-01) was born on November 23, 1945 in Aberdeenshire, Scotland and died on May 12, 2018 (age 72) in North Yorkshire, England. He is reputed to have murdered 12 – 15 men during the span of approximately four years (December 1978 to January 1983) when he was in his mid-thirties.

Figure 08-01: Dennis Nilsen

BACKGROUND

Nilsen was the second of three children; his parents married in May 1942. The marriage lasted for only six years,[1] his parents divorcing when he was approximately three years old. Nilsen's father was reputedly an "absentee" parent, and because they were living with his mother's parents, his grandfather was his primary male role model. Nilsen held his grandfather in very high esteem and was devastated when he died at age 62 in October 1961 when Nilsen was almost six years old.[2]

It appears that Nilsen's grandfather's death was pivotal in his formative years because at that time he became increasingly withdrawn and made a point of avoiding any contact with adult family members who tried to develop an emotional bond with him or show him any warmth.[1] He was resentful of what he regarded as the preferential treatment of his older brother and younger sister by his mother and grandmother, and was jealous of his older brother's popularity.[1]

In the mid-1950s, Nilsen's mother remarried and moved out of her parent's home to live with her new husband in Strichen, a small village in Aberdeenshire, Scotland. Nilsen was approximately ten years old at the time and thought that his stepfather was a harsh disciplinarian who had his favorites (i.e.: not him).[2]

As Nilsen started to experience puberty, he began to realize that he was homosexually inclined. Despite Nilsen's best efforts, his older brother began to suspect as much and subsequently publicly ridiculed him for it on many occasions.[1] This damaged his relationship with his older brother even further and probably only increased his resentment of him.

In 1961 after turning 16 years old, Nilsen applied for and was accepted into the British army,[1] his intention being to train as a chef. He described his experience in the army as being positive, and he thoroughly enjoyed the travel opportunities that it afforded.[2] While stationed in West Germany, Nilsen's sexual fantasies started to find definition. They always involved a sexual partner who was a young male with a trim physique and who was completely passive. The fantasies continued to be refined, and Nilsen described how the sex partner went from being passive to being either unconscious or dead[1]. In 1970 when he was approximately 25 years old and stationed in West Berlin, Nilsen had his first sexual encounter with a female prostitute. He described the experience as being uninspired and unfulfilling.[1]

Nilsen completed his army service in October 1972 and shortly thereafter decided to join the Metropolitan Police in London, England.[3] It was during the summer of 1973 at the age of 28 that Nilsen began visiting gay pubs, which then led to a number of short-term relationships with men. Nilsen eventually decided that a gay lifestyle was not compatible with being a police officer,[3] so in May 1974 he found a job with the civil service.

After a number of failed relationships, Nilsen resigned himself (in 1978) to living alone, having decided that for whatever reason, he was seen to be an undesirable partner,[1,2,4] and in December of that year, he murdered his first victim, a 14-year-old boy by the name of Stephen Holmes.[2]

Nilsen's typical pattern of assault and murder[2] was to convince his victims to go to his residence through the offer of alcohol or a place to sleep. Once there, they were strangled to death or, when rendered unconscious, drowned in the bathtub, a sink or a bucket of water. Once dead, the victims were washed, eventually clothed and kept in Nilsen's residence until decomposition became advanced, at which time they were dismembered. Nilsen would store the bodies under his floorboards[2] until such time as he would have a need for them,[2] seating them on his armchair beside him to watch television and drink alcohol, to have a (one-sided) conversation, or placing them on his bed[8] while he masturbated over them or while he laid beside them. Inevitably the bodies of his victims began to decompose, resulting in an awful stench and the presence of thousands of maggots and flies.[1] At his first residence, Nilsen had a garden and was able to dispose of the bodies by burning them in a bonfire[3,5] (See Figure 08-02). In his second residence, because it was an attic apartment,[6] he dismembered the bodies, stored the torsos and heads in various drawers and closets, and flushed the dissected organs, flesh, hands and feet down the toilet.

On January 26, 1983, Nilsen killed what was to be his final victim.[2] As per his usual routine, he dismembered the body, stored various parts in a closet, a drawer and a tea chest and flushed the flesh, organs, hands and feet down the toilet. Part of his activities prior to disposing materials down the toilet involved boiling the head, hands and feet in a large pot on his kitchen stove.

On February 04, 1983, Nilsen wrote a letter to his landlord complaining of plugged drains[3] (See Figure 08-03). The plumbers who were sent to fix the drains became sufficiently alarmed when they found flesh-like materials and small bones[1,5] that they contacted the police, who in turn took samples for examination. A pathologist identified them as human remains,[7] and the police confronted Nilsen. Interestingly, Nilsen calmly admitted to murder and then proceeded to confess to multiple other deaths.[5] On February 11, 1983, Nilsen was officially charged with murder.

Figure 08-02: Police Forensic Team Examining Firepit

Photo: Inews.co.uk

Figure 08-03: Plumber Examining Plugged Drain

Photo: Irish Daily Mirror

One of Nilsen's more revealing explanations for his murders came from a journal he kept while awaiting his trial. In April 1983, he wrote the following. "It seems necessary for them (his victims) to have been dead in order that I could express those feelings which were the feelings I held sacred for my grandfather… The sight of them (his victims) brought me…temporary peace and fulfilment."[2]

Nilsen's trial began on October 23, 1983. He was charged with six counts of murder and two of attempted murder. On November 03, 1983, he was found guilty and sentenced to 25 years imprisonment.[10] This sentence was later changed to life without parole. He died on May 12, 2018 after surgery for an abdominal aortic aneurysm.

HANDWRITING ANALYSIS - GENERAL PROFILE[12]

Nilsen's emotions ran very deeply, much more so than most people. The very predominant right-hand slant of his writing emphasizes this; 90.9% of his writing had a slant in excess of 125°, and of those a very unusually high level (ie: 12.7%) exceeded 145°. Very few people have such a severe right-hand slant, and this means that Nilsen was subject to strong emotional reactions to most situations in a very quick fashion and without pausing for even a second to consider the consequences. This trait was further exacerbated by his heavy writing (i.e.: thick lines) which is indicative of a person who absorbs the strength of emotional situations to the point that they become part of their personality. They brood for long periods of time about stressful experiences.

Nilsen's intensely felt emotions worked synergistically with his intense sexual appetite to create a major driving force in his personality, and as seen in Figure 08-06, it was a major contributor to his becoming a serial killer. People who have very significant sensory appetites (e.g.: food; sexual) and who over-indulge reveal this trait in their handwriting by having so-called "muddy" writing. See Figure 08-04. Because of their over-indulgence, people with muddy writing experience a build-up of emotional pressure, and this was worrisome for Nilsen because of his already seriously strong emotional responsiveness.

Figure 08-04: General Personality Traits[12]

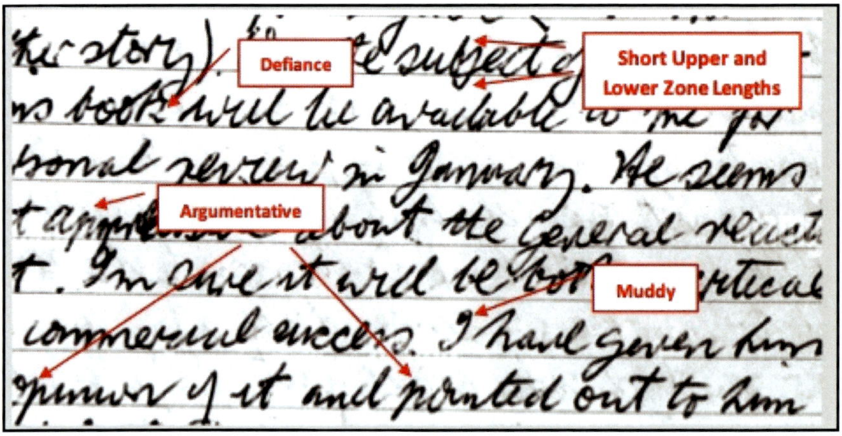

[Handwriting sample with annotations: "Defiance", "Short Upper and Lower Zone Lengths", "Argumentative", "Muddy"]

Note: Defiance – The buckle of a lowercase k is higher or out of proportion to the rest of the writing. Argumentative – The beginning of the downstroke on letter p starts at a point higher than the loop. Defense Mechanisms – Length of upper zone and lower zone loops. See Appendix One. Muddy Writing – Blobs, blotches, cross-outs and partially filled-in circles and loops.

Nilsen was fairly self-conscious, meaning that he routinely worried about what other people thought of his appearance and behavior. This resulted in him feeling rather ill-at-ease in the presence of others, and this perhaps explains why he routinely drank alcohol, to loosen his inhibitions so that he could interact with others more freely.[2] To help deal with his feelings of unease around others, Nilsen also developed three ego defense traits. He could be quite stubborn at times, continuing with an opinion or idea long after he knew that it was wrong; 38.9% of his writing showed this trait, and it was reinforced by his willingness to argue for the sake of arguing (Frequency of Occurrence = 64%; See Figure 08-04) and his inclination to want to challenge or resist authority (i.e.: Defiance). This latter trait was in full display when, while he was in prison awaiting his trial, he objected to wearing a prison uniform, explaining that because he was innocent before being found guilty, he was not to be treated like a prisoner. When the prison guards refused his request, he threatened to wear no clothes at all, and then on one occasion threw the contents of his chamber pot out of his cell, hitting several prison guards in the process.[1,2]

HANDWRITING ANALYSIS - SERIAL KILLER PATHWAY[12]

Nilsen is one of the more complex cases in that it wasn't just a few personality traits that revealed him to be a prime candidate for becoming a serial killer, but the cumulative effect of nine traits:

1. Four traits provided a firm foundation for his anger and rage, as revealed in the following handwriting strokes: Resentment (Frequency of Occurrence (FOO) = 19.1%; Anti-Social Behavior FOO = 2.8%; Dot Grinding FOO = 5.6%; Temper FOO = 14.5%. (See Figure 08-05).
2. Three traits revealed by his emotional and sensory overload, are discussed above (i.e.: Extreme Right-Hand Slant; Heavy Writing; Muddy Writing), and then,
3. Two handwriting characteristics associated with a person's defense mechanisms (See Figure 08-04 and Appendix One).
4. The interaction between these nine traits is outlined in Figure 08-06, Nilsen's personal pathway to murder.

Figure 08-05: Anger-Related Personality Traits[12]

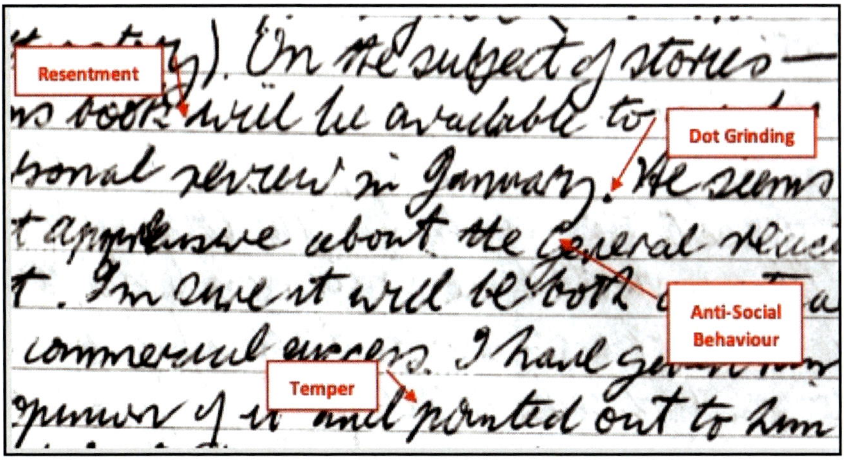

Note: Resentment – Straight approach stroke starting at or below baseline. Dot Grinding – Heavy pressure applied to punctuation. Anti-Social Behavior Stroke – Capitalized letters in place of lower-case letters. Temper – A short, straight initial stroke which joins a downstroke to form a sharp angle – a "tick" mark.

People who exhibit the resentment stroke go through life with a "chip on their shoulder" and so are proactively angry, as was Nilsen's case, about his deep, brooding feelings of injustice that had been inflicted upon him. The FOO rate of the resentment stroke in Nilsen's handwriting reveals him to have a higher-than-average level of the trait. Nilsen's temper was also quite evident in his handwriting and his behavior. Everyone at one time or another has been sufficiently provoked into a show of temper, but this doesn't mean that there will automatically be signs of this trait in their handwriting. For them to show up in a specimen of handwriting, the writer must be predictably predisposed to negatively react to situations that get under their skin, and in Nilsen's case, a FOO rate of 19.1% is quite high, and so the associated anger is very deeply ingrained in his personality. Writers who display dot grinding (at any level) are obsessively resentful by nature because they have been forced to accept something that they did not like, and Nilsen's documented resentfulness of his early childhood experiences certainly validates why this stroke shows up in his handwriting. Writers who display any level of the so-called anti-social behavior stroke are known to engage in actions that are contrary to the normal good graces of behavior expected in public, and this can be a gross understatement when applied to a serial killer. People who are anti-social in the graphological context are against the usual rules of society and will often, when the trait is strong enough, engage in disruptive acts.

Figure 08-06: Pathway to Murder[12]

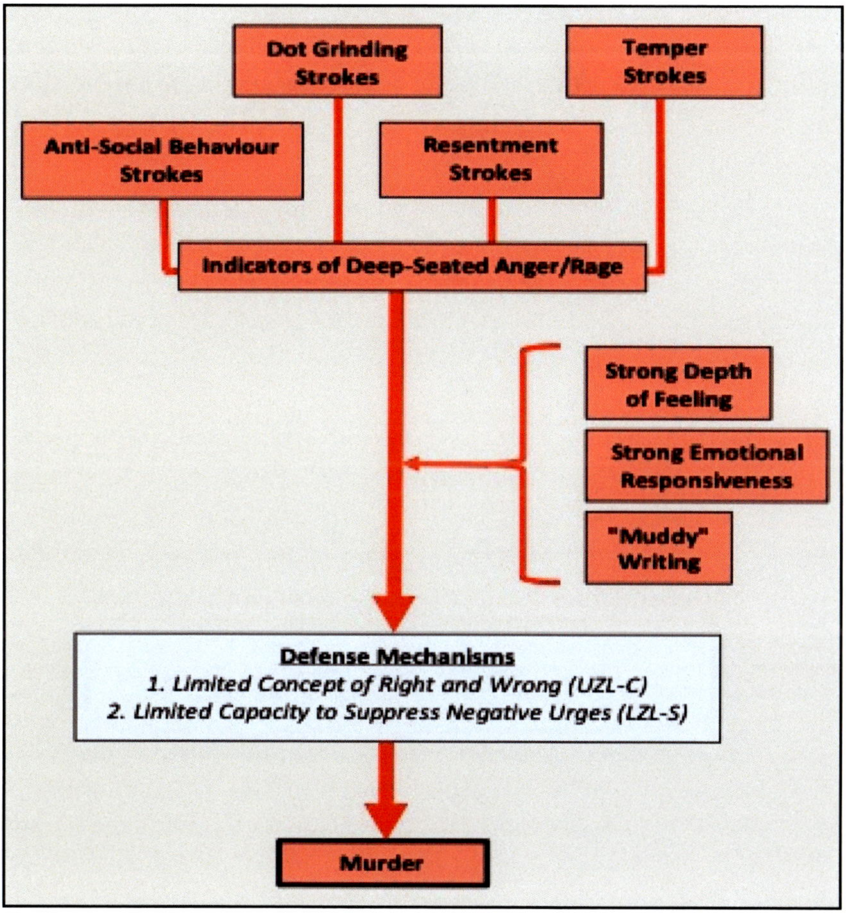

```
    Dot Grinding              Temper
      Strokes                 Strokes
         │                       │
 Anti-Social Behaviour    Resentment
       Strokes              Strokes
         │         │          │
         ▼         ▼          ▼
     Indicators of Deep-Seated Anger/Rage
                  │
                  │          ┐  Strong Depth
                  │          │   of Feeling
                  │◄─────────┤  Strong Emotional
                  │          │   Responsiveness
                  │          ┘  "Muddy"
                  │              Writing
                  ▼
            Defense Mechanisms
    1. Limited Concept of Right and Wrong (UZL-C)
    2. Limited Capacity to Suppress Negative Urges (LZL-S)
                  │
                  ▼
               Murder
```

Nilsen's defense mechanisms, the last line of defense that normally will prevent improper thoughts from being acted upon sadly failed in what they were supposed to do (See Appendix One for an in-depth explanation of the defense mechanisms) because they were of rather limited strength. Weak defense mechanisms are not often seen in the normal population. Normal defense mechanisms are seen in handwriting when the height of upper zone loops (e.g.: *b,h,l*) and lower zone loops (e.g.: *g, y, j*) are greater than twice the average height of the middle zone letters (e.g.: *a, o, n, u, s*). In Nilsen's case, his upper loops were scored at UZL-C = 1.8 and his lower loops were scored at LZL-S = 1.5. See Figure 08-04. People with weak defense mechanisms are not "deep thinkers" and are preoccupied with everyday concerns; they focus on the present rather than looking forward toward the future. They have a very limited perspective on life and are emotionally focused on themselves and their social issues. It was Nilsen's lack of strength in this important part of his personality that, in effect, "put the icing on the cake" in terms of setting the stage for what he was to become.

In Chapter One we saw that the US Federal Bureau of Investigation (FBI) concluded that a serial killer comes into being because of the combination of three factors, and these three factors can be loosely described as the Three N's: Nature, Nurture, Notion. Handwriting analysis can detect the aberrant behaviors associated with the first two factors (i.e.: Nature and Nurture) (See Figure 08-06), but it cannot provide any evidence about the "Notion" factor, which itself can be further broken down into three subsections: Situation, Opportunity, Decision. Details regarding a serial killer's notion can be found in their background information, but this is rarely available. In Nilsen's documented background, however, this information does exist. In a report that touched specifically on the details leading up to and including Nilsen's first kill,[13] we find some information that quite neatly describes the three subsections of his Notion factor. They are:

1. <u>Situation</u>. On December 30, 1978, Nilsen spent much of the day at home, drinking heavily. At some point in time he resolved that he "must at all costs leave his flat and seek company..."[2] and so headed off to the Cricklewood Arms pub.
2. <u>Opportunity</u>. At the pub, Nilsen met Stephen Holmes, whom he invited back to his flat. During the rest of the evening they drank, listened to music, and eventually went to bed together.[13]
3. <u>Decision</u>. The next morning Nilsen awoke and, while watching Holmes sleep, decided that he was to "stay with me over the New Year whether he wanted to or not."[2] Having come to that decision, Nilsen strangled Holmes into unconsciousness using a necktie and then drowned him by holding his head in a bucket of water.

Having killed Holmes, Nilsen kept his body for eight months, storing it under the floorboards of his house and intermittently bringing it out until it had become so decomposed that he then disposed of it by burning it in his back yard. See Figure 08-02. Nilsen was to have chillingly remarked after his arrest in 1983 that, after killing Holmes he had found himself "started down the avenue of death and possession of a new kind of flatmate."[2] It was just over a month after he disposed of Holmes's body that he proceeded with his evolution from being a murderer to a serial killer by killing his second victim,[5] Kenneth Ockenden, a 23-year-old Canadian. Nilsen realized that by killing young men he "had no other thrill or happiness"[11] because it fulfilled a need, a need that would require regular servicing

Nilsen's limited strength defense mechanisms were no match for the combined effect of his overly inflated sexual drive, his anti-social behavior and the significant anger generated by the cumulative impact of his traits identified in Figure 08-05. When asked if he was remorseful of what he had done, his reply was, "I have no tears for my victims…nor those bereaved by my actions."[9]

References

1. Coffey, Russell (2013) Dennis Nilsen: Conversations with Britain's Most Evil Serial Killer ISBN 978-1-782-19459-0
2. 2. Masters, Brian (1985) Killing for Company: The Case of Dennis Nilsen ISBN 978-0-812-83104-7
3. 3. Waddell, Bill (1993) The Black Museum: New Scotland Yard ISBN 978-0-751-51033-1
4. "Serial Killer Who Murdered "At Least" 15 Men Dies in Jail" (May 14, 2018) www.policeprofessional.com
5. Foreman, Laura (1992) Serial Killers ISBN 978-0-783-50001-0
6. Davidson, Lauren (November 12, 2015) "Would You Buy the Former Flat of One of Britain's Worst Serial Killers?" *The Daily Telegraph*
7. "Professor David Bowen (April 12, 2011) www.telegraph.co.uk
8. Wilson, Colin (1992) Serial Murders ISBN 978-1-854-35834-9
9. Persaud, R; Masters, B; Wilson, C. "Murder in Mind: Dennis Nilsen" ISSN 1364-5803
10. Nicholson, David (November 05, 1983) "The Lonely Murderer Who Preyed on Young Drifters" *The Times*
11. "Dennis Nilsen Quotes (Author of The Most Toys)" www.goodreads.com
12. Racher, John (2022) Advanced Graphology: An Encyclopedia of Personality Traits Revealed in Handwriting ISBN 978-1-7773610-1-3 *www.volumesdirect.com*
13. Tweedie, Neil (November 10, 2006) "Nilsen Describes How he Murdered his First Victim" *The Daily Telegraph*

Chapter 9
DOROTHEA PUENTE

DEATH HOUSE LANDLADY[10]

The social workers thought that she was a nice old lady who cared for the homeless.[1,4] They were wrong.

Dorothea Puente (See Figure 09-01) was born on January 09, 1929 and was convicted of three murders while running a boarding house for the disadvantaged in Sacramento, California. She was also charged with six other murders but there was insufficient evidence for a conviction. The murders were committed in the 1980s when she was in her fifties, and she died in prison in March 2011. Unlike many other serial killers who were motivated either by lust, thrill or power, Puente was driven by greed; she rather pragmatically saw her victims as an easy source of income to support her comfortable lifestyle.

Figure 09-01: Dorothea Puente

BACKGROUND

Dorothea Puente led a very troubled life in her early years.[2] Born to a pair of alcoholic parents who worked as itinerant farm laborers picking cotton, she was neglected and abused. She often had to scavenge for food,[3] and this traumatic environment at such an early age most probably set the stage for her history of theft to finance the better things in life. Puente was married on four different occasions (i.e.: 1945, 1952, 1968, 1976), usually to alcoholic and abusive men, and none of these marriages lasted very long.[3] She was engaged to be married shortly after she was released from prison in 1985, but her betrothed soon ended up dead and discarded in a wooden box in a garbage dump.

Puente began her life of crime and her descent towards serial killing in 1948 (See Chart 09-01) when she was 19 years old. She was convicted of using forged cheques that she had stolen from an acquaintance in order to buy some high-end clothing and accessories. Her husband at the time had quickly learned that she loved expensive clothes and left her when she was sentenced to four years in prison for forgery.

In 1952 Puente married husband #2, a merchant seaman who spent long periods of time away from home. Upon arriving home after being at sea for an extended period of time, he would occasionally discover men staying overnight with her.[4] In 1960 Puente was charged with running a brothel.[5]

The pattern of pursuing an expensive lifestyle filled with luxury items was a constant theme in Puente's life. When interviewed after she was convicted of murder, husband #4 complained that shortly after they married (in 1976) he was dismayed to learn that, "She wanted new pantyhose every day. She thought she was rich…"[6]

Chart 09-01: The Evolution of a Serial Killer

Stage	Year	Age	Events
I — Childhood Neglect	1929	0	Born to alcoholic parents — Farm labourers
	1937	8	Father died of tuberculosis
	1938	9	Taken by state children services due to severe neglect
	1938	9	Mother died in motorcycle accident
II — Criminal Career Commences - Theft	1948	19	Arrested for making purchases using forged cheques
	1960	31	Charged with operating a brothel
	1978	49	Charged with illegally cashing 34 state and federal cheques
III — Criminal Career Escalates to Theft and Harm	1982	53	Charged with drugging four elderly men and stealing their valuables
IV — Criminal Career Advances to Theft and Murder	1985	56	Drugged and killed Everson Gillmouth and continued to collect his pension
	1988	59	Police discover seven bodies buried on her boarding house property. Victims were drugged and killed. Puente continued to cash their disability, social insurance and/or pension cheques after their deaths
	1993		Sentenced to life in prison without parole for three murders. Jury could not reach agreement on six other murder charges.
	2011	82	Died of natural causes in prison

Husband #4 was a violent alcoholic, and the marriage lasted for only a few months. In order to sustain her lavish lifestyle, Puente frequented local bars looking for solitary older men who were either on a pension or receiving monthly social security benefits. Once she found a suitable candidate, she would befriend them and, after gaining their trust, begin stealing their cheques and forging their signatures. In 1978 Puente was eventually caught and was convicted of 34 counts of fraud[4] (See Chart 09-01; Stage II).

Trolling bars looking for lonely old men with a steady income from benefit cheques became a pattern of behavior that persisted right up until Puente was apprehended for murder. For instance, in 1982 she was convicted of drugging and robbing four elderly men that she met in taverns.[7] It was at this point that Puente had escalated her assaults from simple theft to drugging her victims (See Chart 09-01; Stage III), presumably because she thought that drugged into unconsciousness, her victims would not be able to identify her as the culprit. This strategy didn't work out quite the way she hoped, however, when one of her victims, a 74-year-old pensioner, was nevertheless able to identify her to police.[7]

Puente was sentenced to five years in the California Institution for Women but was released after three years, a condition of her release being to stay away from the elderly and not to handle government cheques of any kind that had been issued to others. It was during this time in prison where it appears that Puente's income generation strategy took a sinister turn, as evidenced with what happened to Everson Gillmouth (See Chart 09-01; Stage IV).

Gillmouth had a habit of writing letters to women in prison and, having been given her name, he began to write to Puente. What was probably one of the biggest mistakes in his soon-to-be shortened life, Gillmouth let Puente know that he was receiving a generous pension and that he owned an Airstream trailer and a 1980 red Ford pickup. The two became serious pen pals, and Gillmouth told his family that they were going to get married when she got out of prison. In 1985 when Puente received an early release from prison, Gillmouth was there in his 1980 red Ford pickup to greet her,[8] and when he made Puente a signatory on his chequing account,[6] he unwittingly signed his death certificate.

In November 1985, just a few months after her release from prison, Puente hired a local tradesman to do some handyman jobs in her apartment, one of which was to build a coffin-shaped wooden box that she said was for storing books. As part payment for his work, Puente gave him a red 1980 Ford pickup. A few days later, Puente asked the tradesman to transport the box, which now was nailed shut and rather heavy, to a long-term storage facility for her. On the way there, however, Puente changed her mind about putting the box in storage and instead, had the workman unload it at a garbage dump alongside of a river.[8] About three months later, a local sportsman noticed a strange shaped box on the riverbank close to where he was fishing, and because it was emitting a foul odor, he contacted the police. When they opened, the box what they found was the decomposed remains of an old man wrapped in a bedsheet and bound with electrical tape. Because there was no means of identifying the corpse, it was listed as a "John Doe" and put on their unsolved homicide file. Three years later the body would eventually be identified as Everson Gillmouth,[8] but for much of that time Puente continued to access his pension money. Puente wrote letters to his family long after his death, explaining that due to ill health he couldn't come see them.[3] In a particularly cynical and cold-hearted twist, she even sent a "thinking of you" card reputedly signed by Gillmouth himself to his sister about three months after his death.

Using Gillmouth's money, Puente began renting a large house in Sacramento, California and converted it into a boarding house. The first floor was set up for tenants and Puente lived on the second floor.

Puente soon began ingratiating herself to the local social service workers by agreeing to take in homeless clients that would not be accepted by many other establishments, drug and alcohol addicts and those with mental illnesses. To the social workers, Puente was a kind and caring individual who seemed to be able to manage these difficult clients, feed them well and keep them in a clean environment with a cozy bed to sleep in. What the social workers didn't realize however was that shortly after taking these people into her boarding house, she would intercept their mail, take their welfare cheques and cash them herself (using forged signatures) and give the resident a small allowance,[3] keeping the rest of the money for "expenses." It was not uncommon for some of these boarders to leave Puente's place and return to the streets, so when there were not enough placements from social services, Puente would cruise the local bars[1,3,6] looking for homeless people who were on social assistance and invite them to come live at her place.

Things were not always as idealistic as they initially seemed at the boarding house; there were the odd occurrences and disappearances that occasionally caused raised eyebrows. Tenants would disappear without any notice. The social workers who investigated some of these disappearances were told by Puente that they had moved away. This explanation did have a certain ring of truth to it because many of the tenants were transients and had a history of wandering off and returning to the streets. However, during the police investigation of the murders, they learned that several times before a tenant disappeared, Puente would be telling the other residents that the individual wasn't feeling well and that she was taking them upstairs to her apartment area to give them something to help them feel better.[6] Her subsequent explanations about their sudden "departure" usually included mention that they left to go live with a relative. During Puente's murder investigation, the police heard from more than one tenant that Puente had given them drugs that made them sleep all the time.[3]

Figure 09-02: Puento's Boarding House

Daily Mail

And then there was the apricot tree. One resident told police that he thought it odd that Puente wanted a four-foot-deep hole dug so that she could plant a small apricot tree.[1]

In May 1988, Puente's neighbors began to complain about a sick smell emanating from her back yard and the proliferation of flies. Puente explained that it was because of applications of fish emulsion to fertilize her garden. At other times she said that the sewers were backed up or that there were dead rats rotting under the floorboards.[6]

One of the more troubling occurrences, however, was the complete failure of the judicial system that was supposed to be monitoring Puente's activities. One of the conditions of her early release from prison was a court order specifying that Puente was to stay away from the elderly and not to handle government cheques.[6] Between 1985 and 1988, Puente was visited by parole officers at her boarding house on numerous occasions, but shockingly she was never once cited for breaking her parole conditions.[6]

Things started to unravel for Puente in 1988 when she was asked by social worker Judy Moise to take in a mentally disabled man named Alvaro Montoya who was inclined to have conversations with trees.[1] Moise had taken a liking for Montoya because he was a gentle spirit and quite harmless, and so when he suddenly disappeared from Puente's boarding house, she was concerned. Puente told her that he had gone to Mexico to live with relatives, but Moise didn't quite believe this explanation because it seemed to be so out of character for Montoya. Because of her suspicion, she filed a missing person's report with the police, who went to the boarding house to investigate. While they were there a tenant surreptitiously passed a note to one of the officers that said Puente had told him to lie about Montoya. Their suspicions being aroused, they returned a few days later with a search warrant and, acting on a hunch about some recently disturbed soil in the back yard, they uncovered the body of an elderly female. The next day they returned with a forensic unit and eventually recovered six other bodies. They were located in various locations on the property. One was buried under a gazebo, another was found under a garden statue of Saint Francis de Assisi, and another was under...yes...the apricot tree.[1] All the bodies showed various degrees of decomposition, and one of them, later identified as Betty Palmer, was missing the head, hands and lower legs.[1]

Figure 09-03: Police Exhume Bodies at Puente's Boarding House

Fox 40 News

Sadly, Montoya was one of the corpses found in the back yard. What retrospectively added to the tragedy of his death was the fact that in the early days of his tenancy at Puente's boarding house, he had complained to a counselor at a detox center that he was unhappy that Puente had been giving him a medicine that he didn't like to take.[6] The counselor dismissed his concerns and told him that he was better off at the boarding house than at the detox center. During Puente's trial, the counselor told the court, "I told him, 'You'll be safe there.' I was wrong… I've got to live with this for the rest of my life."[6]

Toxicology tests on the corpses all showed traces of the drug Dalmane, a prescription-strength sleeping pill that is particularly potent in elderly people and can be lethal when taken with alcohol or other sedatives. Police found abundant quantities of the drug when they searched Puente's residence, not to mention expensive clothing, a well-stocked liquor cabinet and $100 bottles of perfume.[6]

Figure 09-04: Some of Puente's Victims

Vera Faye Martin | Betty Palmer | Everson Gillmouth

Dorothy Miller | Ruth Monroe | James Gallop

7 of Dorothea Puente's murder victims. | Alvaro "Bert" Montoya | Murdered 1982 through 1988

www.blogspot.com

Shortly after the bodies began showing up, Puente was taken into custody. She was charged with a total of nine murders, one of which was for Everson Gillmouth. Oddly, the jury found her guilty of only three of the deaths; they could not reach a consensus on the other six. During the trial, the prosecutor, John O'Mara, told the jury that Puente's motivation for killing was "a simple matter of predatory greed.[1] She wanted people who had no relatives, no friends, no family. People who, when they're gone, won't have others coming around and asking questions." Unfortunately for Puente, she hadn't counted on a very conscientious social worker who thought enough about one of her clients to take action.

HANDWRITING ANALYSIS - GENERAL PROFILE[9]

Puente's handwriting shows a noticeable and consistent right-hand slant (See Figure 09-05), signifying that she was so sensitive to situations (whether they were emotionally charged or not) that she was inclined to react immediately and without thinking. This is of no surprise to at least one of her neighbors who described an incident that when he walked on her yard without being invited to do so, he was promptly and vigorously sworn at to the degree, as he relates the story, that it was enough to make a sailor blush.[3] In many people who have strong right-hand slants they also have moderating personality traits such as pride in how one behaves in public, but Puente's handwriting doesn't show much in the way of any moderating influences.

Puente had more than her fair share of fears and insecurities, most likely because of her tough childhood. She was rather self-conscious; see Figure 09-05. This was just one of several traits that acted synergistically enough to have Puente in a more-or-less constant state of anxiety in which she worried about the possibility of something bad happening to her. Other traits that contributed to her anxiety levels were her strong emotional responsiveness, her sensitivity to criticism (See Figure 09-05) and her especially strong fear of failure (See Figure 09-06; Self-Underestimation). A particularly strong contributor to her anxiety was her self-pity (See Figure 09-06). Self-pity is a negative trait and is described as an excessive, self-absorbed unhappiness in response to an unfortunate event in one's life. And then there is Puente's strong need to attract the notice of others (See Figure 09-05; Desire for Attention). The desire to be noticed by others is common to everyone. In order to be appreciated we must first be noticed, so all of us desire attention. However, the trait of desire for attention in the graphological context is something more than the entirely normal wish for recognition. It is an urge to actively obtain or demand the attention of others, their approval or their affection. Insecure people crave acceptance and strive very hard to gain the attention of those whose approval they seek. Writers with this trait are often not afraid of the spotlight, and Puente is certainly no exception. While running her boarding house in Sacramento, she portrayed herself as an upstanding member of society[4] who made high profile contributions to various charities and local politicians.

Figure 09-05: General Personality Traits[9]

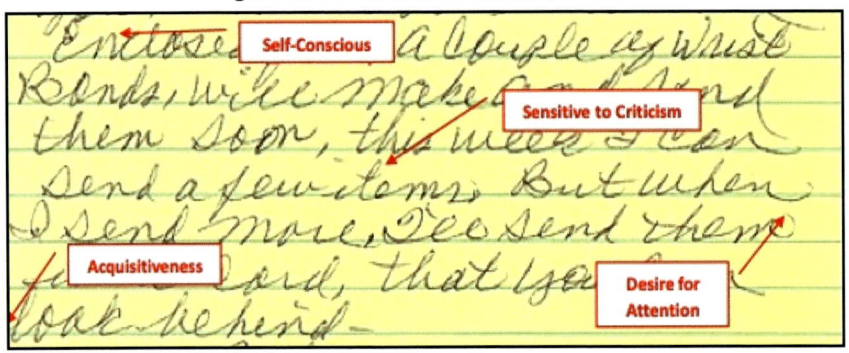

Note: Sensitive to Criticism – Looped d and t stems. Self-Consciousness – Final mound on m and n is higher than rest of letter. Double l's and double t's where second one is higher than the first. Desire for Attention – Final letters at the end of words made with a final stroke that is abnormally long, often curves backward and finish higher than the height of lowercase letters. Acquisitiveness – Hooks found at beginning of a stroke, often at the beginning of a word.

Figure 09-06: General Personality Traits[9]

Note: Vanity – Height of d and t stems are greater than 2.5 times the average middle zone letter height. Self-Underestimation – t-bars set very low on t-stem. Self-Pity – Final stroke of a word turns down, particularly in y, g, j. Deliberate – Separated stems on d and t letters. Stubborn – Wedge shape formation at bottom of d and t stems. Resentment – Straight approach stroke starting at or below baseline. Resentment – Straight approach stroke starting at or below baseline. Defense Mechanisms – Length of upper zone and lower zone loops. See Appendix One.

As mentioned earlier, Puente suffered from an especially strong fear of failure (See Figure 09-06; Self-Underestimation). This trait dovetails with her equally strong trait of shallow goal setting (See Figure 09-07). In Puente's case, 43% of her t-bars show this trait, so it is clear that she found it much easier to resort to crime rather than work hard to get ahead; in her mind theft was a much easier way to get the money to buy the things she wanted.

Given Puente's deprived childhood, it should perhaps come as no surprise that she developed the trait acquisitiveness, that is, the urge to acquire (Figure 09-05). Everyone of course has wants, but when these wants are strong, that is when the appearance of hooks appear at the beginning of a stroke. The detection of acquisitiveness is not all that common; in one study it was seen in only 23% of specimens.

Puente had a rather exaggerated opinion of her appearance; when apprehended for murder she was recovering from extensive facial cosmetic surgery.[1] To be fair, this trait is not uncommon because it is seen to at least some degree in 43% of all handwriting specimens. Having said that, Puente was particularly vain because the trait was seen in 36% of the "d" stems in her handwriting (See Figure 09-06).

HANDWRITING ANALYSIS – SERIAL KILLER PATHWAY

The most critical part of Puente's pathway to murder (i.e.: Figure 09-08) comes from the combination of her anti-social behavior, bolstered by her anger (best represented by the trait of resentment) and allowed to find expression because of her limited defense mechanisms (See Appendix One for an in-depth discussion of defense mechanisms). The traits of vanity and acquisitiveness are what provided a focus for her serial killing but by themselves certainly did not operate as a root cause. Many people have these two traits and do not become criminals or murderers.

Anti-social behavior can, when the trait is strong enough, be expressed in disruptive acts because the writer objects to adhering to the usual rules of society. Puente had anti-social behavior letters in 8.8% of her words in a handwriting specimen (See Figure 09-07). It has been suggested that anti-social behavior as described in the graphological literature has a close similarity to anti-social personality disorder (ASPD) as it is described in the psychiatric literature. Another name for ASPD is sociopathy and is defined as having a long-standing disrespect of the rights of others. It sometimes includes law breaking and can involve physically abusive actions. In the USA the frequency of occurrence of ASPD is estimated at less than four percent of the population, but in convicted criminals the rate can be up to ten times higher.

Puente's anti-social behavior found a very strong boost of negative energy from an interesting combination of two traits that themselves work synergistically to further magnify the reinforcing effect that each one individually would exert; these traits are identified in Figure 09-07. To be obstinate is to adhere to a course of action despite common sense or reason, and this hard-headed determination not to change her mind regardless of the consequences gave Puente the resolve to pursue a murderous solution to her need for money. A significant 79% of Puente's "s" letters showed this trait.

Figure 09-07: Anger-Related Personality Traits[9]

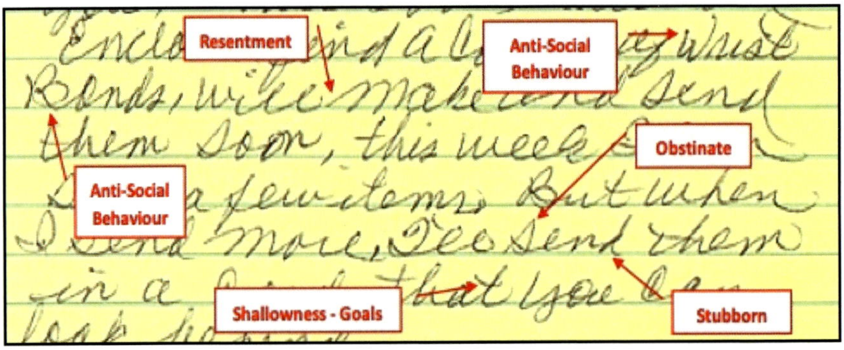

Note: Anti-Social Behavior Stroke- Capitalized letters in place of lowercase letters. Resentment – Straight approach stroke starting at or below baseline. Obstinate – Letter s with point at top. Stubborn – Wedge shape formation at bottom of d and t stems. Shallow Goals – Bent t-bar with ends turned upward.

To be stubborn is to continue in an opinion, idea or action even after one knows that it is wrong, and it is different from being obstinate because it is a defense trait against the fear of a loss of face.

Puente's strong anti-social tendencies were no doubt energized by all of the above-mentioned traits, including the additional effects of defiance and jealousy that show up in a minor fashion in her personality profile. However, they still may not have manifested themselves in the actual action of murder had it not been for the fact that Puente had a very limited set of defense mechanisms to resist these impulses.

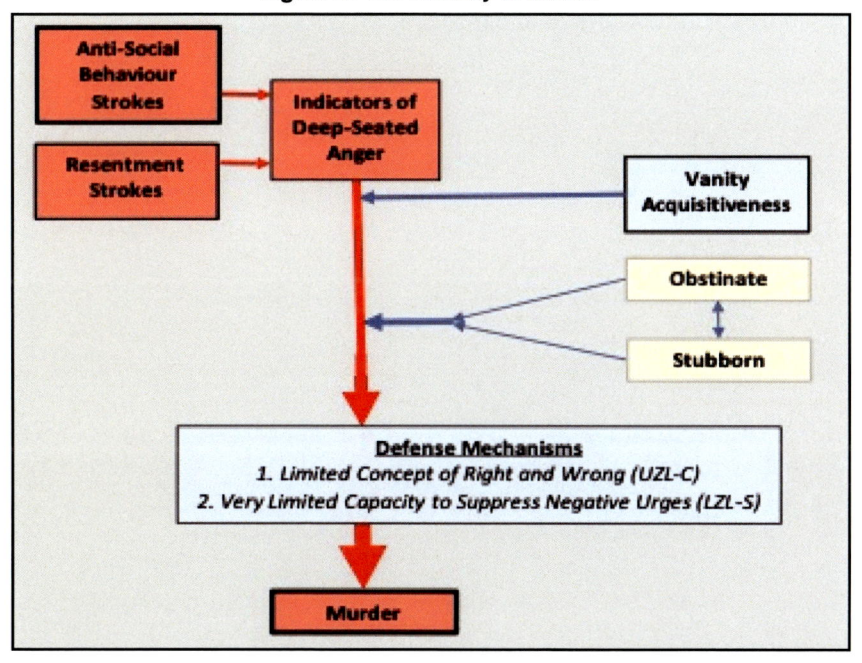

Figure 09-08: Pathway to Murder

Individuals who have inadequate defense mechanisms are those who have shorter than normal upper zone and lower zone loops in their handwriting. See Figure 09-06 and Appendix One. In Puente's case, her upper zone score was UZL-C = 1.6 and the lower zone score was LZL-S = 1.2. Both these scores are well below normal and indicate a significant deficit in both conscientiousness and sublimation.

Why is this so concerning? Upper zone height is one indication of a person's moral and ethical development and has a direct bearing on their personal code of conduct. To be devoid in this area is to be lacking in the capacity or desire to do the right thing. Lower zone extenders are an indication of a person's capacity to develop meaningful relationships with other individuals. To be lacking in this area can mean that the capacity to engage in empathetic behavior is limited. When these two factors are both significantly limited, as in Puente's case, what you have is a person who has very little capacity to think of anything other than what matters to them.

Having limited defense mechanisms is much like having only a minor speed bump in a road instead of a concrete roadblock, and in terms of preventing criminal behavior, it only slowed down the expression of Puente's murderous intent instead of stopping it altogether.

References

1. Bellamy, Patrick "Dorothea Puente: Killing for Profit" www.murderpedia.org

2. Connell, Rich (March 28, 2011) "Dorothea Puente dies at 82; boarding house operator who killed tenants" *Los Angeles Times*

3. Blanco, Juan "Dorothy Puente" www.murderpedia.org

4. Norton, Carla (1995) Disturbed Ground. ISBN 0-380-71188-5

5. Kulczyk, David (2013) California Fruits, Flakes, and Nuts: True Tales of California Crazies, Crackpots and Creeps. ISBN 978-1-61035-194-2

6. Scheeres, Julia "Dorothy Puente" www.murderpedia.org

7. "Guide to the California Superior Court (Sacramento County) case files for the People v. Dorothea Montalvo Puente (criminal case #18056) CNTY0004 www.oac.cdlib.org

8. "Dorothea Puente and the Boarding House of Death" (August 27, 2019) www.absolutecrime.com

9. Racher, John (2022) Advanced Graphology: An Encyclopedia of Personality Traits Revealed in Handwriting ISBN 978-1-7773610-1-3 *www.volumesdirect.com*

10. Ellis, Virginia; Wolinsky, Leo (March 25, 1989) "Death House Landlady Got Drugs From Doctor, Prosecutors Contend" *Los Angeles Times*

Chapter 10
JOSEPH DEANGELO

A BURGLAR WHO BECAME A RAPIST WHO BECAME A SERIAL KILLER

Between 1974 and 1986, Joseph James DeAngelo Junior, while he was in his thirties, went from being a prolific burglar to a repeat rapist and then a serial killer, the first five years of which he was a police officer. DeAngelo is reported to have engaged in approximately 120 burglaries, over 50 rapes and 13 murders,[1,2,3] none of which he was convicted until 25 years later. Because of the statute of limitation on burglaries and rapes in California at the time, DeAngelo was never charged with any of those crimes, but he was convicted of the thirteen murders and sentenced to life in prison without parole in August 2020.

DeAngelo's life of crime had three intriguing aspects to it. First was the obvious escalation in the seriousness of the crimes, the second was the very peculiar fact that the crime spree came to a sudden end in 1986, despite him not being caught or even suspected of having committed the crimes, and third, that even though 25 years transpired from the time of his last crime to the time when he was arrested, the various law enforcement agencies never really stopped trying to find their culprit.

Figure 10-01: Joseph DeAngelo

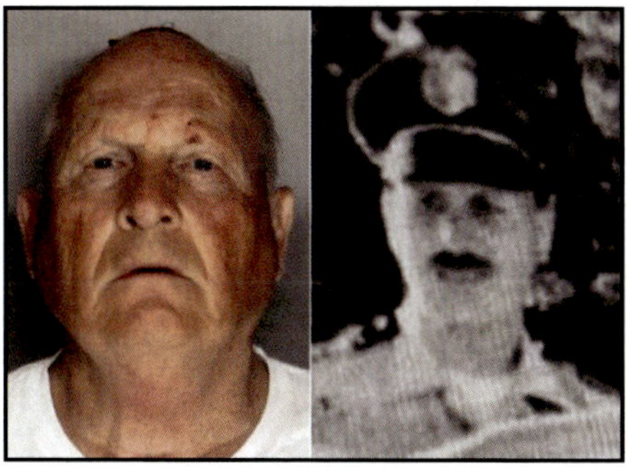

DeAngelo in 2018 and 1978. Photos by CBS News.

BACKGROUND

Joseph DeAngelo was born in November 1945, his father being a sergeant in the US Army, meaning that his early life was spent at various locations in the US and internationally. There is a paucity of information about his upbringing, though there are references to abuse from his father[4] and of witnessing the rape of his seven-year-old sister.[5] DeAngelo's teenage years were spent in California when it was said at his murder trial that he committed burglaries and tortured small animals.[4]

Burglary seems to have been a major theme in the early stages of his criminal career; it began in 1974 when he was 29 years old and lasted for approximately two years. He committed approximately 120 burglaries during that time and was never caught or even suspected of having committed the crimes. What made this situation disturbing was the fact that during that time, DeAngelo was a burglary unit police officer. But then, what better way to know how to evade being caught committing burglaries than working in the police unit responsible for investigating burglaries.

Along with being a rather prolific burglar, DeAngelo was also a bit of an oddity in terms of his behavior. After breaking into a home, he would usually open drawers and closets and either throw items around the rooms or else stage them (See Figure 10-02), often spending an inordinate amount of time in the home. What made his behavior even more unusual was his tendency to only steal items of low value such as single earrings while ignoring cash and items such as valuable jewelry that was often out in plain sight. It seemed like stealing valuables was of secondary interest to the thrill of conducting the burglary itself.

Figure 10-02: Visalia Ransacker Crime Scene

Photo by All That's Interesting

The vast majority of burglaries that DeAngelo committed occurred in the city of Visalia, which led to the press giving the unknown perpetrator the nickname of the "Visalia Ransacker." It was apparent that the burglar's activities were well planned before he would take action, and same day ransackings were a common occurrence. In one such instance, DeAngelo committed twelve separate burglaries in a single day.

It was towards the end of DeAngelo's Visalia Ransacker crime spree that his need for violence began to emerge. In September 1975, DeAngelo broke into a Visalia-area home and was in the process of abducting a teenage girl when her father heard noises and confronted the ski-masked intruder. The girl's father, Claude Snelling, was shot twice and died; the intruder escaped. This crime heralded DeAngelo's advancement into becoming both a rapist and also a murderer, and bear in mind that this was all occurring while he was a police officer. See Figure 10-03 for a complete outline of DeAngelo's activities.

In September 1976, DeAngelo moved to the Sacramento area where his crimes began to include rapes. Over the next three years he committed 51 rapes[3] and acquired the nickname of the "East Area Rapist." As before,

DeAngelo would spend numerous hours carefully conducting extensive reconnaissance of the neighborhoods before selecting a target home. Also as before, DeAngelo would ransack the home and steal small items. He would often spend hours in the homes he attacked, repeatedly raping his victim between taking breaks when he would go into the kitchen to eat a snack and drink beer. If there was a male in the house, he would force his victim to tie him up, blindfold him and gag him. DeAngelo's unusual behaviors continued to grow from his time as a burglar, as evidenced by what transpired during the 37th rape he committed in 1978. While assaulting his victim, he was reported to have repeatedly said "I hate you, Bonnie"[6,7], a reference to Bonnie Colwell to whom DeAngelo was engaged back in 1970. Colwell broke off her relationship in 1971 because of his abusive and manipulative behavior, after which he at one point threatened her with a gun, demanding that she marry him.[8] This wasn't the only example of DeAngelo's peculiar behavior during the commission of his crimes. A number of rape victims also reported that during their ordeal, while their assailant was taking a break, they could hear him crying[9] in another room before returning to assault them again.

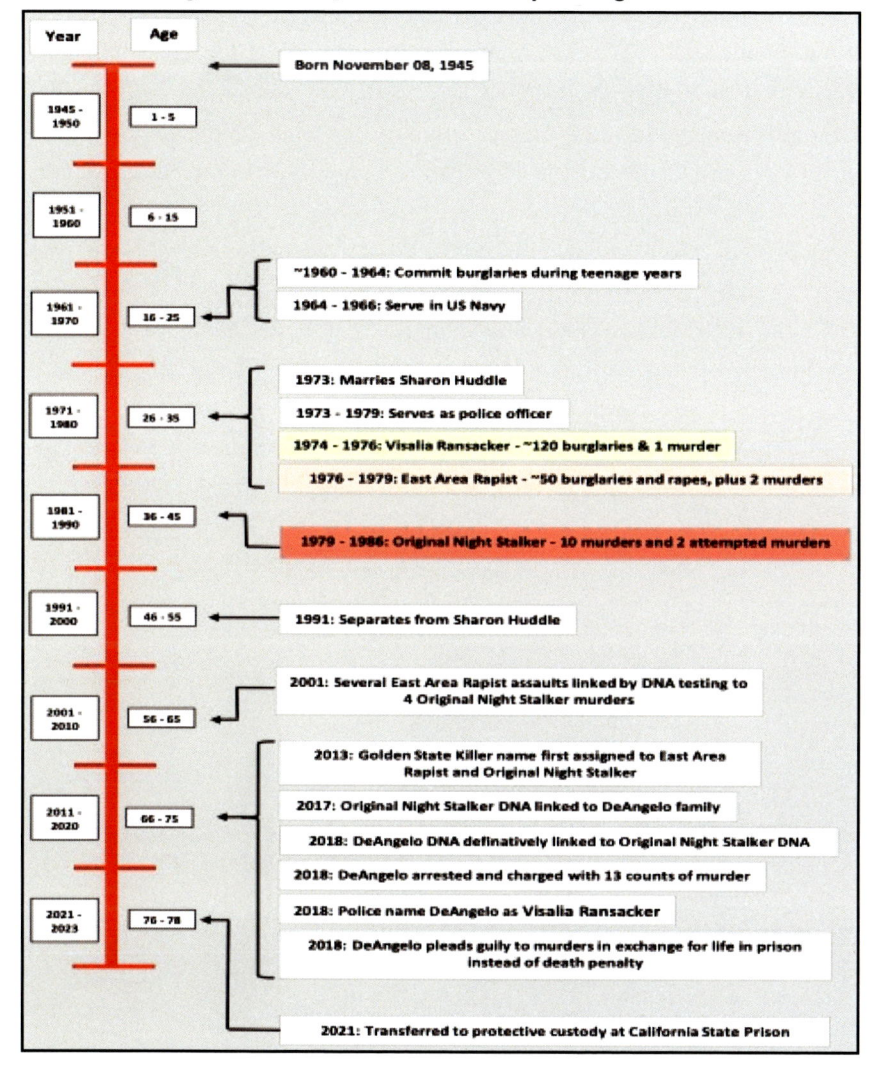

Figure 10-03: Key Milestones in Joseph DeAngelo's Life

Year	Age	Event
		Born November 08, 1945
1945 - 1950	1 - 5	
1951 - 1960	6 - 15	
1961 - 1970	16 - 25	~1960 - 1964: Commit burglaries during teenage years 1964 - 1966: Serve in US Navy
1971 - 1980	26 - 35	1973: Marries Sharon Huddle 1973 - 1979: Serves as police officer 1974 - 1976: Visalia Ransacker - ~120 burglaries & 1 murder 1976 - 1979: East Area Rapist - ~50 burglaries and rapes, plus 2 murders
1981 - 1990	36 - 45	1979 - 1986: Original Night Stalker - 10 murders and 2 attempted murders
1991 - 2000	46 - 55	1991: Separates from Sharon Huddle
2001 - 2010	56 - 65	2001: Several East Area Rapist assaults linked by DNA testing to 4 Original Night Stalker murders
2011 - 2020	66 - 75	2013: Golden State Killer name first assigned to East Area Rapist and Original Night Stalker 2017: Original Night Stalker DNA linked to DeAngelo family 2018: DeAngelo DNA definitively linked to Original Night Stalker DNA 2018: DeAngelo arrested and charged with 13 counts of murder
2021 - 2023	76 - 78	2018: Police name DeAngelo as Visalia Ransacker 2018: DeAngelo pleads guilty to murders in exchange for life in prison instead of death penalty 2021: Transferred to protective custody at California State Prison

Towards the end of his rapist spree, much like what happened during his burglary spree, DeAngelo murdered again. In February 1978, DeAngelo encountered Brian and Katie Maggiore who were walking their dog in the evening. A confrontation ensued, and even though the young couple attempted to flee, they were chased down and shot to death.[10]

Shortly after committing what was to be the last rape in July 1979 that was attributed to the East Side Rapist, DeAngelo moved to southern California where, in October 1979, he made his infamous debut as the Original Night Stalker. See Figure 10-03. And perhaps it was just a coincidence, but it was also in October 1979 that he was fired as a police officer for having been arrested for shoplifting a hammer and dog repellant.[11] DeAngelo's firing was not without its drama; during the process he threatened to kill the chief of police and even went so far as to have done some reconnaissance of the chief's home.

On October 01, 1979, an intruder broke into a couple's home in Goleta, Santa Barbara County and tied them up. When the assailant left the room for a moment and was overheard by the couple muttering to himself that, "I'll kill 'em"[12] the woman started to scream. The would-be killer panicked and fled the scene just as a neighbor responded to the noise.[13] This was the only time that the Original Night Stalker, as he was to become known as, failed in his objective to kill. Just three months later, he would break into a condominium in Goleta and murder the couple living there, after first raping the female victim.

Figure 10-04: Victims of the Original Night Stalker

Daily Mail

During 1980 the Original Night Stalker would murder two couples. In 1981 he killed a couple and murdered the lone female occupant of a home in Irvine, Orange County. The killer then became inactive for five years before killing an 18-year-old girl in her home while her parents were vacationing in Mexico. Like the other female victims, she had been raped and then beaten to death. A map of the Stalker's ten assaults and murders is presented in Figure 10-04. A point to remember is that, at the time of the southern California murders, the police did not realize that they were all committed by the same individual.

TWENTY-FIVE YEARS WOULD PASS BY ....

Even though in retrospect we know that DeAngelo, for some strange reason, stopped killing and raping in 1986, that didn't mean that the police stopped investigating the crimes. But it wouldn't be until 2001, fifteen years after DeAngelo went silent, that the police began to link a number of the murders and some of the East Side Rapist crimes to the same individual by using DNA testing.[14]

DNA testing techniques, and the methods used to analyze the data, had evolved in 2001 to the point where it was becoming an effective investigative tool, and in particular the investigation of cold cases. In December 2017, police were able to put together a complete genetic profile of the person that they then knew was responsible for a number of east side rapes and some of the south California murders. "They did not get a "hit" on the national DNA criminal database because, of course, DeAngelo's profile wasn't in the database. So, what they did was to upload the DNA profile into an international online service (i.e.: GEDmatch) that searches and compares DNA data files from a number of different DNA testing companies. The good news was that they uncovered a number of people who had at least some similarity in their DNA profiles to the one that they uploaded; the daunting news was that it involved approximately twenty-five family trees with thousands of people in them (one of which was DeAngelo). In what was to be a classic case of investigative persistence, the police, with the aid of a professional genealogist, investigated the thousands of individuals associated with the twenty-five family trees, gradually over months of work by five full-time investigators, were able to eliminate all the people on these trees through clues such as age, sex and place of residence until they had a short list of 10-20 people, one of which was DeAngelo. Again, through time-honored but time-consuming investigative work, they were able to narrow the short list down to one individual—DeAngelo.[14] However, this didn't automatically mean that DeAngelo was definitely, without a shadow of a doubt, to be their killer, mainly because they didn't have a specimen of his DNA to run a conclusive match with the profile that they had on file. What they did next was to collect what is referred to as "discarded DNA" from DeAngelo. This was accomplished by obtaining a sample of DNA from DeAngelo's car door handle and another from a tissue in his curbside garbage can.[15] When the DNA profile from these two specimens were compared to the DNA profile that the police had, there was a complete match; 72-year-old DeAngelo was arrested on April 24, 2018.

Approximately two years later (i.e.: March 04, 2020), DeAngelo was in court facing thirteen counts of murder: ten from his killings in southern California plus the three from his time as the East Side Rapist and the Visalia Ransacker. Despite originally planning to seek the death penalty, prosecutors settled for DeAngelo pleading guilty with life in prison and no chance for parole, primarily because they had estimated that if his guilt for all thirteen murders had to be proven in court the process would take up to ten years and cost an estimated $20 million.[17] In November 2020, DeAngelo was sent to the North Kern State Prison in California but was transferred to the California State Prison in February 2021 in order to place him in protective custody.

HANDWRITING ANALYSIS - GENERAL PROFILE[20]

DeAngelo's handwriting reveals that he was quite intelligent based on the combination of high levels of curiosity, analytical ability and attention to detail (See Figure 10-05), and this is substantiated by the fact that he had an associate degree in police science, a bachelor's degree in criminal justice and had taken a number of post-graduate courses. Further evidence of his sharp mind and an attention to detail can be seen by his meticulous planning of his burglaries and rapes, including the selection of numerous escape plans should he be detected during the crimes; this is quite probably why he was never caught.

Figure 10-05 also reveals that his handwriting is fairly heavy. Whenever there is heavy handwriting you know that the writer has a tendency to brood over emotionally charged situations, and because they will remember the circumstances so clearly for quite some time, the emotional impact of these memories tend to become part of the writer's personality. One does not have to look any further than how DeAngelo reacted to when his fiancée in 1971 broke off their engagement.[8] At that time he became enraged and threatened her with a gun, trying to intimidate her into marrying him. And seven years later, he still harbored quite a grudge against her because, as he was raping one of his victims in 1978 he repeatedly muttered, "I hate you Bonnie."[7]

Figure 10-05: Basic Personality Traits[20]

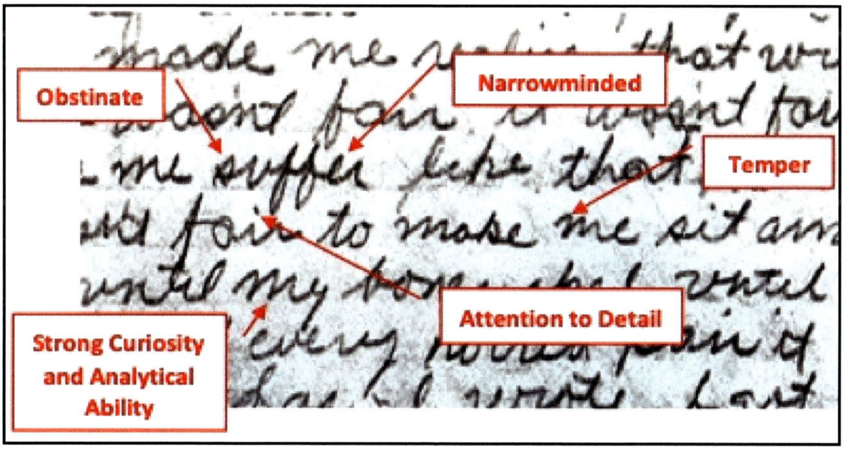

Note: Narrowminded – Letter e that is narrow or completely closed. Obstinate – Letter s with point at top. Temper – A short, straight initial stroke which joins a downstroke to form a sharp angle – a "tick" mark. Attention to Detail – i and j dots placed very close to stem. Curiosity – Tops of humps on m and n letters are pointed. Analytical Ability – Sharp pointed wedges that face downward within m and n letters.

People in the subdivision where DeAngelo lived for a number of years knew him to be a "quirky, angry neighbor."[21] He would often "yell and curse," and his foul language would go "flowing down the cul-de-sac."

"He'd be working outside on his car, and often times he'd get frustrated, and I don't know why but he'd go into a yelling tirade."[21] These frequent outbursts of temper should come as no surprise because his handwriting shows an unusually high level of temper tick strokes, with a frequency of occurrence (FOO) of 14%; see Figures 10-05 and 10-07. It also comes as no surprise that he was quite prone to expressing his temper tantrums, since his defense mechanism that ordinarily works to suppress negative urges was quite stunted. See Figure 10-06. As is explained in detail in Appendix One, his LZL-C score (i.e.: capacity to suppress negative urges) was only 1.3, and any score that is less than 2.0 is indicative of limited capacity in his personality profile.

Figure 10-06: Defense Mechanism Personality Traits[20]

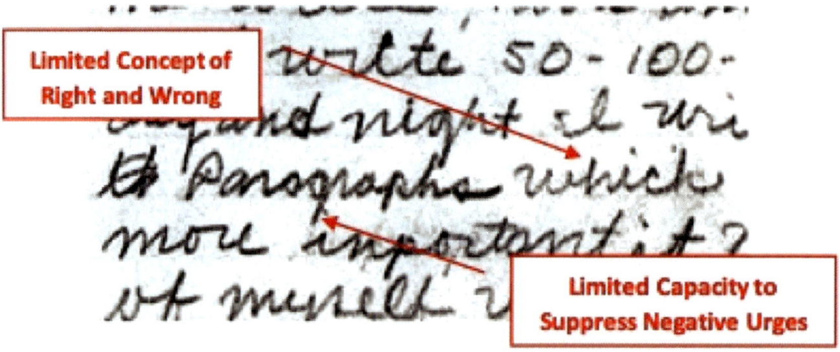

Note: Limited concept of right and wrong – Upper zone strokes in b, k, l and h are less than two times the average middle zone letter height (i.e.: UZL-C). Limited capacity to suppress negative urges – Lower zone strokes in g, y, j and q are less than two times the average middle zone letter height (i.e.: LZL-S).

DeAngelo was quite intolerant of other people's opinions and practices that differed from his own, as is seen by his 77% FOO rate of narrowmindedness strokes. See Figure 10-05. And if this wasn't enough, he would very frequently be found to stubbornly adhere to an opinion or course of action, despite common sense or reason. This obstinance, with an 83% FOO rate (See Figure 10-05), undoubtedly contributed to the observation by his neighbors that he was paranoid and would unreasonably, and without evidence, accuse the neighborhood kids of throwing things at his house and of trespassing on his property.[21]

All in all, it appears that DeAngelo was far from being a pleasant natured individual, even at the best of times.

HANDWRITING ANALYSIS - SERIAL KILLER PATHWAY[20]

As is revealed in Figures 10-07 and 10-08, DeAngelo had more than his fair share of anger/rage personality trait strokes, even for a serial killer. The FOO rate of resentment strokes (i.e.: 34%) places him well towards the upper echelon of severity (See Figure 10-02 in Chapter 12) and this does not even take into account that his handwriting exhibited three additional anger/rage strokes.

DeAngelo's temper was described previously as having a 14% FOO rate. To put this into perspective, 96% of the population have no temper strokes in their handwriting,[20] and of the 4% who do, the average FOO rate is 8%. Everyone at one time or another can be sufficiently provoked into a display of temper, but that doesn't mean that it is an intrinsic part of their personality. However, when temper strokes begin to appear, this is an indication that a display of temper will predictably occur in reaction to negative situations. People who display dot grinding in their handwriting are known to be obsessively resentful and angry in terms of their behavior, regardless of the frequency of occurrence of the trait stroke. The same can be said about individuals who's handwriting shows anti-social behavior strokes. These people will engage in actions that are contrary to the normal good graces of behavior in public, and DeAngelo's profane outbursts in his neighborhood is the perfect example of that.

The cumulative effect of DeAngelo's four above-mentioned strokes is indicative of someone who is overwhelmingly angry with the world. And with stunted defense traits (LZL-S = 1.3; UZL-C = 1.6; See Figure 10-06 and Appendix One), he had very little working for him to curtail his negative behavior.

There was ample evidence of his potential for violence, even without considering his criminal activity. When he was fired from the police force in 1979, he threatened to kill the chief of police.[11] He also threatened to "deliver a load of death"[21] to a neighbor because of their barking dog. In perhaps what was a classic understatement, a forensic psychologist who studies serial killers said of DeAngelo, "he obviously had a lot of anger…"[22]

Figure 10-07: Negative Personality Traits[20]

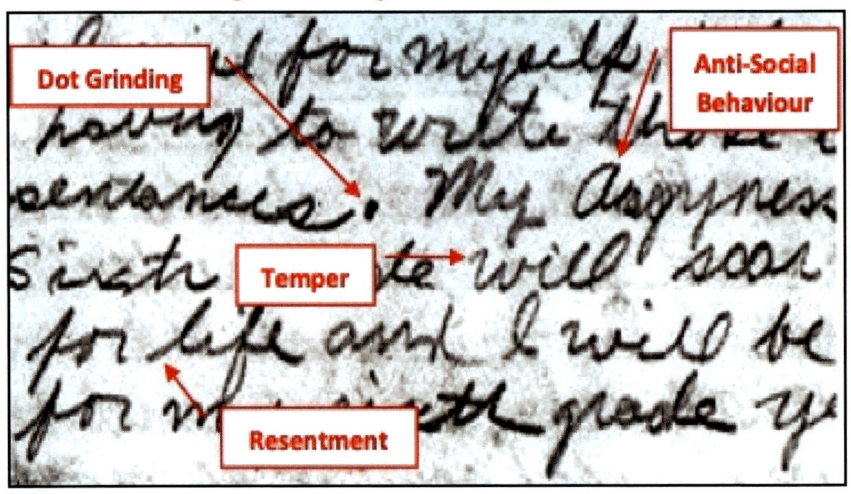

Note: Dot Grinding – Heavy pressure applied to punctuation. Resentment – Straight approach stroke starting at or below baseline. Anti-Social Behavior Stroke – Capitalized letters in place of lowercase letters. Temper – A short, straight initial stroke which joins a downstroke to form a sharp angle – a "tick" mark.

One of the most fascinating yet cryptic comments by DeAngelo regarding his criminal behavior was made during a police interview in April 2018 shortly after his arrest. DeAngelo was alone in an interrogation room when he uttered the following:

> *"He made me. He went with me. It was like in my head, I mean, he's a part of me. I didn't want to do those things. I pushed Jerry out and had a happy life."* [16]

Figure 10-08: DeAngelo's Pathway to Murder[20]

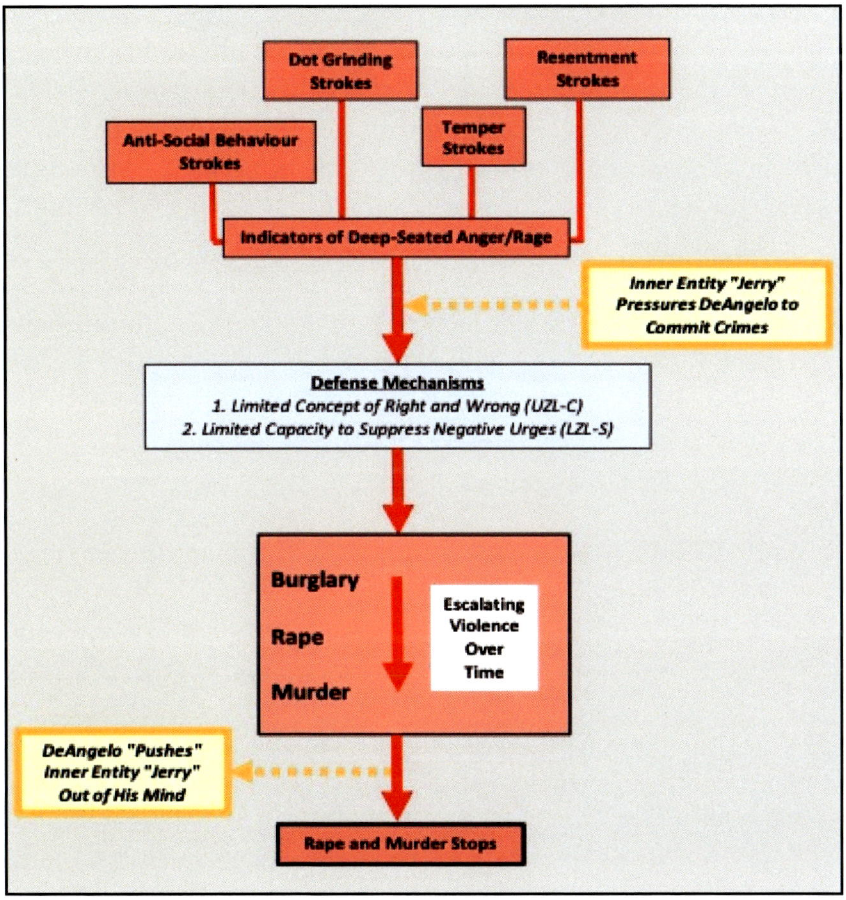

```
        Dot Grinding          Resentment
          Strokes              Strokes
                    Temper
                    Strokes
  Anti-Social Behaviour
       Strokes

    Indicators of Deep-Seated Anger/Rage
                                          ← Inner Entity "Jerry"
                                            Pressures DeAngelo to
                                            Commit Crimes
           ↓
        Defense Mechanisms
  1. Limited Concept of Right and Wrong (UZL-C)
  2. Limited Capacity to Suppress Negative Urges (LZL-S)

        Burglary        Escalating
                        Violence
        Rape            Over
                        Time
        Murder

  DeAngelo "Pushes"
  Inner Entity "Jerry"  ←
  Out of His Mind
           ↓
     Rape and Murder Stops
```

As he talked out loud to himself, DeAngelo made reference to an inner personality by the name of "Jerry" who had been forcing him to commit the crimes that he did, but then he went on to say that he was eventually able to push him out of his mind, after which DeAngelo was able to proceed with a "happy life." DeAngelo's revelation was not totally unique; in Chapter 4 we learned that Ted Bundy made a similar claim[18] of an inner "entity" that coexisted with his "dominant personality." Bundy never went so far as DeAngelo did by assigning a name to this inner entity, but he certainly blamed it for his crimes. DeAngelo also revealed that he somehow was able to rid himself of this evil entity and, having done so, he was able to find peace in having a happy life. It is not too much of a stretch to assume that this claim can be linked to the fact that DeAngelo, in 1986 at the age of 41, abruptly stopped committing murders and led a quiet life for the next 32 years until he was arrested. See Figure 10-08. This ability by a serial killer to unilaterally stop killing is almost unheard of; the vast majority of serial killers never stop until they are arrested because they "have a chronic and overwhelming need to commit murder."[19] As Dr. Scott Bonn, a noted criminal psychologist, has said, "It is important to remember that regardless of the specific motive(s), serial killers are compelled to commit murder—that is, they do it because they want to and need to." [19] Please refer to Chapter 4 for an in-depth discussion of the psychology behind disparate subpersonalities that can exist within a person's mind. Unfortunately DeAngelo never underwent any extensive psychoanalyses, and so we may never know what the true nature was of his mental issues.

References

1. "Golden State Killer pleads guilty to 13 murders" June 29, 2020 *BBC*

2. McNamara, Michelle (February 27, 2013) "In the footsteps of a killer" *City Think, Los Angeles*

3. Hallissy, Erin; Goodyear, Charlie (April 04, 2001) "DNA links to 70's "East Area Rapist" to serial killings / evidence suggests suspect moved to southern California" *The San Francisco Chronicle*

4. Thompson, Don (August 22, 2020) "Apology at sentencing deepens mystery of Golden State Killer" *AP News*

5. Lapin, Tamar (May 14, 2018) "Family of "Golden State Killer" claim he saw men rape his 7 year-old sister" *The New York Post*

6. "The Golden State Killer's ex-financee Bonnie Colwell says she "refuses to wear the blame"" August 03, 2020 *Newsweek*

7. "Golden State Killer's ex-fiancee joins long line of victims confronting him in court" August 19, 2020 *The Los Angeles Times*

8. Sulek, Julia (April 26, 2018) ""I hate you, Bonnie": Golden State Killer likely motivated by animosity toward ex-financee, investigator says" *The Mercury News*

9. "Golden State Killer" June 18, 2020 *Biography*

10. "Joseph DeAngelo pleads guilty to killing Brian and Katie Maggiore" June 29, 2020 *cbslocal.com*

11. Haag, Matthew (April 26, 2018) "What we know about Joseph DeAngelo, the Golden State Killer suspect" *The New York Times*

12. "The Original Night Stalker" Cold Case Files, Season 2, Episode 22 May 28, 2000 *A&E Networks*

13. Crompton, Larry (2010) Sudden Terror ISBN 978-1-4520-5241-0

14. Zabel, Joseph (2019) "The Killer Inside Us: Law, Ethics, and the Forensic Use of Family Genetics" Berkley Journal of Criminal Law SSRN 3368705

15. Arango, Tim; Goldman, Adam; Fuller, Thomas (April 27, 2018) "To

catch a killer: A fake profile on a DNA site and a pristine sample" *The New York Times*

16. "Joseph James DeAngelo Jr. pleads guilty to murder tagged to California's Golden State Killer" June 29, 2020 *USA Today*

17. McDonell-Parry, Amelia (December 07, 2018) "Golden State Killer Trial: Joseph DeAngelo Case Could Last 10 Years" *Rolling Stone*

18. Tron, Gina (November 20, 2020) "Why One Psychiatrist Believes Ted Bundy May Have Had Multiple Personalities" *Oxygen True Crime*

19. Ekua, Hagan (September 15, 2019) "Understanding What Drives Serial Killers" *US*

20. Racher, John (2022) Advanced Graphology: An Encyclopedia of Personality Traits Revealed in Handwriting ISBN 978-1-7773610-1-3

21. Shapiro, Emily; Johnson, Whit; Harrison, Jenna (April 27, 2018) ""Golden State Killer" suspect threatened to kill family dog, yelled and cursed in neighbourhood: Neighbours" *ABC News Live*

22. "Forensic psychologist examines mind of accused Golden State Killer" April 27, 2018 *abc7news.com*

Chapter 11
SAMUEL LITTLE

AMERICA'S SECRET SERIAL KILLER

With over 60 confirmed murders out of 93 that he had confessed to,[1] Samuel Little (See Figure 11-01) is indisputably America's most prolific serial killer, yet he remains largely unknown. Why is that so?

Little was a classic "thrill" serial killer because once the kill had occurred, he lost all further interest in the victim. He once stated during an interview that he "did what I liked to do."[2] The bodies of his victims were either left where they were murdered, or else Little discarded them in remote locations, a number of whom have not been recovered to-date. Even though Little was charged dozens of times for offenses like theft, break and enter, assault, fraud, attempted rape and drug possession in numerous states across the US between 1956 and 2005 and so was quite well known to a number of police agencies, his serial killer activities went on, astonishingly, for 35 years in a completely undetected fashion between 1970 and 2005 and remained that way until he began to confess to them[3] starting in 2018, just two years before he died of natural causes at the age of 80 years in a California prison.

Figure 11-01: Samuel Little

BACKGROUND

Samuel Little's life got off to a rough start even before he was borne. His mother was a teenage sex worker[3] who delivered him while in jail, hence he was sent to live with his grandmother. There isn't much in the way of information about his upbringing, other than the fact that he had discipline problems in high school and eventually dropped out before graduating because of poor academic performance. What was to become a rather ominous forecast of what he was to become, Little admitted that he developed a fascination about women's necks at a young age (possibly as early as in grade school) and that this fetish gradually evolved into fantasies about strangling women, along with sexual overtones.[2] By the time he was in his teens, he was collecting true crime magazines which had stories about women being choked and strangled to death. As the police only learned decades later, this fetish with sexual overtones would remain throughout the rest of his life. Case in point, when Little was extradited to California in 2012 to face a drug possession charge, the police compared his DNA to specimens associated with a number of other California-based crimes and they found a match with three homicides, all from Los Angeles.[3,4] Three women had been killed and their bodies were unceremoniously dumped on the streets. When homicide detectives had investigated these deaths, they collected samples of body fluids; the killer had apparently masturbated on the bodies during the murderous assaults[3] and the specimens were irrefutably linked to Little.

When examining Little's adult life, it is informative to view it as being composed of two relatively distinct parts: there was his day-to-day public activities and then there was what can appropriately be called his "shadowland" activities. These two streams of activities went on for decades and are depicted graphically in the timeline of Little's key milestone events that is presented in Figure 11-02.

LITTLE'S DAY-TO-DAY PUBLIC ACTIVITIES

Little's life of crime began in 1956 when he was just 16 years old.[6] He was caught breaking into a home in Nebraska and ended up spending time in a juvenile detention center. He continued to live on and off at his grandmother's home in Ohio, but in 1961 he was again convicted of break and enter (B&E) and was sentenced to three years in jail. Shortly after his release, he moved to Florida to live with his birth mother but then began to travel around the country, getting by through crime.[7] His day-to-day activities usually focused on finding the means to support his drug and alcohol consumption. By 1975 he had been arrested 26 times in eight states (See Figure 11-04) for a myriad of crimes including shoplifting, armed robbery, fraud, assault and rape.[6]

In 1982 Little was charged with two counts of murder, one in Mississippi and the other in Florida. The first charge was eventually dropped because of a lack of evidence, and he was acquitted on the other charge because the jury was untrusting of the eyewitness testimonies which linked Little with the deceased on the night of her disappearance, primarily because they were sex workers.[7] As it turns out, the Florida murder was in fact one of Little's serial killing, but obviously that never came to light at the time.

In the mid-1980s, Little moved to California where he was soon arrested for beating and strangling two women. Both survived the assaults, but Little was charged and convicted of attempted murder and spent two and a half years in prison.[8] All in all, Little spent approximately ten years in prison, and during that time he often got involved in competitive boxing.[4] It has been speculated that this experience gave him the training that he used when assaulting and killing women.

Little's so-called public life came to an end in 2012 when he was arrested in Kentucky on a drug charge. He was staying at a homeless shelter at the time and was extradited to California. By this time DNA testing had become a commonplace tool for law enforcement, and so after being tested and having his results entered into the California criminal database, the police were surprised to find a match with specimens that had been collected from three female murder victims from 1987 and 1989. In September 1984, Little was found guilty for these three murders and was sentenced to life in prison without any chance of parole.[4,9,10]

Figure 11-02: Key Milestones in Samuel Little's Life

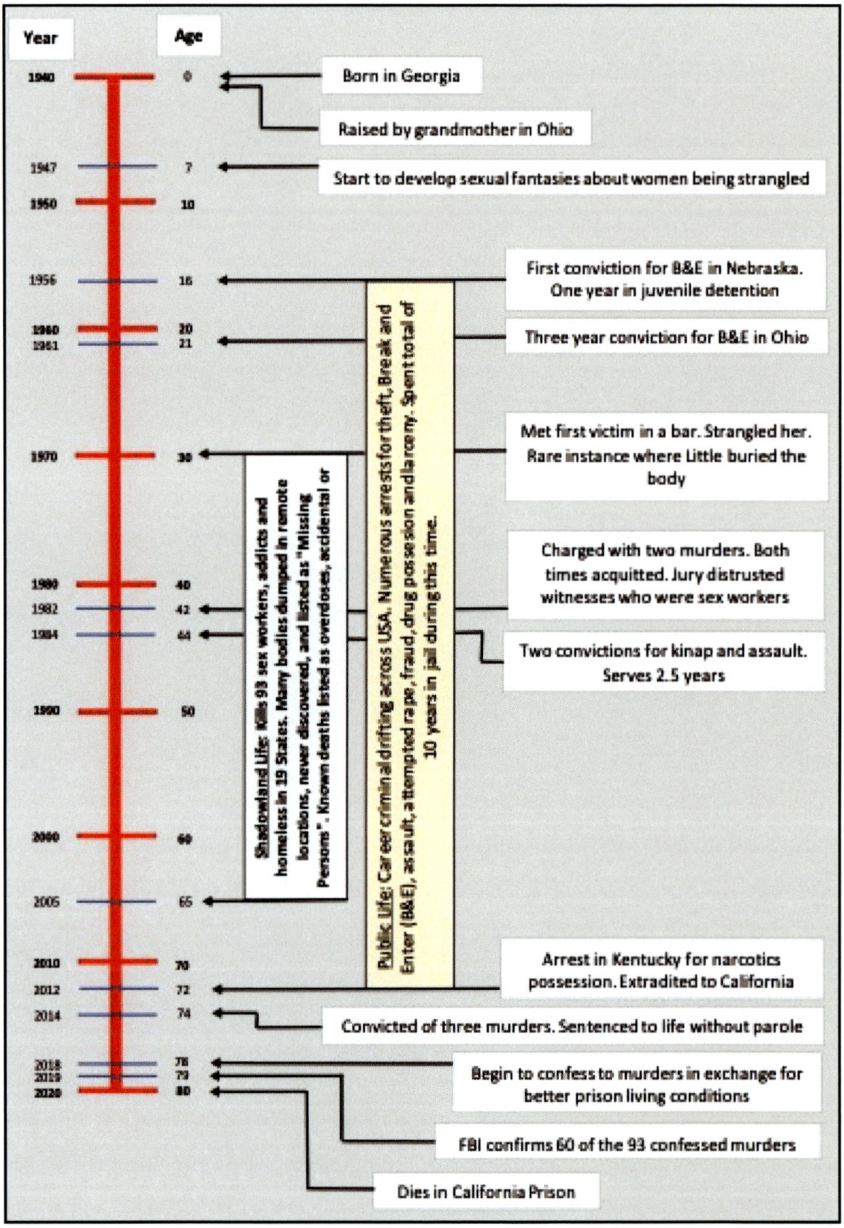

Year	Age	Event
1940	0	Born in Georgia
		Raised by grandmother in Ohio
1947	7	Start to develop sexual fantasies about women being strangled
1950	10	
1956	16	First conviction for B&E in Nebraska. One year in juvenile detention
1960	20	
1961	21	Three year conviction for B&E in Ohio
1970	30	Met first victim in a bar. Strangled her. Rare instance where Little buried the body
1980	40	Charged with two murders. Both times acquitted. Jury distrusted witnesses who were sex workers
1982	42	
1984	44	Two convictions for kidnap and assault. Serves 2.5 years
1990	50	
2000	60	
2005	65	
2010	70	
2012	72	Arrest in Kentucky for narcotics possession. Extradited to California
2014	74	Convicted of three murders. Sentenced to life without parole
2018	78	Begin to confess to murders in exchange for better prison living conditions
2019	79	FBI confirms 60 of the 93 confessed murders
2020	80	Dies in California Prison

Shadowland Life: Kills 93 sex workers, addicts and homeless in 19 States. Many bodies dumped in remote locations, never discovered, and listed as "Missing Persons". Known deaths listed as overdoses, accidental or

Public Life: Career criminal drifting across USA. Numerous arrests for theft, Break and Enter (B&E), assault, attempted rape, fraud, drug possession and larceny. Spent total of 10 years in jail during this time.

146 | JOHN RACHER

LITTLE'S SHADOWLAND ACTIVITIES

Little committed his first murder on New Year's Eve in 1970 in Florida.[11] In what was to become his typical mode of action, he met Mary Jo Brosley at a bar and strangled her to death later that evening after punching her into unconsciousness. Little buried her in a shallow grave in the countryside, but because the effort of finding a suitable spot for a burial and digging a grave was so complicated and time-consuming,[4] in future murders he resorted to simply dumping the body in some remote location or else just leaving it where the assault took place. Little went on to murder three other women in 1971, all of them in Florida. See Figure 11-03.

Little was rather casual in terms of how he conducted his killings. The vast majority involved chance encounters with the assault and murder occurring within just a few hours of the meeting.[2] Little typically used his strength and size to his advantage, aggressively punching and beating his victims until they were unconscious, after which he strangled them to death.[5] He then disposed of the body by taking it to a remote location and unceremoniously dumping it there. Over the years they were left in wooded rural areas, construction sites, dumped in rivers, left along the side of highways or just left where they were killed. A number of his victims' bodies were never found, and so the police and their families only knew that they were missing. Some of the discarded bodies were eventually found, but many of them were so decomposed that they were not able to be identified. And then there were those bodies that were quickly discovered, but because most of Little's victims were either drug addicts or alcoholics, the police often ruled their deaths to have been due to an overdose or accidental.[3]

Figure 11-03: Little's Map of Murders

Australian Broadcasting Corporation.

Little consciously limited his choice of victims to black women who were marginalized and living at the edges of society;[5] only one of his victims was white. In addition to addicts and alcoholics, he would target sex workers and the homeless because, as he explained to police investigators in 2018 and 2019, the deaths or disappearances of these types of people rarely attracted any high-profile media attention,[3,4] nor were they rarely even noticed to be missing by their estranged family members or friends.

Little's shadowland activities went on for 35 years, from 1970 until 2005.[2] When one takes into account that during that period of time he was either in jail or in prison for about 10 of those years, his average kill rate was 3-4 per year. Little stopped killing in 2005 when he was 65 years old. Speculation is that the only reason he stopped when he did was because once he got into his sixties he was lacking the strength and stamina to quickly and successfully subdue any potential victims who were much younger than him.

Of the 65 murders that have been independently confirmed by the FBI, 18 occurred during the 1970s, 26 occurred during the 1980s and 21 occurred in the 1990s. Little had confessed to 93 murders before he died, therefore there are 28 that have yet to be confirmed. The FBI continues to investigate these unconfirmed deaths.

Figure 11-04: Samuel Little's Mug Shots Throughout the Years

Samuel Little: Through the Years

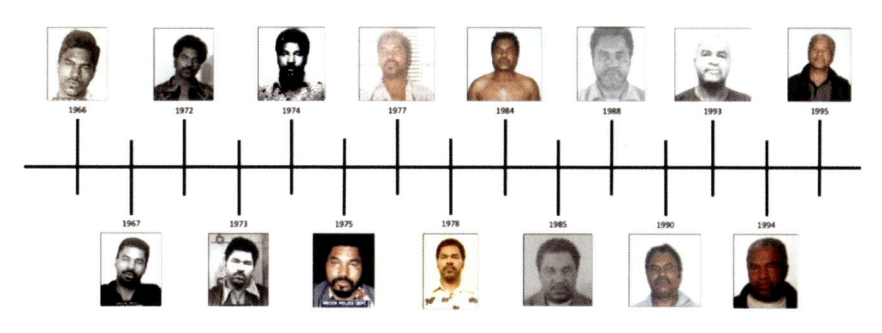

The US Sun

As was mentioned previously, Little was arrested in 2012 and eventually charged and convicted of three murders, all of them in California; he was imprisoned for life in 2014 and sent to the Los Angeles County prison. By this time, police agencies in a number of states began to speculate that Little might have been involved with a number of unsolved cases. Little denied any involvement, just as he continued to proclaim his innocence regarding the three murder convictions, and he steadfastly refused to talk to any investigators who came to the Los Angeles County prison to talk to him. This began to change in 2018, however, when he found himself befriending a Texas State investigator who was looking into an unsolved case dating back to 1994. Over a number of visits, Little gradually began to talk about his murderous past, and beginning in 2018 he began to actually confess to a number of murders; it was only at this time that the police actually realized that what they had was a *bona fide* serial killer. Little didn't confess to every murder he'd ever committed all at once; the information only came out over time and only involved a few murders at a time.[2] Rather than think Little was finally seeking to unburden his soul by confessing, it should be noted that he made these confessions in exchange for a transfer out of the Los Angeles County prison and into another prison where the living conditions were not quite so austere.[3] Little continued to make confessions right up to the time of his death; one month before he died he confessed to two murders in Florida, one of which involved a man who had been wrongfully convicted for the crime.[12] This has left some people speculating that had he not died when he did, more murders may have been revealed over and above the 93 that he had admitted to as of December, 2020.

HANDWRITING ANALYSIS - GENERAL PROFILE[13]

Little was by nature quite effected by his emotions; over 50% of his writing has a strong right-hand slant in excess of 135° meaning that he was inclined to react immediately and without thinking too much about the consequences. In addition, his reaction to emotionally charged situations was a bit inconsistent, making him somewhat unpredictable in his behavior and so people who were acquainted with him for any length of time would be wary, waiting to see if he would react as he usually did versus out-of-the-ordinary outbursts.

One of the police investigators who spent quite a bit of time interviewing Little described him as both a genius and a sociopath.[2] While the sociopath description is undoubtedly accurate, to say that he was also a genius is a bit of an overstatement. Little did have a versatile mind and was able to look at a problem from more than one angle, but he lacked the analytical ability needed to be a deep and perceptive thinker. He had a strong eye for detail (See Figure 11-06), but he wasn't overly organized in his thinking. He was also rather lacking in what is described as stick-to-it-ness, *aka* determination. See Figure 11-05. The trait of determination is defined as the steady focus on working towards a goal, even in the face of difficulty. This lack of determination on Little's part was on display when he remarked to an interviewer that, after finding it to be both time-consuming and tedious to dig a grave when he was disposing of his first murder victim, in subsequent murders he merely dumped the bodies in remote locations. This streak of laziness was also evident in how he wrote the letter "t". Twenty-two percent of his t-bars show the trait of shallowness (See Figure 11-06), indicating that anything that required much effort wasn't, in Little's mind, worth pursuing.

Figure 11-05: General Personality Traits[13]

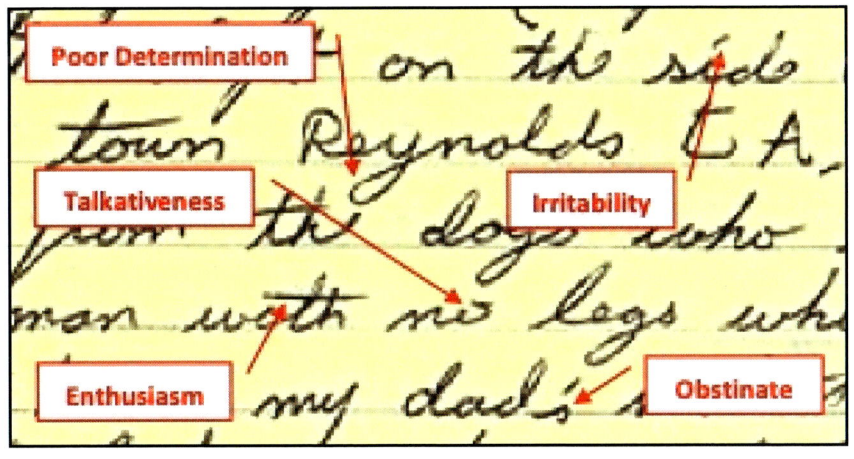

Note: Talkative – Circle letters that are open at the top. Determination – Straight down-stroke in g, y, j, q. Little's lower zone strokes are often bent. Irritation – i and j dots that are dashes. Enthusiasm – t-bars longer than average middle zone letter width. Obstinate – Letter s with point at top.

Figure 11-06: General Personality Traits[13]

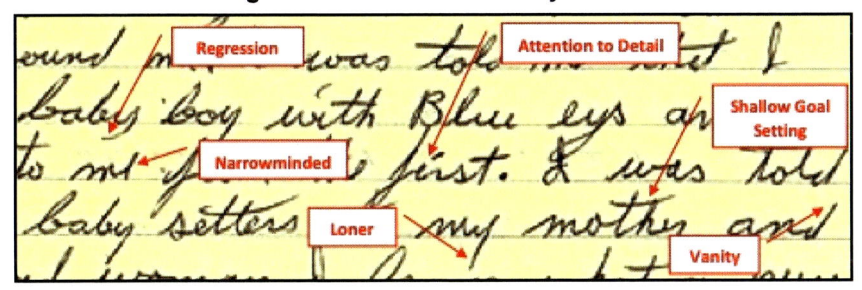

Note: Regression – Lower zone extender of g, y, j turn left and stay there. Attention to Detail – i and j dots placed very close to stem. Narrowminded – Letter e that is narrow or completely closed. Shallow Goals – Bent t-bar with ends turned upward. Loner – Lack of lower zone loop. Single line untraced. Vanity – Height of all of Little's d stems are greater than 2.5 times the height of their corresponding loop.

When engaged in conversation, Little had the natural inclination to want to quickly get to the point, and this trait was reinforced by his strong enthusiasm (See Figure 11-05). People who exhibit this trait of directness can often come across as being rather abrupt, and Little was definitely in this category because of his lack of any sense of diplomacy. This abruptness was made even worse by his quickness to irritability; 64% of his i and j dots exhibit this trait (See Figure 11-05). He also had the propensity to engage in immature behaviors like pouting or exhibiting childishly angry outbursts when he felt slighted in any way. (See Regression – Figure 11-06).

Little was quite vain. The height of all his "d" stems reveal this trait (See Figure 11-06), so it should come as no surprise that whenever he talked about his prowess as a boxer, he often told people that he was a former prizefighter;[7] nothing could have been further from the truth however.

Like many other serial killers, once Little expressed an opinion about something, he would often stubbornly adhere to it even in the face of overwhelming evidence to the contrary (See Obstinate; Figure 11-05). Eighty-three percent of his s letters showed this trait, underscoring just how strong a force it was in his personality. The driving force behind obstinance is a desire not to be seen to be wrong or to suffer a loss of face, and Little's aforementioned vanity only reinforced this behavior. To make things even worse, he was also quite narrowminded (See Figure 06). Eighty-seven percent of Little's e letters showed this trait, meaning that he was quite intolerant of other people's opinions that differed from his, and especially if it involved the inflated opinion he had of himself.

The sum total of Little's general personality profile indicates that he wasn't the most likeable sort of person to be around. Did this perhaps weigh on his conscious in some way? Probably not, because one other trait to take note of is Little's loner trait; see Figure 11-06. Little was quite happy with his own company and had little need for social interactions or relationships. He preferred to be and work alone and considered himself to be a private person.

HANDWRITING ANALYSIS - SERIAL KILLER PATHWAY[13]

Little's pathway to murder (Figure 11-07) was simple and straightforward. His personality was fueled with a high degree of rage, as seen by the fact that there are four different behavioral traits, all of them negative. First and foremost is his resentment. With the highly unusual level of resentment strokes (i.e.: 38% of all words; Figure 11-06), Little was something of a powder keg of anger that could quickly be ignited whenever someone offended him, and with his very high level of vanity, Little's strong reservoir of resentment would be directed at anyone who he even suspected was belittling the high opinion he had of himself.

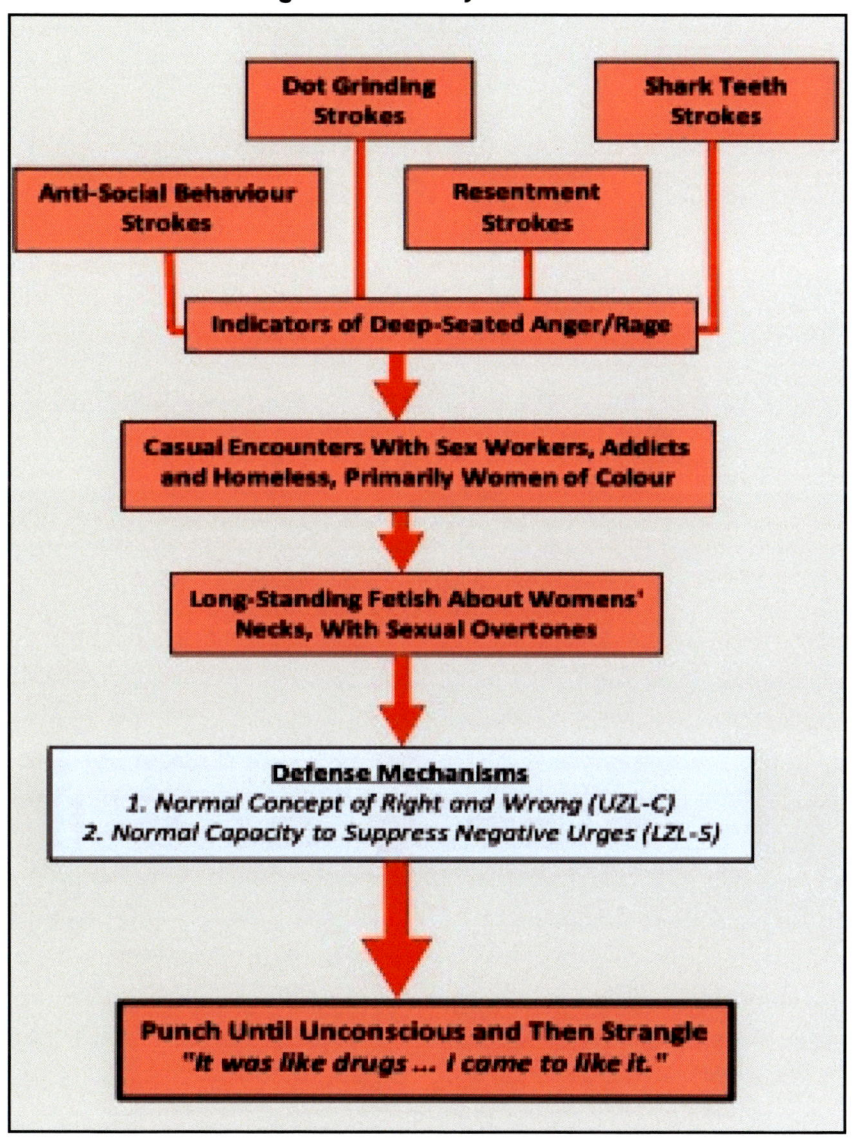

Figure 11-07: Pathway to Murder[13]

```
        Dot Grinding              Shark Teeth
          Strokes                   Strokes
              │                        │
  Anti-Social Behaviour    Resentment
       Strokes              Strokes
         │                    │
         └──────┬─────────────┴────────┘
                ▼
     Indicators of Deep-Seated Anger/Rage
                │
                ▼
  Casual Encounters With Sex Workers, Addicts
   and Homeless, Primarily Women of Colour
                │
                ▼
     Long-Standing Fetish About Womens'
         Necks, With Sexual Overtones
                │
                ▼
            Defense Mechanisms
   1. Normal Concept of Right and Wrong (UZL-C)
   2. Normal Capacity to Suppress Negative Urges (LZL-S)
                │
                ▼
     Punch Until Unconscious and Then Strangle
       "It was like drugs ... I came to like it."
```

"It was like drugs ... I came to like it."

Reinforcing the resentment was the trait associated with dot grinding (Figure 11-09). Whenever this type of stroke is seen in handwriting, and no matter how infrequently it occurs, we know that the writer can be obsessively resentful of anything that they do not like but are being forced to accept. The painful bitterness associated with this stroke can result in an obsessive dwelling upon how the writer was, in their way of thinking at least, wronged.

Figure 11-08: Anger/Rage-Related Personality Traits

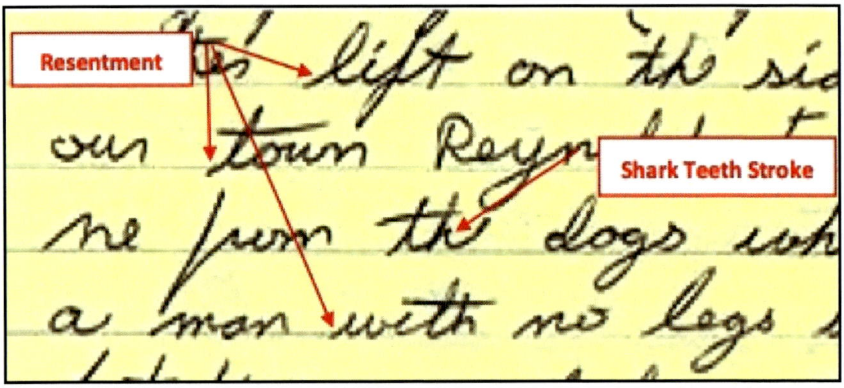

Note: Resentment – Straight approach stroke starting at or below baseline. Shark Teeth Stroke – Retraced hooks on mounds of m, n, h.

The anti-social stroke seen in Little's handwriting (Figure 11-09) indicates that he was naturally predisposed to engage in actions that are contrary to the usual rules of society and which can often manifest themselves in disruptive or violent behavior. Even though this stroke is seen in only 2% of Little's handwritten words, it is nevertheless a sign that this behavior is an intrinsic part of his personality and, disturbingly, reinforces even more the disturbing level of resentment that is there. Finally, there are the so-called shark teeth strokes (Figure 11-08). This is the last of the three negative traits that all work collectively and cumulatively to reinforce the already high level of anger seen with the resentment in Little's personality. People who display shark teeth strokes seek to portray an exterior of friendliness and trustworthiness while they prepare to assault (in Little's case physically and not just verbally) their intended target.

Figure 11-09: Anger/Rage-Related Personality Traits

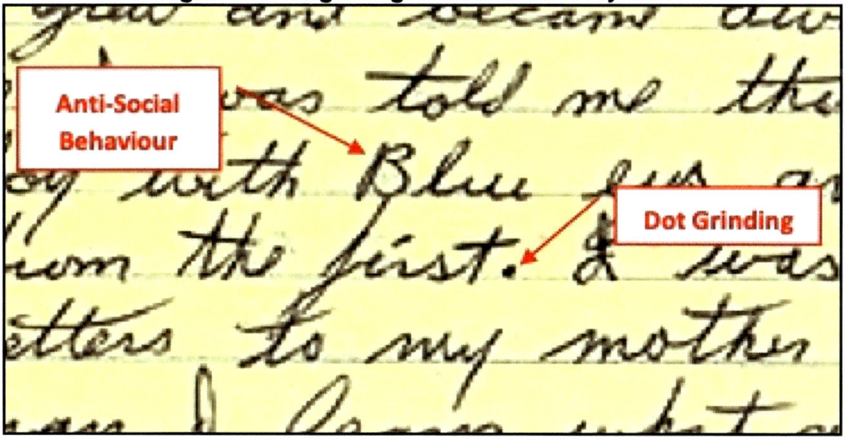

Note: Anti-Social Behavior Stroke – Capitalized letters in place of lowercase letters. Dot Grinding – Heavy pressure applied to punctuation.

Little's last line of defense against inappropriate urges from actually being acted upon was not up to the task; see Appendix One for additional details. His handwriting indicates that he had a normal level of conscientiousness and sublimation (i.e.: UZL-C = 2.5; LZL-S = 2.0), but, as has been seen with other serial killers, the strength of his negative traits overwhelmed his defenses.

In his last few years of life, Little suggested to a few interviewers that he thought that God wanted him to end the misery of his victims' lives by killing them.[5] Even though this conveniently alleviates Little of the actual responsibility for killing and places it on a higher authority, most experts agree that this is a common form of rationalization that serial killers often take, and so very little credence has been placed in his statement; the psychiatric assessments that Little had undergone support this conclusion.

So, back to our original question. Why, while being confirmed by the FBI as America's most prolific serial killer as of 2019, is Samuel Little largely unknown? T. Theodore in an article written in 2022[4] speculated that Little isn't well known because, unlike Ted Bundy and John Gacy who have received a huge amount of coverage by the press, book publishers, TV documentaries and movie directors, Little didn't confess to his crimes until much later and because his victims weren't college-age women and young men; they were marginalized sex workers, drug addicts and the homeless. Allan Branson, however, had a different point of view. In his 2013 article[14] entitled, "African American Serial Killers: Over-Represented Yet Underacknowledged," Branson says that the disparity is because the "media shows little reticence in portraying black males as low-level criminals, but rarely portray them as serial killers."

References

1. Warren, David (June 07, 2019) "Prosecutor: More than 60 deaths now linked to serial killer" *Associated Press*

2. Rogers, John (December 31, 2020) "Samuel Little, believed to be most prolific serial killer in US history, dies at 80"

3. Pak, Eudie (December 05, 2019) Samuel Little Biography *www.The-Biography.com*

4. Theodore, T. (April 27, 2022) Samuel Little (Serial Killer Biography) *Practical Psychology*

5. Biswas, Shuvrajit (July 21, 2022) Where is Samuel Little Now? *The Cinemaholic*

6. "Timeline retraces the whereabouts of a career criminal, alleged serial killer" (April 07, 2013) *Associated Press*

7. Abdollah, Tami (April 07, 2013) "More cases connected to L.A. serial killer suspect" *Honolulu Star-Advertiser*

8. Kim, Victoria (September 01, 2014) "Women's testimony called "blueprint" to serial killer suspect's behavior" *Los Angeles Times*

9. Havens, April (September 04, 2014) "Former Pascagoula prostitutes testify of escapes from convicted serial killer Samuel Little" www.gulflive.com

10. Gerber, Marisa (September 25, 2014) "L.A. serial killer gets 3 life terms, screams, "I didn't do it!"" *Los Angeles Times*

11. Lowery, Wesley; Knowles, Hannah; Berman, Mark (November 30, 2020) "How America's deadliest serial killer went undetected for four decades" *The Washington Post*

12. Bul, Lynh (November 29, 2018) "Serial killer Samuel Little says a 1972 unsolved Maryland case is among 90 he got away with, police say" *The Washington Post*

13. Racher, John (2022) Advanced Graphology: An Encyclopedia of Personality Traits Revealed in Handwriting ISBN 978-1-7773610-1-3 *www.volumesdirect.com*

14. Branson, Allan (February, 2013) "African American Serial Killers: Over-Represented Yet Underacknowledged" The Howard Journal of Criminal Justice Vol 52, Issue 1

Chapter 12

HANDWRITING STROKES ASSOCIATED WITH SERIAL KILLERS

TWO OUT OF THREE AIN'T BAD

After having examined the ten serial killers' handwriting specimens for up to 108 different handwriting trait-strokes, ten were found to occur at a much higher level of frequency than what is seen in the normal population. Not surprisingly, eight of them can be described as anger/rage-related; see Figure 12-01.

When analyzing handwriting specimens using the trait-stroke methodology, there are two aspects to consider. First is the presence or absence of a particular stroke, and that is what has been measured in Figure 12-01. The second is the strength of the trait, as indicated by its frequency of occurrence (FOO), and this information is provided in Figure 12-02 for each of the ten serial killers featured in this book.

Understanding how to interpret trait-stroke data is best accomplished by way of an example. For instance, the trait-stroke of dot grinding is seen in five of the ten (50%) specimen results listed in Figure 12-02. When the strength of this trait-stroke for the ten serial killers is examined, we see that its frequency of occurrence (FOO) ranges from a low of 2.6% (i.e.: Samuel Little; Chapter 11) to a high of 5.6% (i.e.: Dennis Nilsen; Chapter 8). You will recall that dot grinding (i.e.: heavy pressure applied to punctuation; See Figure 05-07; Kendall Francois) is indicative of feelings of extreme resentfulness that is expressed by being angry. Dot grinding is one of the six anger/rage-related trait-strokes that are of the "low frequency – high intensity" type. Whenever any of these six trait-strokes (i.e.: Anti-Social; Dot Grind; Shark Teeth; Harpoons; Maniac "d"; X-Stroke) are seen, they are to be interpreted as revealing a serious level of anger/rage in the writer who produced them, regardless of their FOO.

Figure 12-01: Detection of Anger/Rage-Related Strokes

	Serial Killers	Normal Pop'n
Resentment	100%	53%
Temper	70.0%	4.0%
Anti-Social	40.0%	< 1.0%
Dot Grind	50.0%	< 1.0%
Shark Teeth	20.0%	< 1.0%
Harpoons	30.0%	< 1.0%
Maniac "d"	10.0%	< 1.0%
X-Stroke	10.0%	< 1.0%

As indicated in Figure 12-01, resentment strokes are seen in 53% of the normal population's handwriting, and when they occur it is at an average FOO rate of 13% (See Figure 12-03). *All ten* of the serial killers featured in this book have resentment strokes, and if this isn't significant enough by itself, when we look at their individual FOOs (See Figure 12-02) we see that they *all exceed* the normal population's average FOO. In fact, two of our featured serial killers have resentment stroke FOOs in excess of 40% (i.e.: Kendall Francois – 45.1%: Richard Cottingham – 53.8%). This level of frequency is indicative of a huge amount of anger/rage bottled up in their personalities. In an effort to validate whether or not this level of detection (i.e.: 100% of specimens) and high FOO rates hold true for all serial killers, eleven additional serial killer specimens were examined for resentment strokes; see Appendix 02 and Figure 12-03. *All eleven* exhibited resentment strokes, and so this single trait-stroke is definitely a prime indicator of serial killers.

Chart 12-02: Frequency of Occurrence (FOO) of Anger/Rage-Related Handwriting Strokes

Serial Killer	GS	AW	TB	KF	RC	EW	DN	DP	JD	SL
Chapter	2	3	4	5	6	7	8	9	10	11
Resentment	18.3%	20.0%	43.8%	45.1%	53.8%	23.2%	19.1%	20.4%	34.3%	37.6%
Temper	1.8%	1.7%	1.6%	-	-	-	11.1%	0.9%	14.3%	0.9%
Anti-Social	-	-	-	-	-	-	2.8%	8.8%	2.9%	1.7%
Dot Grind	2.8%	-	-	4.8%	-	-	5.6%	-	3.0%	2.6%
Shark Teeth	-	8.6%	-	-	-	-	-	-	-	5.6%
Harpoons	5.5%	-	19.6%	-	-	2.1%	-	-	-	-
Maniac "d"	-	-	11.1%	-	-	-	-	-	-	-
X-Stroke	-	8.3%	-	-	-	-	-	-	-	-

Legend: GS = Gerard Schaefer; AW = Aileen Wuornos; TB = Ted Bundy; KF = Kendall Francois; RC = Richard Cottingham; EW = Elizabeth Wettlaufer; DN = Dennis Nilsen; DP = Dorothea Puente; JD = Joseph DeAngelo; SL = Samuel Little.

The temper stroke is the second most frequently seen anger/rage-related stroke in the normal population at only 4%, but in the ten featured serial killers, seven had it, and two of serial killers revealed very strong tendencies (i.e.: Dennis Nilsen – 11.1%; Joseph DeAngelo – 14.3%). In Chapter 10 we saw ample evidence that DeAngelo had serious temper issues, as expected with such a high FOO. Given that the temper stroke is detected at a much higher rate in serial killer writing, that makes it a strong indicator.

The remaining six trait-strokes listed in Figure 12-01 and described as "low frequency – high intensity" are rarely seen in the normal population's cursive handwriting with rates of less than 1.0%. In fact, of the six, the maniac "d" stroke and the X-stroke occur at even lower rates (i.e.: less than 0.1%). In our ten featured serial killers, however, they were all detected at exponentially higher rates than what is normally the case, making their presence in writing to be a clear differentiator.

What conclusions can we draw based on the observations made regarding the ten handwriting specimens outlined in Figure 12-02? Certainly, resentment strokes with a very high FOO rate are a clear indicator on their own about the writer being a serial killer, and in this book a FOO rate that is ≥30% is the breakpoint; see Figure 12-03.

Two trait-strokes that are non-anger/rage-related and which can be closely correlated with serial killers are the obstinance and narrowmindedness strokes. In the general population, high levels of obstinance (i.e.: >75% FOO) occur

24.1% of the time, whereas with the ten serial killers featured in this book, that level of obstinance was observed in 70% of the specimens. For narrow-mindedness, 27.6% of the population show high (i.e.: > 75%) FOO rates, but in the serial killers the rate was 60%. Four of the ten serial killers listed in Figure 12-04 showed high levels of both trait-strokes, and nine out of the ten (i.e.: 90%) had a high level of abstinence or narrowmindedness or both. While neither of these traits can be directly associated with anger or rage, both of them can certainly be regarded as negative personality traits.

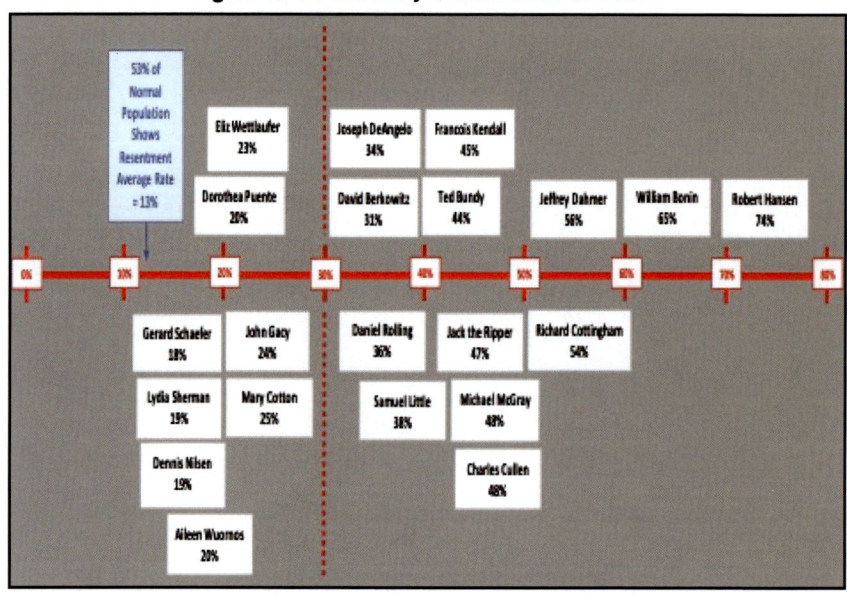

Figure 12-03: Intensity of Resentment Strokes

Name	%
53% of Normal Population Shows Resentment Average Rate = 13%	
Eliz Wettlaufer	23%
Joseph DeAngelo	34%
Francois Kendall	45%
Dorothea Puente	26%
David Berkowitz	31%
Ted Bundy	44%
Jeffrey Dahmer	56%
William Bonin	65%
Robert Hansen	74%
Gerard Schaefer	18%
John Gacy	24%
Daniel Rolling	36%
Jack the Ripper	47%
Richard Cottingham	54%
Lydia Sherman	19%
Mary Cotton	25%
Samuel Little	38%
Michael McGray	48%
Dennis Nilsen	19%
Charles Cullen	48%
Aileen Wuornos	20%

Based on the information gathered, if you are examining the handwriting of a known serial killer, then the following will be observed:

1. There is a 100% probability that the specimen will have resentment strokes with a FOO rate of > 15%, and a 62% probability that the FOO rate will be > 30%.
2. There is a 70% probability that the specimen will have temper strokes.
3. There is a 90% probability that the specimen will have at least one of the six "low frequency – high intensity" stroke types, and a 60% probability that there will be two or more types.

4. When the obstinate and narrowmindedness strokes are considered together there is a 90% probability that at least one of them will have a FOO rate of > 75%.

An extremely important point to take note of is that even though the above criteria are applicable when you are looking at the handwriting specimen of a known killer, *the reverse is not true*. If you are looking at a specimen of handwriting from a neighbor, a relative or a complete stranger and you see these tell-tale strokes, that does not automatically mean that they are a serial killer. The reason is simple, and it is explained by what we learned about serial killers in Chapter 1 "The Definition of a Serial Killer." In this chapter, it was said that in order for an individual to become a serial killer there must be the combined effect of three factors: nature, nurture and notion (the Three N's). Nature refers to genetics, nurture involves the individual's upbringing and social development (or lack thereof), and notion refers to the decision to actually proceed with killing. The effects of two of the three factors—nature and nurture—will be expressed in how an individual writes, but notion is NOT.

Figure 12-04: Other Strokes Frequently Seen in Serial Killers' Handwriting

Serial Killer	GS	AW	TB	KF	RC	EW	DN	DP	JD	SL
Chapter	2	3	4	5	6	7	8	9	10	11
Obstinate	90%	100%	83.3%	30.8%	33.3%	81.8%	23.8%	78.6%	82.9%	81.3%
Narrowminded	80%	39.4%	100%	15%	79.2%	32.5%	78.4%	70%	77.1%	86.7%

The distinction is perhaps best explained through an analogy. Let's say that a friend of yours receives a train ticket to travel from London, England to Moscow, Russia. The ticket can be redeemed at any time, so your friend must decide when to travel, or whether to travel at all. However, just because your friend has a ticket does not automatically mean that they are a traveler. They only become a traveler when they decide to take the trip and then actually board the train. Then and only then do they become an actual traveler.

The same is true about finding the tell-tale trait-strokes listed above in a specimen of handwriting (*aka*: a ticket), and the person exhibiting these trait-strokes does not become a serial killer until they act on the notion to do so. Up until then, all that can be said is that they have the potential, given the right circumstances, to become an actual serial killer. There are people who can have these trait-strokes in their handwriting and yet never become a killer. It might well be said that they are not the nicest people you could ever meet, but being a troubled or unpleasantly-natured person doesn't automatically make them a killer.

By way of example, refer to the specimen of handwriting in Figure 12-05 below. To maintain confidentiality, let's pretend that this individual's last name is *Btfsplk*. Mr. *Btfsplk* is the chief librarian at a large, well-known organization based in southern Ontario in Canada. If you had access to a large specimen of his cursive writing you would be able to determine that the FOO rate of his resentment strokes was 32.1%, his anti-social strokes had a 20.2% FOO rate, his harpoon strokes occurred 0.9% of the time, and he was quite narrow-minded with a 75.8% FOO rate. Using the criteria for assessing a serial killer's handwriting, you might assume that Mr. *Btfsplk* is to be feared because he is a serial killer. But nothing could be further from the truth.

True, Mr. *Btfsplk* has a number of inner demons that undoubtedly trouble his soul, but he is not a serial killer. He lives in a small rural town, he has a PhD in English Literature, he's married and is the father of two boys.

Figure 12-05: Handwriting Specimen – Is This Person a Serial Killer?

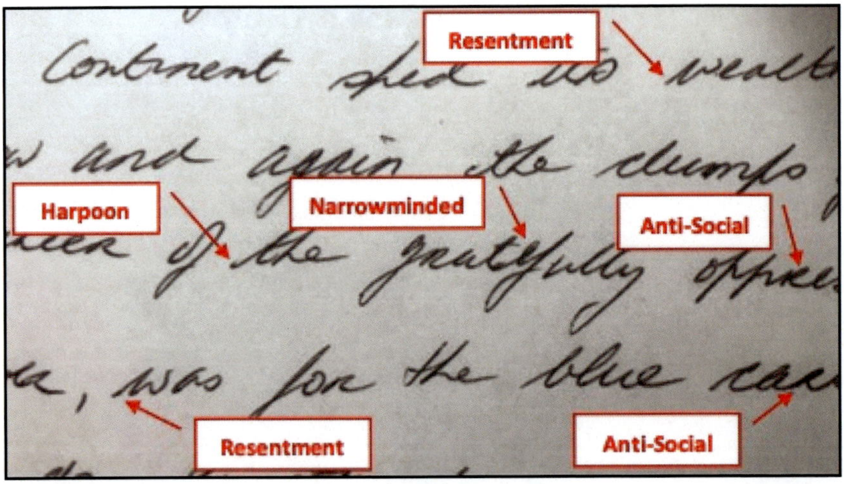

Note: Resentment – Straight approach stroke starting at or below baseline. Anti-Social Behavior Stroke – Capitalized letters in place of lowercase letters. Harpoon – Resentment stroke that begins with a hook or temper tick. Narrowminded – Letter e that is narrow or completely closed.

Nature, Nurture, Notion… The Three N's. It takes all three to make a serial killer. You can have two of the three—Nature and Nurture—but that doesn't automatically make you a killer. It's the third factor—Notion—that you've really got to watch out for, and that can only be determined from an examination of an individual's background. Two of our featured serial killers (i.e.: Aileen Wuornos – Chapter 03; Dennis Nilsen – Chapter 08) have sufficiently well documented histories that the notion which set them off on their journey as serial killers can be identified.

As I pondered the particularly critical role that notion plays in terms of a person taking that final step towards becoming a serial killer, it made me think of the American musician "Meatloaf" and his 1977 hit song "Two Out of Three Ain't Bad." The title of the song nicely captures the reality that a person's nature and nurture aren't totally bad by themselves in terms of someone becoming a serial killer.

Appendix One
THE LAST LINE OF DEFENSE

A person's mind has two different types of defense mechanisms to prevent them from engaging in a socially unacceptable fashion, and both can be identified in a person's handwriting. This appendix describes how graphologists go about identifying and quantifying these defense mechanisms and explains how they function in terms of limiting unacceptable behaviors. Analyzing the handwriting of serial killers is an effective way to understand how defense mechanisms function and what their limitations are.

<u>Conscientiousness</u> is a personality trait revealed by the length of upper zone strokes (i.e.: UZL) as seen in the letters "b, k, l, h", and <u>sublimation</u> is a trait that can be rated based on the length of lower zone strokes (i.e.: LZL) as seen in the letters "g, y, j, q". These two traits are the last line of defense that strive to dissuade someone from engaging in inappropriate or socially unacceptable behaviors. Upper zone (UZ) strokes are an indication of the writer's philosophical, theoretical and spiritual beliefs that are then expressed in their standards of conduct, the principles by which they comport themselves and their conscience. If the UZ strokes are less than two times the average middle zone height (MZH) then, as Dr. Helmut Ploog describes in his book, *Handwriting Psychology* (2013), their level of conscientiousness is stunted.[14] When the UZ strokes are significantly less than two times the MZH (e.g.: 1.2) then this is an indication that the writer has a poorly developed sense of what is right or wrong and they are relatively unmotivated by a sense of responsibility to only do good in the world. Scores obtained with the number (UZL÷MZH) are referred to as UZL-C.

Lower zone (LZ) strokes reflect a writer's practical side and is the area of gratification for biological imperatives such as food, sex and possessions. It is the area where either the release or suppression of anger originates, where dreams and fantasies exist and where the energy of the personality is sourced. In her book, *The Complete Idiot's Guide to Handwriting Analysis, Second Edition* (2007), Sheila Lowe describes the LZ as the basement of a personality where dark thoughts can reside.[15] When these dark thoughts try to come up and out of the basement, then in a normal personality the defense mechanism of sublimation is activated. Sublimation is sort of like a gatekeeper that exerts a "cleansing" effect to channel the psychic energy associated with dark thoughts into something that is more socially acceptable. For example, let's say that your manager has unfairly criticized your work. Your inner urge may be to punch him in the nose, but instead you go for a long and vigorous walk during your lunch hour to "let off steam." Sublimation converted your thoughts of anger and violence by burning off the energy as you walked up the steepest hill you could find. Ploog (2013) uses the same descriptors for describing the LZL as he does with the UZL,[14] so as the number (LZL÷MZH) drops below 2.0 it can be said that the ability to sublimate gets weaker and weaker. Scores obtained with the number (LZL÷MZH) are referred to as LZL-S.

As previously mentioned, the length of the UZ and LZ strokes is measured and evaluated based on their size relative to the average height of the middle zone lowercase letters such as "a, c, e, n, s, o, u". Any UZ or LZ strokes that are greater than two times the average MZH are considered to be normal and reflective of a healthy personality. To explain the dynamics of conscientiousness (i.e.: UZL-C) and sublimation (i.e.: LZL-S) in more practical terms, let's say that you are looking at a specimen of handwriting in which the average UZL is 1.5 times the MZH (i.e.: UZL-C = 1.5) and the average LZL is only 1.2 times the MZH (i.e.: LZL-S = 1.2). What these scores are telling you is, this is an individual who is inclined to act on any dark thoughts that may be lingering in their basement, and who is not at all constrained by feelings about morality in terms of what is right or wrong.

When a writer's defense mechanism scores are well above 2.0 then they have, in essence, a roadblock made of reinforced concrete against the expression of unacceptable behavior. However, if the UZL-C and LZL-S scores are well below 1.5 (for example) and the level of anger or resentment residing in the basement of their psyche is high enough, the writer can be said to have a significantly limited capacity that is only equivalent to the size of a minor speed bump in the road, and this level of restraint or control is usually not enough to stop any unacceptable behavior from occurring.

What range of scores can you expect from normal individuals? In a database of client personality profile results for over 200 individuals that the author maintains, the highest scores were UZL-C = 3.9 and LZL-S = 4.0. Most scores were similar to the following: UZL-C = 2.1 and LZL-S = 2.2, but it was not at all unusual to find scores like UZL-C = 1.8 and LZL-S = 1.5. The lower scores are not necessarily indicative of a flawed personality; all it indicates is that the individual is overly pragmatic in their day to day thinking and their attitude towards life and people in general. The majority of people included in this database had few questionable personality traits dwelling in their basement, and those that were there typically had low frequencies of occurrence. That being the case, even with defense mechanism scores that are below 2.0, they are not necessarily a detriment to society and those around them because their defense levels are adequate in curtailing whatever minor negative behaviors that are part of their personality. It is only when these basement dwellers are numerous and/or at very high frequency levels that they warrant concern. To underscore this point, the following four examples from serial killers are presented.

Example #1. Dennis Nilsen (See Chapter 08) was a British serial killer who murdered 12-15 men between 1978 and 1983, and his defense mechanism scores were UZL-C = 1.8 and LZL-S = 1.5. Nilsen's limited strength defense mechanisms were no match for the combined effect of his overly inflated sexual drive, his anti-social behavior and the significant anger generated by the cumulative impact of his temper, resentment, argumentativeness, jealousy and domineering attitude. See Figure A01-01.

Figure A01-01: Dennis Nilsen[16]

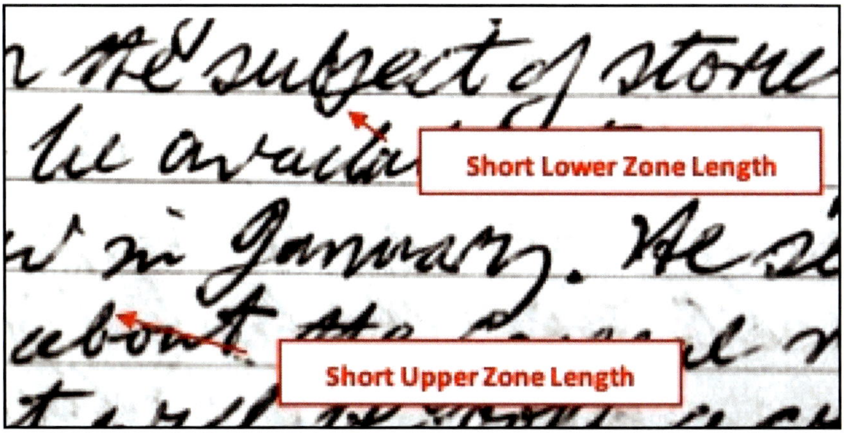

Example #2. Dorothea Puente (See Chapter 09) ran a boarding house in Sacramento, California, USA and is claimed to have murdered nine people between 1985 and 1988. Her defense mechanism scores were UZL-C = 1.6 and LZL-S = 1.2. Unlike many other serial killers who were motivated either by lust, thrill or power, Puente was driven by greed; she saw her victims as an easy source of income to support her comfortable lifestyle. Puente's defense mechanism scores were even weaker than Nilsen's, and like Nilsen, she had an abnormally large number of negative traits that collectively were able to overwhelm her last line of defense and so find expression in her actions. See Figure A01-02. To put things into perspective, Puente's anti-social behavior was seen in 9% of her written words and this is worrisome by itself, since the trait is rarely seen in the general population and when it is, the level is in the less than 2% range. Puente also had a very high level of resentment; 20% of all words had that stroke. Resentment strokes occur in less than 50% of the population, and when they do, the strokes usually occur less than 5% of the time.

Figure A01-02: Dorothea Puente[16]

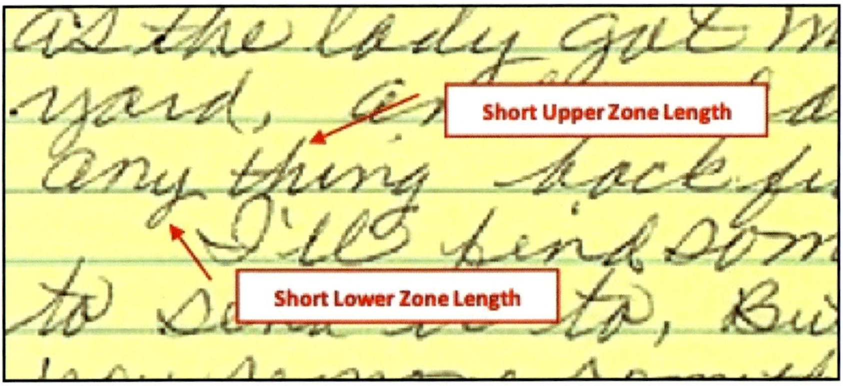

Example #3. Not all examples of defense mechanism score interpretations are quite so straightforward as the previous two might suggest; take the Canadian Elizabeth Wettlaufer for example (See Chapter 7). This serial killer was convicted of eight counts of murder, four counts of attempted murder and two counts of aggravated assault that occurred between 2007 and 2016. Her victims were all elderly patients in long term care institutions and who were under her care (Wettlaufer was a nurse); they were all injected with lethal doses of insulin. What made this case of serial killing interesting was the fact that had Wettlaufer not voluntarily sought out the police to confess to her crimes, they would have gone completely unnoticed; all the deceased were initially thought to have died of natural causes.

Wettlaufer's confession demonstrates that she must have had a functional sense of morality. In her confession to the police, she categorically stated that she "knew right from wrong" yet she obviously couldn't control her urge to kill. When you look at her defense mechanism scores however, the situation becomes clear. Her UZL-C score was 2.1 and her LZL-S score was 1.3; see Figure A01-03. Her UZL-C score validates what she acknowledged in her confession, that she did really understand the difference between good and bad. Her LZL-S score indicates that there was little in the way of sublimation of her negative drives. Wettlaufer had a history of mental instability, had a great deal of anger (a whopping 23% of her handwritten words showed the resentment stroke) and she was subject to what she called "red surges" of rage. Wettlaufer was a bit of an oddity, a serial killer with a conscience.

Figure A01-03: Elizabeth Wettlaufer[16]

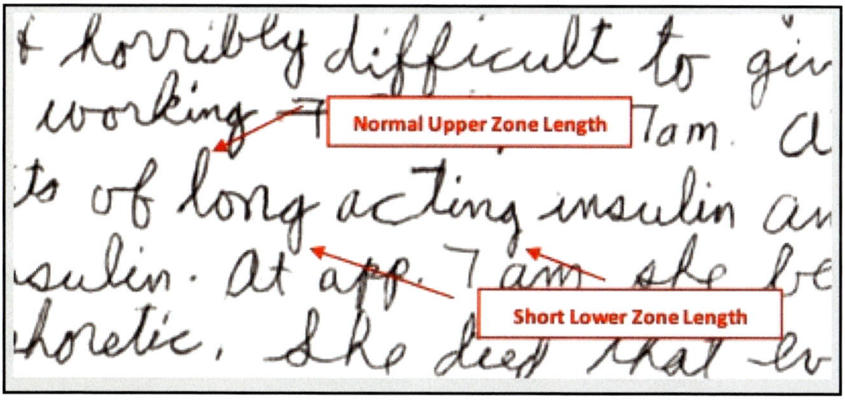

Example #4. Ted Bundy is perhaps one of the most disturbing of all serial killers who, between 1974 and 1978, kidnapped, raped and murdered at least 30 young women in the USA. His motive to kill was not for sexual gratification, but for the overwhelming need to control and possess his victims, to have power over them. One of the defense lawyers assigned to his case described him as "the very definition of heartless evil."[1] You would think that someone as bad as Bundy would obviously have defense mechanism scores that would be very, very low. You would be mistaken however, because his UZL-C score was 2.0 and his LZL-S score was 2.2. How could this be?

Bundy's case is, from a graphological perspective at least, very revealing when it comes to understanding the limitations of a personality's defense mechanisms. Under normal circumstances with a typical human being, his defense mechanism scores would have been enough to curtail any socially unacceptable behaviors. Bundy, however, was anything but normal because he had some monstrously negative traits dwelling within his very dark basement. Bundy's handwriting (See Figure A01-04) shows an astonishingly high level of resentment; 43.8% of the words he wrote had the resentment stroke. And if that were not enough, an additional 19.6% of his words had the harpoon stroke. Harpoon strokes look like resentment strokes that begin with a temper tick. Whenever you see a harpoon, you know that you are dealing with a person who has major resentfulness and who is capable of acts of physical aggression. Even the presence of just a few harpoons is to be taken seriously, and Bundy had an almost unprecedented number of them. And then there were the maniac "d" strokes. In the specimen of Bundy's writing that was examined, the right-hand slant of two of the 18 "d" letters was markedly more pronounced (i.e.: greater than 10%) than the average degree of slant of the rest of his writing. When a maniac "d" is seen, it is indicative of a person who can have sudden, uncontrolled and violent actions followed by a rapid return to normal behavior, and this is an almost exact description of the assaults that Bundy would engage in.

When one considers the combined effect of these three extremely negative traits, it should be of no surprise that Bundy's defense mechanisms were overwhelmed. Going back to our roadblock analogy, the cumulative effect of Bundy's negative personality traits would be something like having one of Britain's main battle tanks, a Challenger 2, crashing through the concrete roadblock without even slowing down.

It is also worth noting that Bundy was not a pure killer in terms of being a threat to every woman that he encountered. Bundy only attacked women that he did not know and had never met before. He had numerous female acquaintances and was in a number of serious relationships with partners who saw nothing disturbing in his personality and described him as "kind, solicitous and empathetic."[2] This is indicative of someone who did have the capacity to function normally, at least when it suited him.

Figure A01-04: Ted Bundy[16]

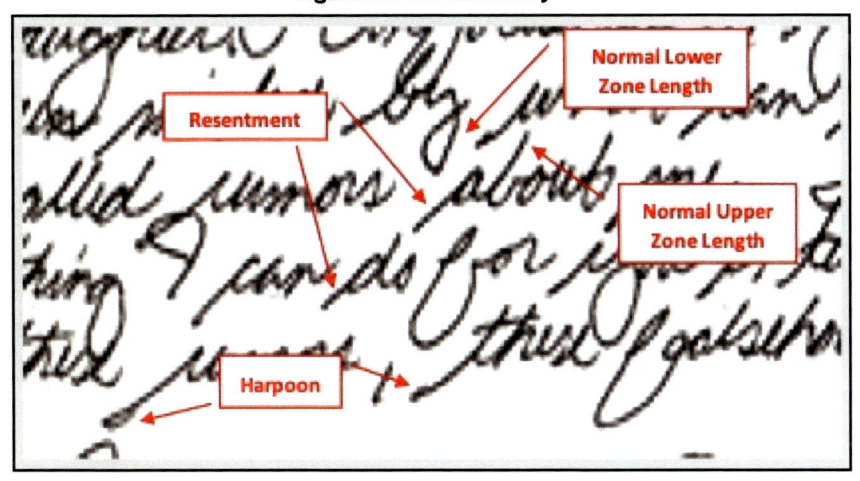

Labels on image: Resentment; Normal Lower Zone Length; Normal Upper Zone Length; Harpoon

AN EXAMPLE OF VERY LOW DEFENSE MECHANISMS

Not everyone who has defense mechanism scores that are well below the level of 2.0 is a serial killer.

That's not to say, however, that they are upstanding citizens either. Take Sherri Papini as an example.

On November 02, 2016, 34-year-old Sherri Papini went for her daily jog[3] in Redding, California, USA after dropping her two children off at daycare; her husband Keith had already left for work. The first sign of trouble arose when the daycare center called Mr. Papini and told him that his wife had failed to pick up the children. When he was unable to contact her, the police were called, and what ensued was a massive three-week search across several US states.

Twenty-two days after her disappearance, on the morning of November 24, Ms. Papini was finally located wandering alongside of a road approximately 240 km from her home.[4] She had numerous bruises, her nose was broken, her hair had been cut off, she had ligature marks on her wrists and ankles, she had lost a lot of weight,[5] and she appeared to have been branded on her left forearm. She told the police that she had been tortured but not sexually abused.

Ms. Papini described her assailants as two Hispanic females in a dark-colored SUV and armed with a handgun.[6] They forced her into their vehicle, and she was taken to a house where she was kept chained in a small, dark closet. She told police that her captors had said that a cop had ordered her abduction and that he was going to "buy" her from them. She had no idea why they eventually dropped her off on the roadside.

Descriptions of the two Hispanic women were widely circulated and a number of people were interviewed because they were identified as resembling the women in the police press releases. Male and female DNA was found on Ms. Papini's clothing which didn't match her or her husband, but they also did not match anyone in the police datafiles. The California State police mounted an exhaustive investigation into Ms. Papini's abduction,[7] but as time went on, some within the police force began to wonder about her evasive behavior when certain topics were brought up. This and her "over the top theatrics"[8] about what happened to her led them to begin investigating Ms. Papini herself. The big break in the case came early in 2020 when the police requested a familial DNA search on the specimens collected from Ms. Papini's clothing at the time of her abduction, and the male DNA was eventually linked to her ex-boyfriend James Reyes. Over the course of numerous interviews, Mr. Reyes explained that even though their romantic relationship had ended in 2006, Ms. Papini had gotten back in touch with him in 2015 and then in 2016 asked him to help her escape from what she described as an abusive relationship with her husband. Mr. Reyes explained to the police that Ms. Papini had fabricated the entire abduction scenario and had in fact come to live with him the entire time that she was reported as missing.[9] Mr. Reyes was of the belief that they could eventually become romantically involved again, but after a couple of weeks Ms. Papini said she missed her kids and wanted to go home. Mr. Reyes's story was corroborated by his brother and his wife who had visited Mr. Reyes at his home a number of times and had met Ms. Papini there. He also explained that in order to add credence to her abduction story, Ms. Papini starved herself and persuaded Mr. Reyes to assist her with her self-inflicted injuries.

In August 2020, the police interviewed Ms. Papini and confronted her with the evidence they had accumulated. She denied everything and stuck with her original narrative; her husband later accused the police of insensitively harassing his wife. On March 03, 2022, Ms. Papini was formally arrested[10,11] on several charges including having made false statements to law enforcement officers; if convicted on all counts, she would have been imprisoned for up to 25 years. Six weeks after her arrest, Ms. Papini signed a plea deal admitting that she had orchestrated the entire hoax.[12] On September 20, 2022, Papini was sentenced to 18 months in jail, over twice what the prosecutors had recommended. The presiding judge in the case felt that the sentencing recommendation made by the prosecutors was insufficient. "She caused innocent individuals to become targets of a criminal investigation.[13] She left the public in fear of her alleged Hispanic capturers who purportedly remained at large,[13]" and she also "fraudulently collected more than US$300,000 in Social Security disability income.[13]" Her own sister's words were probably the most damning of all. In a Facebook post that was then passed along by the media,[13] Sheila Koester stated that "Sherri could intentionally mislead her own beautiful children, her devoted husband, Keith, our families, the authorities, and all of you for so long is beyond comprehension." She went on to say that, "Sadly, despite what she has expressed to the media, she feels no remorse or guilt for the untold damage she has caused nor for taking advantage of criminal, financial, and mental health resources that should have gone to help real victims in need. It deeply pains me to say this, but my sister is very disturbed."

Sherri Papini's UZL-C score was 1.1, and her LZL-S score was, amazingly, 0.9. Scores this low are extremely rare, especially the LZL-S score that indicates that her lower zone lengths were, on average, even smaller than her middle zone letter heights. See Figure A01-05. Papini fortunately didn't have any seriously worrisome traits like resentment or temper, but she did have a very strong and obsessive desire to be seen as someone unique and special. Because there was absolutely nothing working to neutralize her impulses (i.e.: LZL-S) and next-to-no capacity to be influenced by feelings of what is right or wrong (i.e.: UZL-C), the expression of her desire for fame found full bloom.

The two personality traits of conscientiousness and sublimation are the last line of defense that work to prevent unacceptable thoughts or urges from being acted upon. What we have seen however is that they are not all-powerful, especially if the personality under consideration also has a number of strong negative traits. For that reason, the effect of the defense traits should never be considered in isolation but as part of a holistic assessment of all traits that are operational within a personality, and all of the serial killer cases presented in this book reflects this approach.

Figure A01-05: Sherri Papini[16]

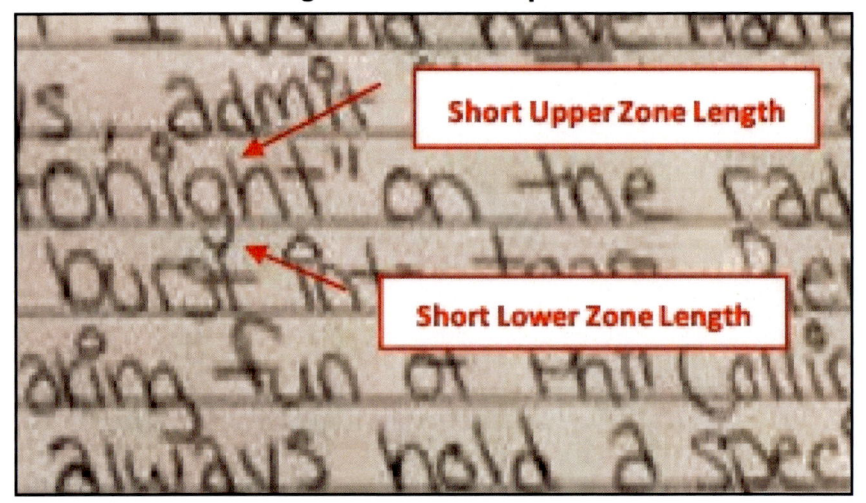

References

1. Nelson, Polly (1994) Defending the Devil: My Story as Ted Bundy's Last Lawyer ISBN 978-1635617-91-7

2. Rule, Ann (2000) The Stranger Beside Me ISBN 978-0-451-20326-7

3. "Missing California 'Super Mom' Found Alive, Bound by Road, Sheriff Says" (November 24, 2016) ABC News.

4. "Sheriff: Sherri Papini Was Kidnapped; Captors Still at Large" (November 24, 2016) CBS Sacramento

5. "Sherri Papini's husband might have compromised kidnapping probe with public comments, sheriff says" (November 30, 2016) Los Angeles Times.

6. "Full Text of Nov 30 Press Conference About Sherri Papini's Abduction" (November 30, 2016) CBS Sacramento

7. Carlson, Adam (April 03, 2017) How Detectives Continue to Dig on the Case of Calif. Mom Who Said She Was Abducted on a Jog. People Magazine

8. Dowd, Katie (March 06, 2022) FBI affidavit unravels astounding claims about California mom Sherri Papini *SFGate.com*

9. Fieldstadt, Elisha (April 21, 2022) Sherri Papini's theatrics are what got her caught, detectives say. US News

10. Martinez, Christian (March 03, 2022) Sherri Papini, accused of faking 2016 kidnapping, injured herself to further her hoax, feds say. Los Angeles Times

11. And one, Dakin (March 08, 2022) California woman's alleged fake abduction cost the public hundreds of thousands of dollars, authorities say. CNN

12. Stanton, Sam (April 12, 2022) "California 'Super Mom' will admit her 'kidnap' was all a hoax, accept plea deal" Yahoo! News

13. Mannie, Kathryn (September 20, 2022) Sherri Papini sentenced for faking own kidnapping, misleading police for 4 years. Global News

14. Ploog, Helmut (2013) Handwriting Psychology – Personality Reflected in Handwriting ISBN 978-1-4759-7021-0

15. Lowe, Sheila (2007) The Complete Idiot's Guide to Handwriting Analysis Second Edition ISBN 978-1-59257-601-2

16. Racher, John (2022) Advanced Graphology: An Encyclopedia of Personality Traits Revealed in Handwriting ISBN 978-1-7773610-1-3

Appendix Two
A QUICK LOOK AT 11 MORE SERIAL KILLERS

William Bonin[4,11] was an American serial killer and sex offender who was active in California between May 1979 and June 1980. Best known as the Freeway Killer because he discarded most of his victim's bodies along a variety of freeways in southern California, Bonin murdered at least 21 young men and boys. What made him different from many serial killers is the fact that in a number of instances he had an accomplice. Estimated frequency of occurrence of resentment stroke: 65%.

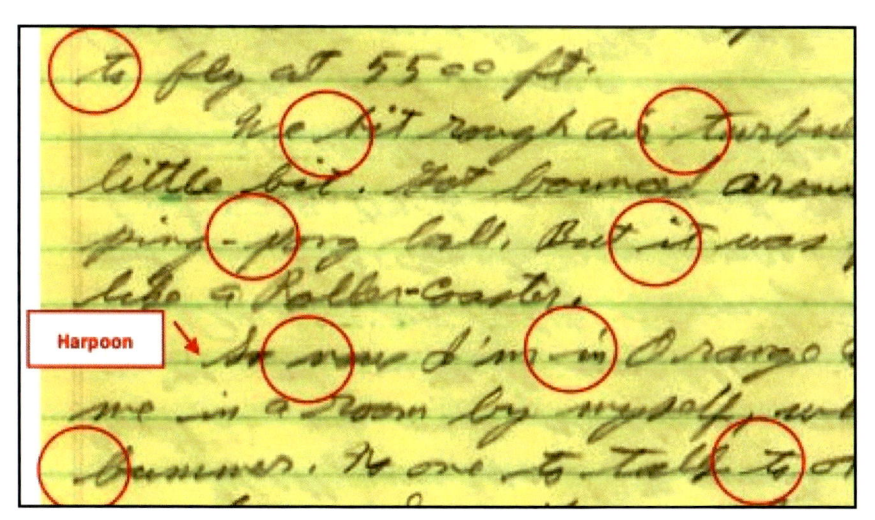

Charles Cullen[3,11] was a troubled child who attempted suicide for the first time when he was only nine years old. He told investigators that his childhood was miserable because, among other things, he was frequently bullied at school. After a stint in the USA Navy, he trained as a nurse and, starting in 1988, proceeded to kill at least 40 of his patients (29 murders were eventually confirmed) over the next 16 years, usually by fatal injections of a variety of drugs such as digoxin and insulin. Estimated frequency of occurrence of resentment stroke: 48%.

Jack the Ripper[1,11] was a serial killer of female prostitutes in the east end of London, England in 1888 and who remains unidentified to-date. He typically cut the throats of his victims and then proceeded to mutilate their abdomen and internal organs. The number of murders committed by Jack the Ripper is uncertain, though at least five have been most likely linked to him. Estimated frequency of occurrence of resentment stroke: 47%.

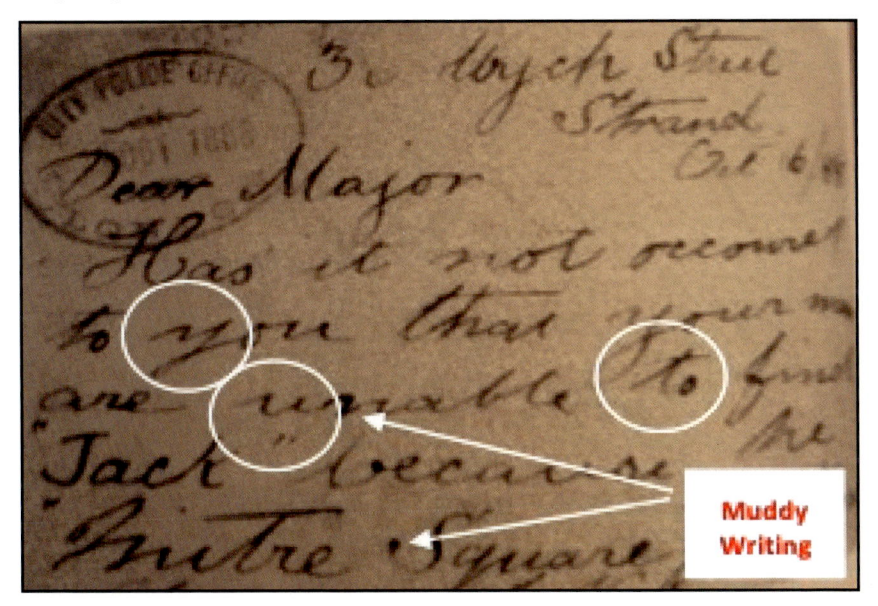

Daniel Rolling[2,11] was an American serial killer who murdered five young female students over four days in August 1990 in Gainesville, Florida. Rollings was terribly abused by his father who told him he was unwanted right from the time he was born. His father routinely abused and beat Rollings, his mother and his brother. Rolling raped and then stabbed his victims to death. In one particularly disturbing instance, he decapitated his victim and then positioned the body so that it was sitting on the edge of her bed facing a shelf where he placed her head. Estimated frequency of occurrence of resentment stroke: 36%.

John Wayne Gacy[5,11] raped, tortured and killed at least 33 young men and boys between 1972 and 1978; all of whom were murdered in his home in suburban Chicago, USA. Most of the bodies were buried in the crawl space beneath his home, but some were dumped in a near-by river. What made Gacy so disturbing was the fact that he was a regular performer at local children's hospitals as "Pogo the Clown" or "Patches the Clown". Estimated frequency of occurrence of resentment stroke: 24%.

David Berkowitz[6,11] is best known by his nickname Son of Sam" and who pleaded guilty to eight shootings that occurred in New York City between 1976 and 1977. The nickname came about because he (falsely) claimed that the reason for his murders was because he was obeying the orders or a demon that spoke to him through his neighbor Sam's dog. Estimated frequency of occurrence of resentment stroke: 31%.

Lydia Sherman[7,11] also known as the Derby Poisoner, was an American serial killer who, between 1864 and 1871 poisoned six of her children, two children who were under her care and three of her husbands; her usual choice of poison was arsenic. Estimated frequency of occurrence of resentment stroke: 19%.

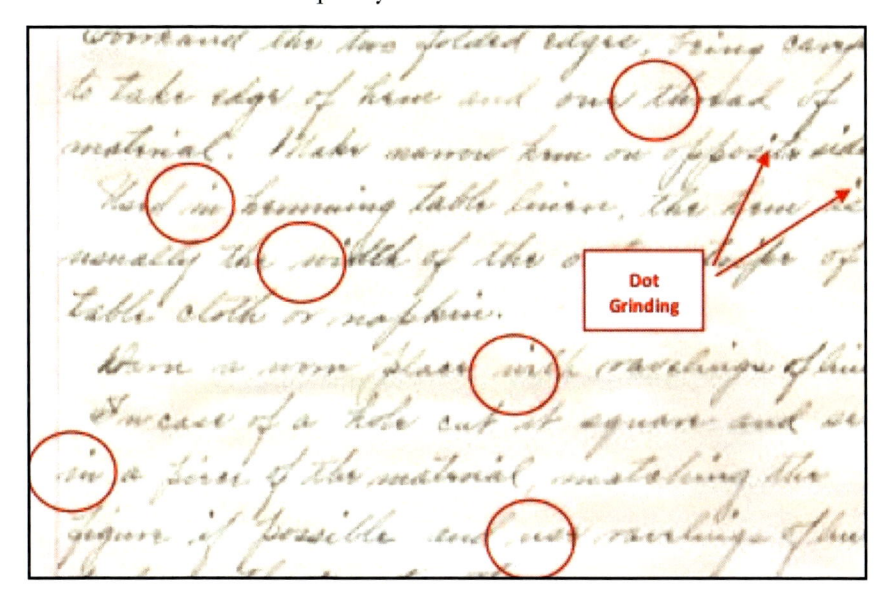

Mary Cotton[8,11] was an English killer who, despite being convicted for one count of murder, is generally regarded as being a serial killer for poisoning three of her four husbands with arsenic for their insurance money. She is also believed to have also poisoned 11 of her 13 children. Estimated frequency of occurrence of resentment stroke: 25%.

Muddy Writing

Robert Hansen[9,11] was an American serial killer who raped and murdered at least 17 women in Alaska. At the age of 21, while in prison for arson, he was diagnosed as someone who was obsessed with obtaining revenge on society because of people whom he felt had wronged him. Hansen's victims were prostitutes whom he abducted and raped. What made him even more sinister was the fact that he would then take them into a secluded forest area where he would turn them loose and then hunt them down and kill them either by shooting or stabbing them. Estimated frequency of occurrence of resentment stroke: 74%.

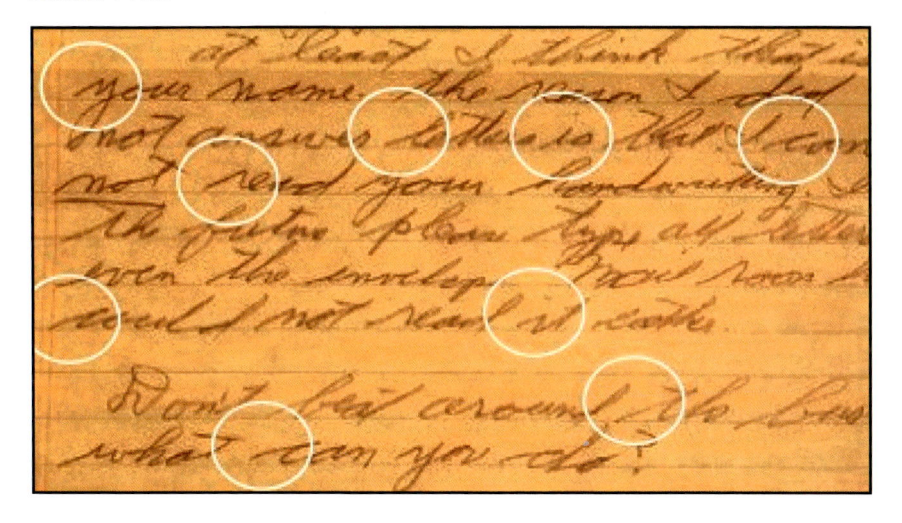

Jeffrey Dahmer[10,11] otherwise known as the Milwaukee Cannibal or the Milwaukee Monster, was responsible for the deaths of 17 men and boys whom he murdered and dismembered between 1978 and 1991. A number of his murders also involved necrophilia and cannibalism. Estimated frequency of occurrence of resentment stroke (including harpoons): 56%.

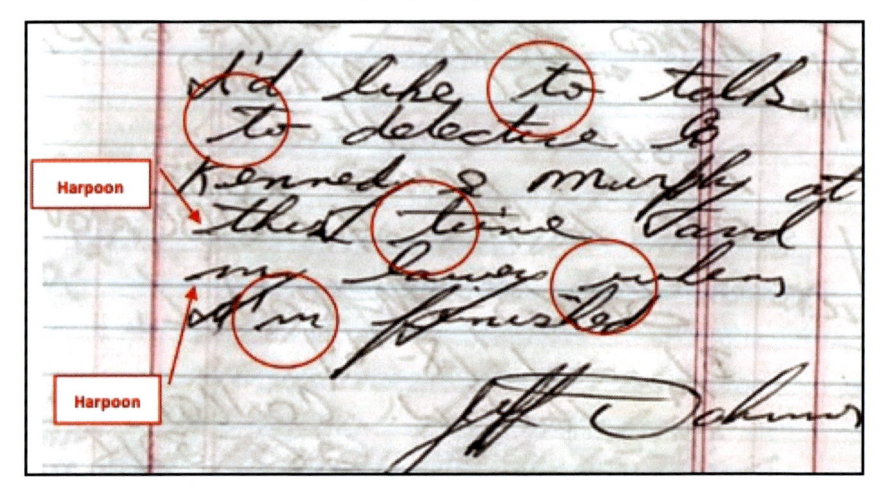

Michael McGray[11,12] was a Canadian serial killer who murdered seven individuals between 1985 and 1998. McGray is best known for singlehandedly exposing several serious shortcomings in how the Canadian prison system was administered. While serving time in prison in 1991 for a robbery conviction, McGray received a three-day weekend pass to stay in a halfway house in Montreal. During his brief time there, he met two men in gay bars, accompanied them to their apartments, and fatally stabbed both to death. Estimated frequency of occurrence of resentment stroke (including harpoons): 48%.

References

1. Haggard, Robert (1993) "Jack the Ripper as the Threat of Outcast London" Essays in History vol 35 University of Virginia

2. "Rolling's confession to Shreveport murders" (October 27, 2006) NBC News

3. Graeber, Charles (April 29, 2007) The Tainted Kidney New York Magazine

4. California Murderer Gets Death Sentence (March 13, 1982) The New York Times. Associated Press

5. "John Gacy: Businessman, Clown, Mass Killer (May 01, 1982) The Ottawa Citizen

6. Abrahamsen, David (1985) Confessions of Son of Sam ISBN 0-231-05760-1

7. Schechter, Harold (2014) Fatal: the poisonous life of a female serial killer ISBN 978-1-476-72912-1

8. Armstrong, Neil (October 31, 2016) "Dark Angel: the gruesome true story of Mary Ann Cotton, Britain's first serial killer" The Daily Telegraph

9. Krajicek, David (August 30, 2014) "Robert (Bob the Baker) Hansen blamed his tortured adolescence for the rape and murder of dozens of women in Alaska in 1970's" New York Daily News 10.

10. Ellens, J. Harold (2011) Explaining Evil, Volume 1 ISBN 978-0-313-38715-9

11. Racher, John (2022) Advanced Graphology: An Encyclopedia of Personality Traits Revealed in Handwriting ISBN 978-1-7773610-1-3

12. Weaver, Jackson (July 12, 2019) Who is serial killer Michael Wayne McGray? CBC News Online

Appendix Three
HANDPRINTING AND THE ZODIAC KILLER

"Zodiac" is the name that an unidentified serial killer (See Figure A03-01) gave himself during the relatively brief yet incredibly intense period of almost 11 months between December 1968 and October 1969 when he murdered five people in the San Francisco area.[1] He in fact had intended there to be seven murders, but two of his victims miraculously survived, and it was their reports that provided much of the information about this killer's appearance.

Perhaps it was because the killer sent letters to a variety of local newspapers taunting the police and providing clues about the murders in the form of cryptograms (See Figure A03-02). Perhaps it was because the killer left bizarre messages at some of the crime scenes (See Figure A03-06) and occasionally wore disturbing disguises during some of the murders (See Figure A03-05). Whatever the reason, the Zodiac Killer became a fascinating topic[2] to millions of people both at the time of the crimes 50 years ago, but also to this day, as evidenced by a still-active website that is devoted to him (i.e.: www.zodiackiller.com).

The Zodiac letters to local newspapers present an interesting challenge as it pertains to the subject of this book. Because these letters were all hand printed and were not prepared using cursive writing (See Figure A03-02), can his existence as a serial killer be determined, since it is cursive writing that is what is almost exclusively used identify the various strokes that are seen in the writing of serial killers? The following analysis seeks to answer this question.

Figure A03-03: Zodiac Killer Police Composite Sketch

BACKGROUND

The Zodiac's first murders[3] occurred on December 20, 1968 when he shot two high school students when they were parked on a lover's lane sometime between 10:15 and 11:00 P.M. David Faraday and Betty Lou Jensen were on their first date, and instead of attending a Christmas concert at their high school like they told their parents, they went to visit a friend and then hung out at a local restaurant before going to Lake Herman Road. See Figure 03. Based on the crime scene evidence it appears that someone had approached their car and ordered them to get out. The assailant shot Faraday in the head as he exited the vehicle and then turned and shot Jensen, who by that time was out of the car and attempting to run away. Jensen's body was found approximately 30 feet from the car face down, with five gunshot wounds to her back. At around 11:00 P.M. a neighbor heard a commotion and went to investigate. When she saw what happened she immediately called the police.

At the time they occurred, these two murders were considered to be a case of random homicide and were not attributed to Zodiac until the following summer when he sent letters to local newspapers claiming responsibility.

Figure A03-02: Zodiac Killer Cryptogram

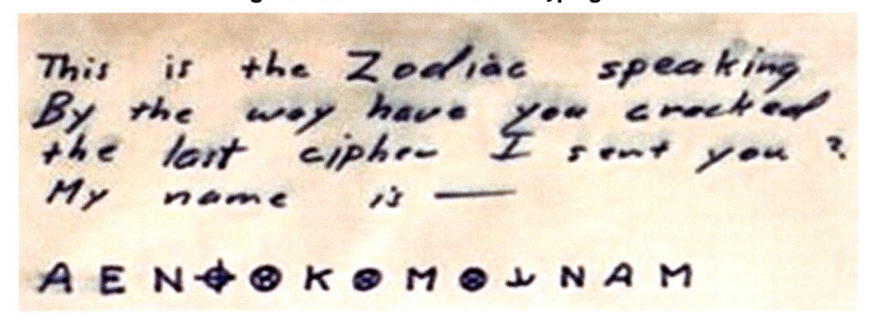

```
This is the Zodiac speaking
By the way have you cracked
the last cipher I sent you?
My name is ———

A E N ⊕ ⊙ K ⊙ M ⊙ ⌐ N A M
```

Just before midnight on July 04, 1969 (six months after the Lake Herman Road murders), Michael Mageau and Darlene Ferrin went to the Blue Rock Springs Park (See Figure A03-05), approximately four miles from the Lake Herman Road murder site to spend some time alone. It was not to be however, because shortly afterwards a car drove into the parking lot and eventually came to a stop behind their car. The young couple noticed that the driver of the second car got out and approached their vehicle on the passenger side and were alarmed to see that he was carrying a flashlight and what appeared to be a handgun. Standing beside their car, the assailant fired five shots through the window, hitting both Mageau and Ferrin numerous times. Perhaps assuming that the teens were both dead, the killer started to return to his car, but upon hearing Mageau crying out in pain, he returned and shot both of them again.

According to Vallejo Police Department records, a phone call was received at approximately 12:40 P.M. The caller informed the police of the shooting[3] and claimed responsibility for doing it. The police rushed to the scene, and both teens were quickly transported to hospital. Ferrin was pronounced dead, but Mageau somehow survived, despite being shot in the face, neck and chest.[3] Because the person who placed the call also claimed responsibility for the Lake Herman Road murders, the police now had the first indication that a repeat killer was on the loose.

Three weeks after the Blue Rock Springs Park shootings had occurred, three near-identical letters were received by the *Vallejo Times Herald*, the *San Francisco Chronicle* and the *San Francisco Examiner*. The writer of these letters claimed to have been the shooter at Lake Herman Road and Blue Rock Springs Park. In each letter was part of a cryotogram, and when the three were put together, they formed a 408-symbol message that the writer claimed would contain his identity. The writer of the letters demanded that they be published on each papers' front pages; failure to comply would result in the writer embarking on a killing spree the following weekend. The police and the newspapers were rather skeptical of the messaging and the threat, but the San Francisco Chronicle did publish their third of the cryptogram on page four the day after receiving it. The threat of the killing spree never materialized, and the other two newspapers eventually published their portions of the cryptogram. Less than a week after the 408-symbol cryptogram was published, it was deciphered.

Figure A03-03: Map of Location of Zodiac Murders

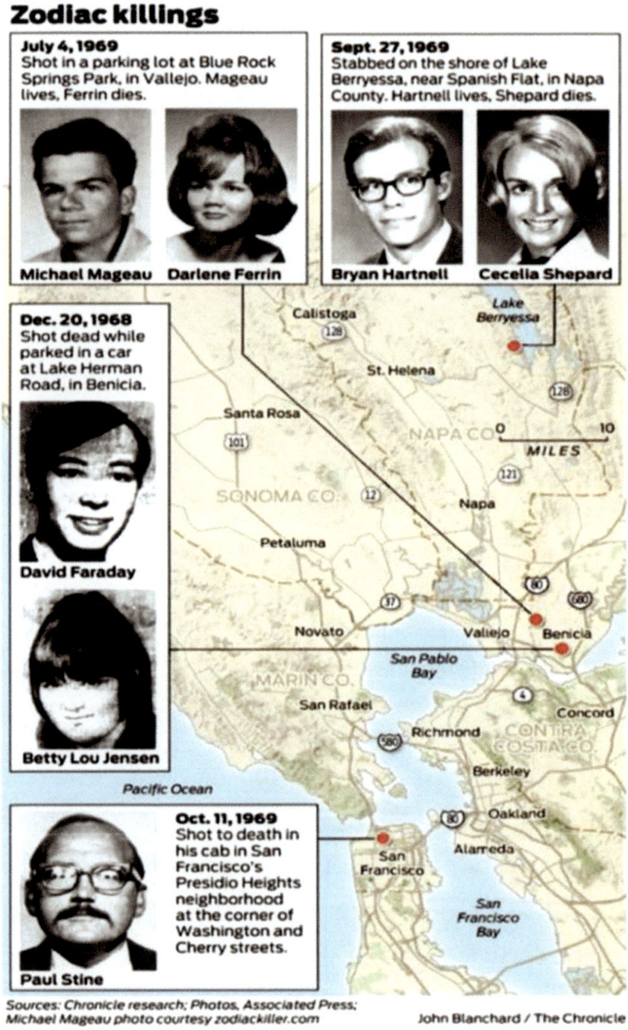

Perhaps not surprisingly, the writer didn't reveal his identity, but he did explain that the reason for his killing was to collect slaves for his afterlife.[3]

On August 07, 1969, another letter had been received at the San Francisco Examiner.[3] In it the writer revealed details of the Lake Herman Road and Blue Rock Springs Park murders that had not been revealed to the public, thereby confirming that he definitely was the assailant. See Figure A03-04. In this letter, the writer for the first time alluded to himself as the "Zodiac."

Figure A03-04: Zodiac Letter to Newspaper

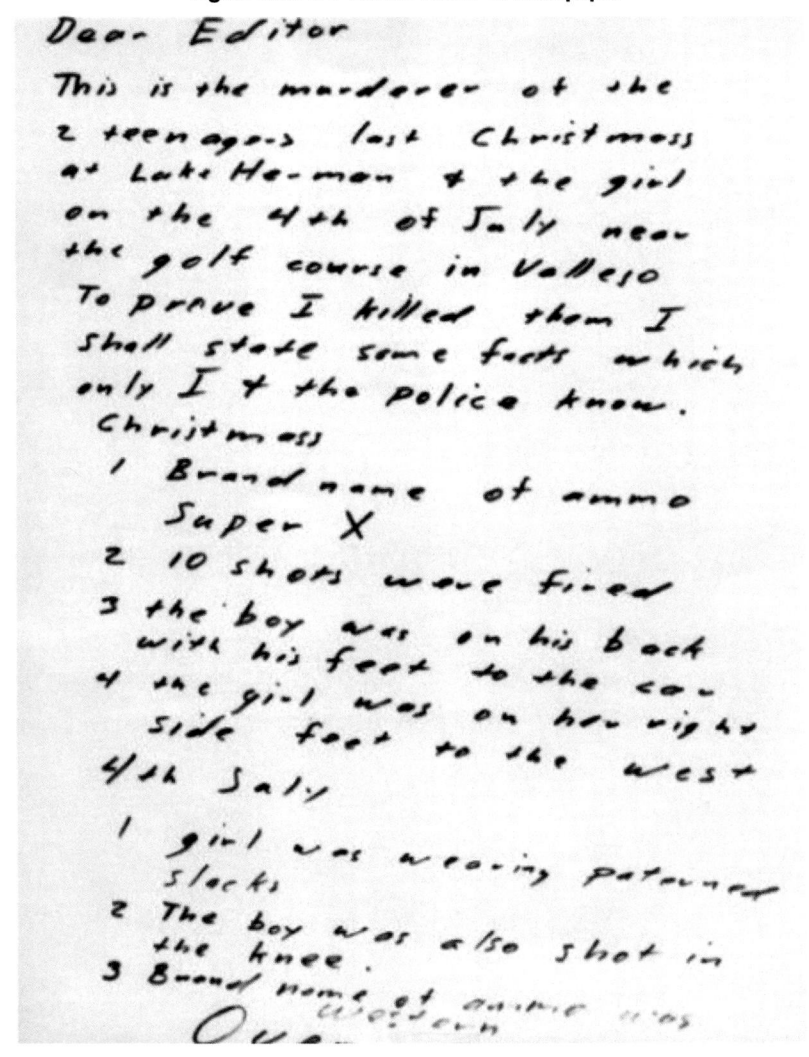

```
Dear Editor
This is the murderer of the
2 teenagers last Christmoss
at Lake Herman + the girl
on the 4th of July near
the golf course in Vallejo
To prove I killed them I
shall state some facts which
only I + the police know.
Christmoss
   1 Brand name of ammo
     Super X
   2 10 shots were fired
   3 the boy was on his back
     with his feet to the ca-
   4 the girl was on her right
     side feet to the west
4th July
   1 girl was wearing patterned
     slacks
   2 The boy was also shot in
     the knee.
   3 Brand name of ammo was
     western
   Over
```

In the afternoon of September 27, 1969, two college students—Bryan Hartnell and Cecelia Shepard—were enjoying a picnic lunch at Lake Berryessa (See Figure A03-03) when they were confronted with a bizarre-looking male walking towards them. He had on a black hood with sunglasses and was wearing what looked like a type of bib with a cross-circle symbol painted on it (See Figure A03-05). He was pointing a handgun at them while carrying some plastic clothesline in his other hand. After tying the college students' hands behind their backs, he pocketed the gun, drew a knife out and stabbed both of them repeatedly in the back. Hartnell was stabbed six times and Shepard was stabbed ten times.[4]

Having stabbed his victims and left them for dead, Zodiac then went to where they had parked and wrote a message on their car door. See Figure A03-06.[5] Zodiac left the park and, at approximately 7:40 P.M., called the Napa County Sheriff's office to report his latest assault. Unbeknownst to him, however, the screams of his victims had been heard by a man and his son who happened to be fishing nearby. When they investigated, they found Hartnell and Shepard, barely alive. After the police arrived, the young couple were rushed to hospital. Shepard died two days later without having regained consciousness, but Hartnell survived.[6]

Zodiac's last murder that can conclusively be attributed to him occurred on October 11, 1969, just two weeks after the Lake Berryessa assaults. Paul Stine, a 29-year-old cab driver, picked up a fare (a white male) at approximately 10:00 P.M. close to Union Square in San Francisco. See Figure A03-03. He was asked to drive to Presidio Heights, but when he arrived, he was shot once in the back of the head. The assailant then took his wallet, his car keys and ripped off a piece of his blood-stained shirt. The police initially thought that this was a routine robbery that went horribly wrong, but just two days later, Zodiac sent a letter to the *San Francisco Chronicle* claiming responsibility for the killing; he included part of Stine's blood-stained shirt as proof.[7]

Figure A03-05: Zodiac Killer Disguise

Note: Drawing based on description of assailant by Bryan Hartnell.

Figure A03-06: Zodiac Killer Message Left at Crime Scene

Note: Cross-Circle Symbol – How Zodiac identified himself. 12-20-68 refers to Lake Herman Road murders. 7-4-69 refers to Blue Rock Springs Park murder and attempted murder. Sept 27-69- 6:30 by knife refers to the assault he had just committed.

After Stine's murder, a number of letters, cards, etc. have been written over the years and sent to various individuals and newspapers, all purporting to be from the Zodiac Killer. While some of them are thought to be authentic, a number were not. By the mid-1970s, the Zodiac killings had become a source of fascination to untold numbers of people and was destined to achieve an almost cult-like status. Over the years, various individuals have claimed to have been Zodiac, or personally knew Zodiac, or had received confessions from people who said they were Zodiac. Psychics have claimed to have information about the Zodiac. But then, 50 years later, some hard news broke. A small team of code-breakers announced that they had decrypted another of the Zodiac's messages, and this was confirmed by the FBI[8] as being authentic. The big letdown, however, came when the team lead, David Oranchak, described the message as "more of the same attention-seeking junk from Zodiac" and that it really didn't reveal anything of any investigative value about him.

The most recent bit of Zodiac news occurred on October 06, 2021 when a group known as the Case Breakers announced that they had identified Zodiac as being Gary Francis Poste,[9,10] who died in 2018 at the age of 80. The Case Breakers is a team of over 40 detectives, journalists and military intelligence officers who take on cold cases. The FBI disagreed however.[11] And while they were somewhat diplomatic about rejecting the Case Breakers' claim by saying that there was "no new information to report" about Zodiac, Tom Voigt, an author and Zodiac Killer investigator, was a bit less circumspect, simply describing the announcement as "bullshit."[12]

HANDPRINTING ANALYSIS[13]

We learned from the information presented in Chapter 12 that there are eight different handwriting strokes that are associated with a writer's level of anger and rage, and if the writer is a serial killer, then you will definitely find at least one of these strokes in their handwriting. But what if the only notes from a serial killer that are available for analysis are handprinted and not handwritten; can you still find telltale strokes? The answer is a qualified yes, since what we see in Zodiac's handprinted letters only indicates the presence of some of the strokes.

The eight strokes that are indicative of anger/rage are as follows:

1. Resentment stroke
2. Temper stroke
3. Anti-Social Behavior stroke
4. Dot Grinding stroke

5. Harpoon stroke
6. Shark Teeth stroke
7. Maniac "d" stroke
8. X-Stroke

The problem with handprinted letters is that printing typically does not include an initial stroke that leads into the letter itself (See Figure A03-07), and that being the case, then the resentment, temper and harpoon strokes will not be seen, even if the person who printed the letters has significant anger or rage issues that, had they written their letters, would have been present. In the Zodiac Killer's handprinted note presented in Figure A03-08, we see that he displays two of the eight anger/rage-related strokes: dot grinding and maniac "d", and their respective FOO rates (i.e.: 5.7% and 80%) are even more revealing. In fact, the 80% FOO rate of maniac "d" strokes is unprecedented.

Figure A03-07: Written vs. Printed Letters

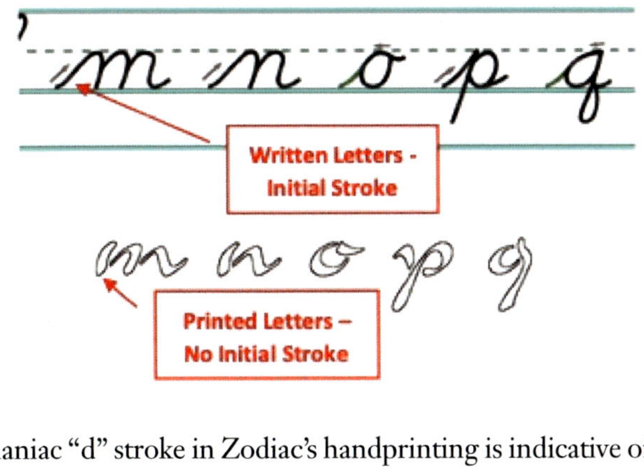

The maniac "d" stroke in Zodiac's handprinting is indicative of an astounding level of pent-up rage[13,14] typified by sudden, uncontrolled, violent actions followed by a rapid return to normal behavior. To fully appreciate the full magnitude of Zodiac's 80% FOO rate, a more in-depth explanation is presented.

The slant of the upper zone portion of letters like b, d, h, k, l and t is measured in a clockwise fashion using the baseline of the letter under consideration as the starting point. See Figure A03-09.

In order to determine the presence and magnitude of the maniac "d" stroke in Zodiac's handprinting, the degree of right-hand slant of 20 letter d's and 32 other letters (i.e.: b, h, l, t, k) were measured. Of the twenty letter d's, the average slant was 148° with a range of 134° to 156°. The 32 other upper zone stem letter measurements yielded an average of 128° with a range of 114° to 141°. The bar chart in Figure A03-10 quite clearly demonstrates that the letter d's are a very distinct subset of the upper zone stem letter measurements. In order to ensure continuity and accuracy in assessing the presence and magnitude of the maniac "d" strokes between different specimens of handwriting, a letter "d" is not categorized as a maniac "d" stroke unless it is 10% or more larger than the average for that specimen's other letters;[13] in the Zodiac's case, a letter d must therefore be at least (128° * 1.1) = 141°. Using this criterion, sixteen of the twenty (80%) letter d's from the Zodiac handprinted specimen were determined to be maniac "d" strokes.

With only five murders to his name, the Zodiac certainly wasn't the most prolific and therefore most infamous of serial killers, but what he lacked in numbers he more than made up for in style. For decades he was arguably the most famous of serial killers, and still commands an interesting level of attention to this day. Three different police agencies still have him on an active investigation list. Even for graphologists, Zodiac holds an almost unique position of infamy because he is the ultimate poster child when it comes to his maniac "d" strokes.

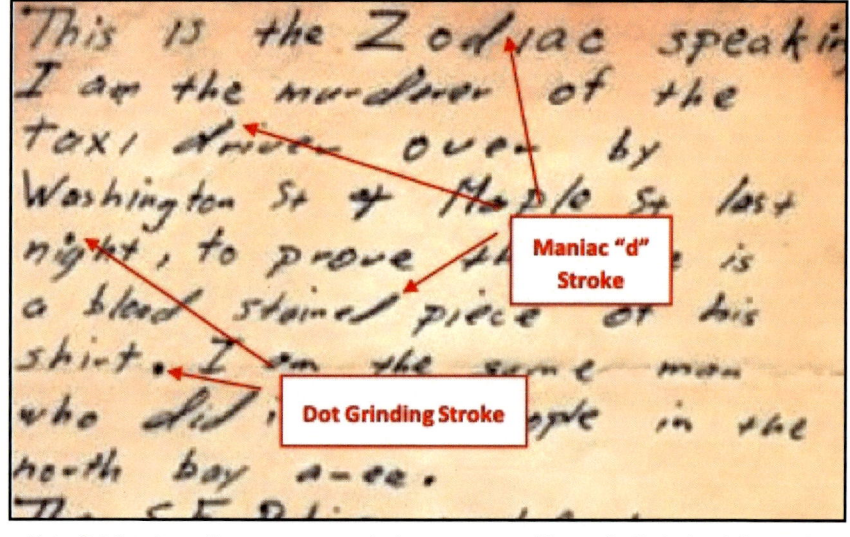

Figure A03-08: Zodiac Killer Handprinting

Note: Dot Grinding – Heavy pressure applied to punctuation. Maniac d – Right-hand slant of the letter "d" stem is markedly more pronounced than the rest of the writing.

Figure A03-09: Evaluating the Right-Hand Slant of Letters

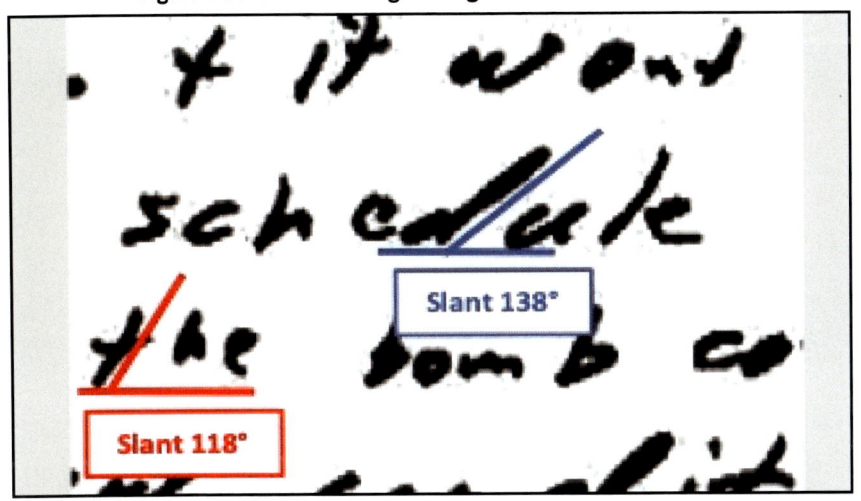

Slant 138°

Slant 118°

Note: Slant is measured in a clockwise direction from the baseline.

Figure A03-10: Degree of Slant of Zodiac Killer's Letters

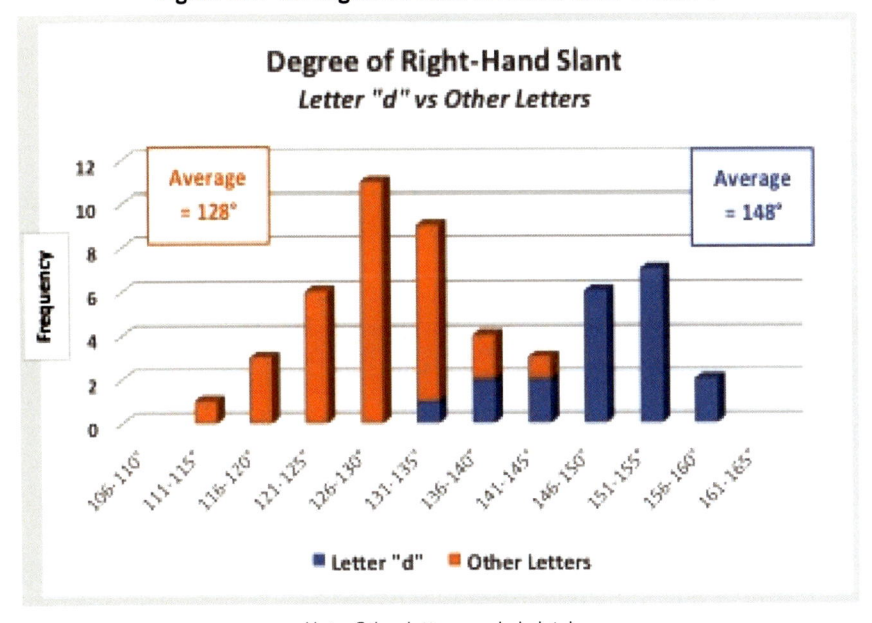

Note: Other letters are b, h, l, t, k

References

1. "Zodiac Killer – Crimes, Letters, Codes, DNA" www.zodiackiller.com

2. Fagan, Keving (December 11, 2020) "Zodiac '340 Cipher' cracked by code experts 51 years after it was sent to the S.F. Chronicle" The San Francisco Chronicle

3. Graysmith, Robert (1976) Zodiac ISBN 978-0-425-09808-0

4. "Zodiac the Killer" (October 27, 1969) The Tuscaloosa News

5. "Message written on Hartnell's car door" (April 20, 2010) www.zodiackiller.com

6. "Girl dies of stabbings at Berryesa" (September 30, 1969) San Francisco Chronicle

7. "Definite Zodiac Victim Paul Stine" www.zodiackiller.com

8. Zodiac Killer: Code Breakers solve San Francisco Killer's Cipher (December 12, 2020) BBC

9. "Zodiac Killer Finally Identified!!! But 3 Years Too Late" www.tmz.com

10. Casiano, Louis (October 06, 2021) "Cold case team says Zodiac Killer ID'd, linking him to another murder" *Fox News*

11. "'The case remains open": FBI rebuts claim Zodiac Killer case is solved" (October 18, 2021)*NBC News*

12. Kreps, Daniel (October 06, 2021) ""Hot Garbage": Zodiac Expert Calls "Bullshit" on Possible ID of Infamous Serial Killer" *Rolling Stone*

13. Racher, John (2022) Advanced Graphology: An Encyclopedia of Personality Traits Revealed in Handwriting ISBN 978-1-7773610-1-3 www.volumesdirect.com

14. Lowe, Sheila (2007) The Complete Idiot's Guide to Handwriting Analysis Second Edition ISBN 978-1-59257-601-2